"Totally outstanding and inspirational."
Revd Dr Canon Andrew White

"This second volume of stand-alone Bible studies offers a feast of good things, whether you are using them in a group or in your own quiet time.

Pen has a gift of being able to pack a lot into very few words. Her commentaries alone offer much food for thought, while the questions she poses open up many avenues for discussion.

It's a wonderful resource for people who appreciate a starting point and then the freedom to explore, meander and digress."
Jackie Harris, editor, *Woman Alive*

"Pen Wilcock has done it again! In this second volume of Bible studies she helps us reflect on Scripture, apply it to our lives, and connect with the life-giving grace and mercy of God. Her studies are thought-provoking, inspiring, and relevant. They help me remember who God is, what His great purposes are in the world and how I fit into them faithfully. What more could we ask for?

Use these Bible studies on your own, in a group, or as part of your church's discipleship program and you will grow in faith, in community, and in understanding of how to live out a relationship with Jesus Christ in the world today."
Revd Malcolm Duncan, lead pastor, Dundonald Elim Church

Penelope Wilcock has pastored ten Methodist congregations, worked as a school chaplain and a hospice chaplain, been involved in ministry with prisoners, and initiated a Fresh Expression of Church. She blogs at Kindred of the Quiet Way (*www.kindredofthequietway.blogspot.co.uk*) and is a regular columnist in *Woman Alive* magazine.

She believes in the hidden working of the gospel in the context of the daily lives of ordinary people as the revolution that will change the world.

Penelope lives a quiet life on England's Sussex coast.

By the same author

Fiction

The Hawk and the Dove series (Lion Fiction):
The Hawk and the Dove
The Hardest Thing to Do
The Hour Before Dawn
Remember Me
The Breath of Peace
The Beautiful Thread
A Day and A Life

Thereby Hangs A Tale (Kingsway)
The Clear Light of Day (David C. Cook)

Pastoral resources

Spiritual Care of Dying and Bereaved People (SPCK; revised and expanded edition, BRF)
Learning to Let Go (Lion)

Christian lifestyle

The Road of Blessing (Monarch)
The Wilderness Within You: A Lenten Journey with Jesus, Deep in Conversation (Monarch)
In Celebration of Simplicity (Monarch)
100 Stand-Alone Bible Studies: To Grow Healthy Home Groups (Monarch)
52 Original Wisdom Stories: Short Lively Pieces for the Christian Year (Monarch)

100

MORE STAND-ALONE BIBLE STUDIES

Nurturing and nourishing your home group

Penelope Wilcock

MONARCH
BOOKS

Published by
Lion Hudson Limited
Wilkinson House, Jordan Hill Business Park,
Banbury Road, Oxford OX2 8DR, England

ISBN 978 0 85721 833 9
e-ISBN 978 0 85721 834 6

First edition 2018

Acknowledgments

Scripture quotations marked "NIVUK" are taken from the *Holy Bible, New International Version Anglicized*. Copyright © 1979, 1984, 2011 Biblica, formerly International Bible Society. Used by permission of Hodder & Stoughton Ltd, an Hachette UK company. All rights reserved. "NIV" is a registered trademark of Biblica. UK trademark number 1448790.

Other Bible versions used:

Scripture quotations marked "KJV" are taken from the Authorized (King James) Version. Rights in the Authorized Version are vested in the Crown. Reproduced by permission of the Crown's patentee, Cambridge University Press.

Scripture quotations marked "GNB" are taken from the Good News Bible published by the Bible Societies and HarperCollins Publishers, © American Bible Society 1994, used with permission.

Scripture quotations marked "NRSVA" are taken from the New Revised Standard Version Bible: Anglicised Edition, copyright © 1989, 1995 the Division of Christian Education of the National Council of the Churches of Christ in the United States of America. Used by permission. All rights reserved.

Scripture quotations marked "RSV" are taken from the Revised Standard Version of the Bible, copyright © 1946, 1952, and 1971 the Division of Christian Education of the National Council of the Churches of Christ in the United States of America. Used by permission. All rights reserved.

Scripture quotations marked "TLB" are taken from The Living Bible, copyright © 1971 by Tyndale House Foundation. Used by permission of Tyndale House Publishers Inc., Carol Stream, Illinois 60188. All rights reserved. The Living Bible, TLB, and the The Living Bible logo are registered trademarks of Tyndale House Publishers.

Scripture quotations marked "NET" are taken from the NET Bible® copyright ©1996–2006 by Biblical Studies Press, L.L.C. http://netbible.com. All rights reserved.

Scripture quotations marked "ESVUK" are taken from The Holy Bible, English Standard Version® (ESV®), copyright © 2001 by Crossway, a publishing ministry of Good News Publishers. Used by permission. All rights reserved.

Scripture quotations marked "ERV" are taken from the Easy-to-Read Version, copyright © 2006 by Bible League international.

Scripture quotations marked "DLNT" are taken from the *Disciples' Literal New Testament* copyright © 2011 Michael J. Magill. Published by Reyma Publishing. All rights reserved.

Scripture quotations marked "AMP" are taken from The Amplified Bible, copyright © 2015 by The Lockman Foundation, La Habra, CA 90631. All rights reserved.

A catalogue record for this book is available from the British Library
Printed and bound in the UK, August 2018, LH27

Contents

About this book

Less is more in group work

100 More Stand-Alone Bible Studies can be an aid to personal devotion and could be very useful for a quiet-day context, but is primarily intended as a resource for your home group. In the introduction to volume 1 (*100 Stand-Alone Bible Studies*), you will find detailed notes on home-group leadership and preparation, and how to use these studies.

The happy experience of many years of leading retreats, quiet days, and small groups has impressed on me the vital lesson that "less is more".

Most leaders (myself included) fall into the trap of fearing inadequacy – wanting to be sure enough material is offered, and the subject is thoroughly covered with no stone left unturned. People go home with distended souls – inspirational resource material pressed down, shaken together, and running over from every spiritual orifice.

It's not necessary.

You need a clock, because people have babysitters waiting and schedules to fulfil. Say what the time frame will be, and keep to it.

You need confidence – to wait, to give space for silence, to be at warm peace with people's tears if their sharing touches on deep places in their psyche and they can't help crying.

You need trust – that the Holy Spirit will show up, that people will have enough experiences and opinions they want to share to fill up the time, and that they have the inborn skill to meet with God in their discussions without anxious chaperoning.

You need a certain spaciousness in your spirit – an inner freedom. A home-group leader who feels a concern to monitor and promote religious orthodoxy will not support spiritual formation. Of course people's views on life will be exploratory, sometimes surprising, even heretical. Christ who holds all truth within himself can be trusted to find them, to sit alongside them, to guide them. The home-group leader is there to listen, to offer, to suggest – not to be an accredited Thought Police officer.

People want to be beheld, heard, affirmed, and loved; but they also want to contribute, to shape the thing themselves, without being much curtailed or interrupted.

Though these Bible studies seem at first sight a bit skinny, a little "lite", this is deliberate. You see, they are not intended to be the *substance* of your meeting. They are the bones not the meat; the structure not the content: the framework. The content of the meeting is the interaction, the discussion, the passion, the laughter, the friendship, the discoveries, the adventure, the excitement of doing theology, and with increasing boldness exploring faith.

Home groups, and Christian faith, are about encounter with each other and with the living God. All the questions are open, designed to draw people out. There are no right answers. The questions are not a form of testing but an invitation to explore, and the brief commentaries in each study offer some food for thought to get you started.

This collection of studies sets out to help build a bridge between the eternal gospel and its lived context in contemporary life. Together the studies form a comprehensive overview of the Christian way of discipleship.

Sacred moments

Baptism 1

BIBLE PASSAGES

Matthew 28:18–20, GNB

Jesus drew near and said to them, "I have been given all authority in heaven and on earth. Go, then, to all peoples everywhere and make them my disciples: baptize them in the name of the Father, the Son, and the Holy Spirit, and teach them to obey everything I have commanded you. And I will be with you always, to the end of the age."

1 Peter 3:20–21, NRSVA

... God waited patiently in the days of Noah, during the building of the ark, in which a few, that is, eight people, were saved through water. And baptism, which this prefigured, now saves you – not as a removal of dirt from the body, but as an appeal to God for[1] a good conscience, through the resurrection of Jesus Christ ...

Colossians 2:12, NRSVA

... [Y]ou were buried with him in baptism, you were also raised with him through faith in the power of God, who raised him from the dead.

Commentary

The sacred moment of baptism is the outward sign of the invisible grace of new creation. It's more than a new start. We make new beginnings all the time – moving from junior school to high school, changing jobs, moving house; change is just part of life, so we are always starting over. This is something deeper.

There's a sense of separation from all that went before and all that will be from now on – a complete divide. Our verse from Colossians speaks of baptism as a death; whoever and whatever we were, that is *over*. A whole new life is born in us as we discover and develop our new identity in Christ.

There's also a sense of transition – that baptism is a burial, or like the ark carried on the floodwater, sealed against the outside word. This has the same feeling as a caterpillar drawn, impelled, to make its chrysalis and withdraw within it. Once inside, it completely dissolves. It becomes nothing but a liquid. But that fluid contains the blueprint of wonder – the possibility of a butterfly.

---

1   Or "a pledge to God from a good conscience".

Interestingly, you must absolutely not try to help an emerging butterfly get out of its chrysalis. Well-meaning bystanders who step in to help things along discover to their dismay that the struggle is not without purpose. It's all part of the development of a functioning butterfly. Without those struggles, it will never fly properly.

I wonder if the same applies to us. We enter the experience of baptism – the washing clean, dying to the world, embracing union with Christ, losing ourselves in him, taking on a new identity. Perhaps the struggles and temptations that often follow – that will certainly follow sooner or later – are not a downside, an avoidable misfortune, but part of the necessary process of our new development; the part that makes sure our faith can fly.

Questions

- Have you been baptized? If you have, what can you remember (or what do you know) about your baptism? What was the context? What does it mean to you? Did you have sponsors or godparents? Have they been a big part of your life? If you haven't been baptized, was that a conscious choice? Can you share why?

- Suppose you had never been baptized, and you were planning to take this step now. Where would it take place? What elements would you like to build in to the occasion? Who would you like to be present, and who would baptize you? Are there any songs and readings with special meaning that you would like to include? Would you like to give a testimony? What would you like to mention if you did?

- The sacred moment of baptism signifies being born again – into a completely new life as part of the family of Christ. How do you feel about this? Is it easy for you to believe it? How can you integrate into this reality of new creation the sad truth that we still continue to mess things up, to stumble and fall? What's the difference between the before and after, in your opinion?

Prayer

Loving Father, we thank you from the bottom of our hearts that you welcome us into your family as we are united with Jesus by faith. Thank you for forgiving us, for accepting us. Thank you for the chance to begin again.

As we travel, step by step along this new and living way, please walk with us. Talk to us, show us which path to take at every crossroads, reveal yourself to us in the ordinary circumstances of life.

By your grace, may we trust you enough to keep faith with you and bear witness to your love every day of our lives, until the great moment comes when you take us home to yourself, and we at last get to meet you fully, face to face. Amen.

Baptism 2

BIBLE PASSAGES

Acts 2:38–39, NIVUK

Peter replied, "Repent and be baptised, every one of you, in the name of Jesus Christ for the forgiveness of your sins. And you will receive the gift of the Holy Spirit. The promise is for you and your children and for all who are far off – for all whom the Lord our God will call."

Mark 10:13–14, NIVUK

People were bringing little children to Jesus for him to place his hands on them, but the disciples rebuked them. When Jesus saw this, he was indignant. He said to them, "Let the little children come to me, and do not hinder them, for the kingdom of God belongs to such as these."

Acts 16:31–33, ESVUK

And they said, "Believe in the Lord Jesus, and you will be saved, you and your household." And they spoke the word of the Lord to him and to all who were in his house. And he took them the same hour of the night and washed their wounds; and he was baptized at once, he and all his family.

Luke 3:16, RSV

John answered them all, "I baptize you with water; but he who is mightier than I is coming, the thong of whose sandals I am not worthy to untie; he will baptize you with the Holy Spirit and with fire."

1 Corinthians 12:13, NIVUK

For we were all baptised by one Spirit so as to form one body – whether Jews or Gentiles, slave or free – and we were all given the one Spirit to drink.

Commentary

As we consider these scriptural texts, all of them either about baptism or often read out at baptisms, three categories begin to emerge – the baptism of children, the baptism of adults, and baptism in the Holy Spirit as distinct from in water.

The church has seen much fierce dispute about the biblical legitimacy of infant baptism, and these texts show why: those who hold opposing views can find support for their perspectives in the Bible.

Jesus did tell his disciples to let the little children come to him and not get in their way – and is not baptism exactly coming to Jesus, to embrace and be embraced by him? The jailer Paul met at Philippi did ask him, "What must I do to be saved?"[2] Paul did say that if he believed in the Lord Jesus he would be saved – he *and his household*. But did he mean the household would be saved if the jailer believed, or that they had the same opportunity of salvation? Either way, it seems his family had little choice about their baptism! This encourages us to accept infant baptism as a valid path of faith.

Others stoutly defend the inclusion of repentance as a necessary prerequisite for baptism, without which it is meaningless – so they feel it can never be offered to those too young to make a choice.

And the baptism in Holy Spirit is seen by some as an every-believer experience – the outcome of accepting Christ as saviour – while others see it as a further step on the way of discipleship, a choice of its own to be embraced.

Questions

- Do you have a strong conviction in favour of adult or infant baptism, or do you feel either way is equally blessed? What are your reasons?
- Does the faith family in which you currently worship follow the same practice as the one in which you were brought up (if you went to church as a child)? What changes of mind have you undergone about baptism, or noticed in others?
- What does the phrase "baptism in the Holy Spirit" mean to you? Would you say you have experienced this, or not, or aren't you sure? What experiences have you had that feel like a baptism in the Holy Spirit? What do you think John the Baptist meant by it? Is that the same as we mean when we use the phrase today?

Prayer

O God of love and power, we come to you for cleansing, renewal, and peace. Immerse us in your free Spirit until our lives overflow with your grace. May we be so saturated with your presence that the healing power of your shalom touches others and leads them into freedom, into joy. For we ask it in Jesus' name. Amen.

---

2   Acts 16:30.

Eucharist 1

BIBLE PASSAGES

Luke 22:19–20, NET

Then he took bread, and after giving thanks he broke it and gave it to them, saying, "This is my body which is given for you. Do this in remembrance of me." And in the same way he took the cup after they had eaten, saying, "This cup that is poured out for you is the new covenant in my blood."

John 6:53–56, ERV

Jesus said, "Believe me when I say that you must eat the body of the Son of Man, and you must drink his blood. If you don't do this, you have no real life. Those who eat my body and drink my blood have eternal life. I will raise them up on the last day. My body is true food, and my blood is true drink. Those who eat my body and drink my blood live in me, and I live in them."

1 Corinthians 10:16–17, NRSVA

The cup of blessing that we bless, is it not a sharing in the blood of Christ? The bread that we break, is it not a sharing in the body of Christ? Because there is one bread, we who are many are one body, for we all partake of the one bread.

Commentary

The greatest, and deepest, most beautiful mystery of the church's life is the Eucharist. Here is the beating heart of the celebration of our salvation, the place where broken humanity is knit together and remade. In the homeliness of a shared meal, humbly God comes to us, enters us, and becomes one with us, makes his communion with us.

In the agony of dying, Jesus cries out, "My God, my God, why have you forsaken me?" As in that act of self-offering he opens the work of salvation, so in this intimate meal the broken shards of his crucifixion fuse into the triumph of their meaning. Here his broken body is re-membered; his brokenness meets ours, and the miracle happens. The seemingly unbounded propensity of humanity for cruelty, ugliness, and sin is turned back. Here darkness is rolled back by the light from the dawn of creation, the eternal world.

We are what we eat; what we take refuge in takes refuge in us; what we make common cause with determines who we become. Evil cannot co-exist with the presence of Christ. John Wesley called the Eucharist a "converting and sanctifying ordinance".

This touching place should never have been made for church members only – for initiates, for the accepted, accredited in-crowd – it was not intended as an élitist thing. It is for everyone: for sinners, for the broken, puzzled, and lost. It is for doubters and little children. It is not our table but the table of the Lord. Here he is food and host and guest. Here he melds with us into one luminous continuum of grace.

Here, if anywhere on earth, we touch the living God.

One time when I was called to visit an aged woman so deeply depressed she had to be hospitalized, I heard her story – the burrowing anguish that ravaged her soul. She believed herself to be inherently, irremediably wicked. Evil. When I asked her, did she believe Jesus to be good, she affirmed – oh yes, most certainly. So I explained how in the Eucharist Jesus comes right into us, becomes part of us as we eat the bread of his broken body and drink the wine of his blood, to remember him. We invite him in. And where such light, such goodness, comes in, evil is driven out. I asked her, would she like to make her Communion and share with me in the Eucharist. She responded with a heartfelt "Yes". So we broke and ate the bread and shared the cup of wine in her small, austere hospital room. And after that she was well again.

Questions

- What is the experience of making your Communion like for you? Does it feel important and special, or just a regular church event? Some people find it boring because it can be more formal than non-Communion services. How about you? If it doesn't feel very special to you, what might make it feel more meaningful?
- Can you think of an occasion when you attended a really wonderful Eucharist? What happened?
- In many churches, participating in the Eucharist is open only to church members (of all denominations or just those of that particular church); in others it is open to seekers as well. Often, children may not participate. How do you feel about those rules? Should there be rules about participation, and, if so, what should they be?

Prayer

Thank you, Jesus, for your great love. Thank you for coming to be with us, for sharing life with us, for dying our death, and for opening a new and living way for us to cross into the presence of God. Help us by your grace to enter fully into the mystery of your love, to be made whole by becoming one with you, and to be remade and renewed as we remember you. Amen.

Eucharist 2[3]

BIBLE PASSAGES

Acts 2:44–47, TLB

And all the believers met together constantly and shared everything with each other, selling their possessions and dividing with those in need. They worshiped together regularly at the Temple each day, met in small groups in homes for Communion, and shared their meals with great joy and thankfulness, praising God.

1 Corinthians 11:20–22, TLB

When you come together to eat, it isn't the Lord's Supper you are eating, but your own. For I am told that everyone hastily gobbles all the food he can without waiting to share with the others, so that one doesn't get enough and goes hungry while another has too much to drink and gets drunk. What? Is this really true? Can't you do your eating and drinking at home to avoid disgracing the church and shaming those who are poor and can bring no food? What am I supposed to say about these things? Do you want me to praise you? Well, I certainly do not!

1 John 4:20, TLB

If anyone says "I love God," but keeps on hating his brother, he is a liar; for if he doesn't love his brother who is right there in front of him, how can he love God whom he has never seen?

Luke 24:28–31, TLB

By this time they were nearing Emmaus and the end of their journey. Jesus would have gone on, but they begged him to stay the night with them, as it was getting late. So he went home with them. As they sat down to eat, he asked God's blessing on the food and then took a small loaf of bread and broke it and was passing it over to them, when suddenly – it was as though their eyes were opened – they recognized him!

Commentary

Our Bible passages bring out the Eucharist as not just a ritual but a way of life. It's the wellspring of being family, belonging to one another, being the community of love Jesus died to bring to birth.

---

3   For further study, see also "The Body of Christ" in the section of *100 Stand Alone Bible Studies* called "John".

The opening chapters of Acts show us a group of people living in freedom and generosity, sharing everything, with no needy people among them. By contrast, Paul speaks sharply to the Corinthians about a haughty and competitive spirit developing – wanting to be right, take precedence, get in first, grab the best.

John, in his letter, avers that it's simply impossible to enter the mystery of God and become one with him while simultaneously despising and detesting one's human brothers and sisters. And, in Luke's story of the road to Emmaus, it is when the two disciples invite their new friend to stay the night with them and share their evening meal that they find Christ revealed in the stranger they met on the road.

The word "eucharist" means thanksgiving. The word "communion" means one-with. The inward and invisible grace of this sacred moment, this *mysterion*, has to do with accepting vulnerability. As we meet intimately with the presence of Jesus and allow his broken body to be the healing of our broken lives and souls, so we are set free to live from his unconditional love in our relationships with one another. As the power of the Eucharist ripples out in ever-widening circles, we realize its implications for our family lives, the kind of neighbours we are, and our national and international political relationships. Our attitudes to the poor, those living with illness and disability, those fleeing from war zones and seeking refuge, must all proceed from this central Eucharistic mystery: Christ in our midst. We are to receive but also to *become* the body of Christ, the Eucharist.

Questions

- If we liberate the Eucharist from its context as a religious ritual, into a wider understanding of healing communion between people, can you think of an occasion in your life with the characteristics of Eucharist – humility, vulnerability, acceptance, understanding, and healing? Take a moment to think back and find such a rare and precious instance.

- Many Christians strongly believe we should keep politics out of religion. What are your feelings about that? If we do try to separate those two aspects of our life, in what ways should we express our faith as a Eucharistic community in the sphere of citizenship?

- The church is a very quarrelsome family. Is this a matter for shame or a sign of health – inclusiveness? What part could Eucharistic worship play in helping to bring healing and understanding to those currently opposed to one another in what is meant to be a communion of love and humility?

Prayer

Lord Jesus, must your body forever be broken, forever be nailed to the cross? We ask your forgiveness for the ways we, personally and individually, have contributed to your torture and death. We confess that sometimes we, too, have driven the nails home. Forgive us, for we did not know what we were doing. We could not possibly have known. Then, open our eyes, loving Lord, to see as you see. Give us the insight, the perspective of mercy and gentleness, that will bring healing and wholeness to the way we live every day. Amen.

Reconciliation 1

BIBLE PASSAGES

2 Corinthians 5:18–19, KJV

And all things are of God, who hath reconciled us to himself by Jesus Christ, and hath given to us the ministry of reconciliation; To wit, that God was in Christ, reconciling the world unto himself, not imputing their trespasses unto them; and hath committed unto us the word of reconciliation.

Psalm 32:5, RSV

I acknowledged my sin to thee,
    and I did not hide my iniquity;
I said, "I will confess my transgressions to the Lord";
    then thou didst forgive the guilt of my sin.

Acts 3:19, NIVUK

Repent, then, and turn to God, so that your sins may be wiped out, that times of refreshing may come from the Lord ...

James 5:16, NIVUK

Therefore confess your sins to each other and pray for each other so that you may be healed.

Commentary

How wise and how beautiful it is that the confession and forgiveness of sins should be identified as one of the sacred moments of the church. That word, "absolution" (its roots are Latin – *ab* = "from" and *solvere* = "loosen"), means the detachment, setting free, from sin. Some of the church's sacred moments are milestones, not intended to be repeated – baptism, confirmation, marriage, ordination. The others – reconciliation, the Eucharist, and the anointing of the sick – are part of the week-by-week rhythm of the church's life, to be both administered as needed and integrated into the ordinary pattern of the Christian way, humbly admitting our need of one another and of God.

At various times and in a number of congregations in church history, confession of sin has been a semi-public affair. In the Catholic (and Anglican) Church, confession is made to a priest who represents both the community and the authority of Christ. But some Christian groups practise open confession of sin to one another, and John Wesley encouraged this within the small-group structure of the Methodist society. He laid down that at every such meeting the following four questions be addressed: What known sins have you committed since our last meeting? What temptations have you met with? How were you delivered? What have you thought, said, or done, of which you doubt whether it be sin or not?

Dietrich Bonhoeffer regarded confession to one another as essential. He says, "In confession the breakthrough to community takes place."[4] He describes sin as isolating, bringing loneliness. He speaks of fellowships of the pious where everyone keeps up the appearance of goodness, making sure their sin is hidden. He says, "Many Christians are unthinkably horrified when a real sinner is discovered among the righteous. So we remain alone with our sin, living in lies and hypocrisy. The fact is we are sinners!"

The world of politics shows us how destructive of trust and community lies and lack of transparency can be. The Christian practice of confession and absolution, in the sacred moment of reconciliation, not only restores our peace and our relationship with God but is instrumental in building honest and wholesome community.

Questions

- How do you feel about confessing sins? Would you be comfortable confessing to a pastoral leader? How about making regular confession in a small group? What can you identify as the positive aspects, and what drawbacks can you think of? Why do you think confession, once a common practice in various Christian groups, is now mostly no longer practised?

- Can you think of a time when – as an adult or as a child – you owned up to doing something wrong and felt better as a result?

- In some families they practise what is called the "unqualified apology", where instead of saying "I'm sorry I burnt the dinner, but you distracted me by asking me to help bring the logs in", you say simply, "I'm sorry I burnt the dinner". No "but". People report that this greatly improves the quality of their relationships. What has been your experience of apologizing or being apologized to? When did it go well and when not? Why do you think that was?

Prayer

Father, we rely on the steadiness of your love and forgiveness. So often we stumble and fall, leaving ourselves no option but to ask you for another chance, a new start.

---

4   Dietrich Bonhoeffer, *Life Together*, first published by Christian Kaiser Verlag in 1939.

In our dealings with one another, give us the grace to learn from you. Help us to be humble in contrition and generous with others who have messed things up. For we ask it in the name of Jesus, friend of sinners. Amen.

Reconciliation 2[5]

BIBLE PASSAGES

John 17:20–23, NIVUK

"I pray ... for those who will believe in me ... that all of them may be one, Father, just as you are in me and I am in you. May they also be in us so that the world may believe that you have sent me. I have given them the glory that you gave me, that they may be one as we are one – I in them and you in me – so that they may be brought to complete unity. Then the world will know that you sent me and have loved them even as you have loved me."

Ephesians 2:14, NRSVA[6]

For he is our peace; in his flesh he has made both groups into one and has broken down the dividing wall, that is, the hostility between us.

1 John 1:5–10, RSV

God is light and in him is no darkness at all. If we say we have fellowship with him while we walk in darkness, we lie and do not live according to the truth; but if we walk in the light, as he is in the light, we have fellowship with one another, and the blood of Jesus his Son cleanses us from all sin. If we say we have no sin, we deceive ourselves, and the truth is not in us. If we confess our sins, he is faithful and just, and will forgive our sins and cleanse us from all unrighteousness.

Commentary

A wise woman[7] once said, "Reconciliation can be initiated in an instant. It's also a process." Do you see a repeating theme emerging as we consider our sacred moments? We touch them in the mysteries of specific liturgical occasions and life events, but that's just the tip of the iceberg. Attached to the mysteries encountered in sacred moments is the transformation of day-to-day living. With baptism we die to self and rise to Christ, and this will manifest in a life made new – not a reversion to old habits. With the Eucharist we make our communion with God through

---

5   For further study, see "His work of reconciliation" in the section of *100 Stand-Alone Bible Studies* called "Learning from the life of Jesus".

6   See also Romans 5:9–11.

7   Alice Wilcock, 2010, quoted in the frontispiece of *The Hardest Thing to Do* by Penelope Wilcock, published by Lion Fiction in 2015.

Christ's broken body and shed blood, and find that the ripples of this union and identification flow into every aspect of our lives, constituting a calling to live as a holy people belonging to one another.

So, with reconciliation, we see that its implications extend beyond the sacred moment of confession and absolution. That is an unconditional gift like all God's grace, but it doesn't make sense, it isn't properly activated, until it is expressed in reconciliation with one another *in ongoing relationship* – the dismantling of barriers of distrust and suspicion that divide us.

What about wise boundaries and toxic relationships? Well, reconciliation is a mystery, not a business merger. To wish another well with all one's heart, to seek their good not their harm, to protect their real interests, to do them no ill and speak no ill of them – these foster reconciliation and bear the seeds of peace. But some relationships are better protected by silence and distance than by proximity. Some individuals are so deeply scarred and their perspective is so dangerously awry that one cannot be the person to bring them God's embrace. Even so, within the scope of mystery's depth and breadth, we are one with them because Christ has brought us together by his death. For now, we may have to travel different roads, but our common journey is into the heart of God; to get there we must cross the bridge and pass along the way that Christ has opened. We are, in every real sense, one.

Questions

- Where (or what) is your true community? With whom are your heart's roots? How did that come about? What brought you and bound you together? What fostered the closeness? How did you overcome the differences and divides?

- Can you tell us about a time when you had to really work at a relationship? Where something so serious happened that a rift divided you, but it was healed. What happened?

- Are there any relationships in your life where you have just had to agree to differ and go your separate ways? How do you feel about those divisions? What did you do to make things as peaceful and kind as they could be? Do you think there are any final touches of healing you'd like to apply?

Prayer

God of love, we dare do no less than add our "Amen" to the heart cry of Jesus – that we might be one with him, with you, and with one another – so that the whole world might believe and be drawn into this communion of love. Transform us, Lord, by your indwelling Spirit, that this miracle may come about in our hearts and lives. Amen.

Confirmation 1

BIBLE PASSAGES

Jeremiah 31:29–31, NIVUK

In those days people will no longer say,

"The parents have eaten sour grapes, and the children's teeth are set on edge."

Instead, everyone will die for their own sin; whoever eats sour grapes – their own teeth will be set on edge.

"The days are coming," declares the Lord, "when I will make a new covenant with the people of Israel and with the people of Judah."

1 Corinthians 13:11, NRSVA

When I was a child, I spoke like a child, I thought like a child, I reasoned like a child; when I became an adult, I put an end to childish ways.

Mark 8:27–29, RSV

And Jesus went on with his disciples, to the villages of Caesarea Philippi; and on the way he asked his disciples, "Who do men say that I am?" And they told him, "John the Baptist; and others say, Elijah; and others one of the prophets." And he asked them, "But who do you say that I am?" Peter answered him, "You are the Christ."

2 Timothy 1:5–6, NRSVA

I am reminded of your sincere faith, a faith that lived first in your grandmother Lois and your mother Eunice and now, I am sure, lives in you. For this reason I remind you to rekindle the gift of God that is within you through the laying on of my hands...

Commentary

Confirmation is one of the sacred moments of the Orthodox and Catholic Churches, and an important step of faith formation in the Anglican Church. Because John Wesley was to his life's end an Anglican, Methodists traditionally have Reception into Membership (of "the Society", not of "the Church") as their equivalent, but have begun to call this "Confirmation" in recent decades. Lutherans have "Affirmation of Baptism", Presbyterians have "Confirmation", and the URC has "Re-affirmation of Baptism & Admission to Church Membership". Those churches that practise adult baptism have no need of a separate service of confirmation.

So, even in the denominations practising infant baptism, there is a common recognition of the necessity for a further profession of faith before entering church membership. It is a serious matter, nothing is assumed, and Christian faith has to be personal and individual. It is a living, heart-to-heart relationship with Jesus, a step of personal commitment. Being part of the faith community is a Christian essential, but so is each member's own profession of faith. Following the crowd is not enough.

In the Old Testament, tribal belonging within the people of God was the key. "Son of Abraham" could mean "Isaac" or "Ishmael", but could equally mean any of the children of Israel in every age. So sin was also a communal matter – and could be inherited.[8] The doctrine of the fall relies on this concept – that the consequences of Adam and Eve's choices pass on to succeeding generations.

So our verse from Jeremiah represents a break from traditional thinking; a time to come when a person would no longer inherit blessing or curse, but when all must stand on their own feet and take individual responsibility for their faithfulness.

This comes into sharp focus as Jesus asks his disciples, first, "Who are other people saying I am?" – then, "But who do *you* say I am?"

The passage from Timothy is above all the foundational text for the church's tradition of confirmation, incorporating the three elements of development within the faith community under the wing of others, stepping into personal profession of faith, and laying on of hands by a church leader to receive the Holy Spirit.

So, though the tradition of confirmation is not biblical as such, its spirit and its logic are congruent with biblical teaching.

Questions

- If you have come to a definite personal faith in God, can you pinpoint the time that happened, or did it come gradually? What about faith in Jesus? Did that come to you separately or at the same time? Were you confirmed? If so, how old were you; what do you remember about it? Did you feel different? If you were not confirmed, what comparable step of faith did you make, at what age? If you have never undertaken such a step, what are your reasons? Are you unsure about what you believe, or do you disagree with some things the church asks you to believe, or have you never been invited to take such a step, or … ?

- How do you believe the Holy Spirit comes into a person? Do you have to ask? Does there have to be laying on of hands by a church leader?[9] Do you feel confident that you have received the Holy Spirit?

- What do you think of the possibility of further steps of commitment – renewing the promises of faith either on a regular basis or after a time of struggle and doubt?

---

8 See Psalm 51:5; Numbers 14:18; Exodus 20:5; Genesis 3:13.

9 You might like to look up Acts 10:44–46.

Prayer

Faithful God, you were in Jesus calling us to follow and showing us the way. Send your Holy Spirit into our hearts to fill us with your grace, your love, truth, and power. Help us to live what we believe; give us insight into the deeper spirituality that lies behind the complexities of human society and material being. For we ask it in Jesus' name. Amen.

Confirmation 2[10]

BIBLE PASSAGES

Acts 1:8, RSV

"You shall receive power when the Holy Spirit has come upon you; and you shall be my witnesses in Jerusalem and in all Judea and Samaria and to the end of the earth."

Isaiah 6:8, RSV

And I heard the voice of the Lord saying, "Whom shall I send, and who will go for us?" Then I said, "Here am I! Send me."

1 John 1:1–3, RSV

That which was from the beginning, which we have heard, which we have seen with our eyes, which we have looked upon and touched with our hands, concerning the word of life – the life was made manifest, and we saw it, and testify to it, and proclaim to you the eternal life which was with the Father and was made manifest to us – that which we have seen and heard we proclaim also to you, so that you may have fellowship with us; and our fellowship is with the Father and with his Son Jesus Christ.

Matthew 5:13–16, ESV

"You are the salt of the earth, but if salt has lost its taste, how shall its saltiness be restored? It is no longer good for anything except to be thrown out and trampled under people's feet.

"You are the light of the world. A city set on a hill cannot be hidden. Nor do people light a lamp and put it under a basket, but on a stand, and it gives light to all in the house. In the same way, let your light shine before others, so that they may see your good works and give glory to your Father who is in heaven."

Commentary

Their critics often complain that modern devotional songs express a "Jesus and me" mentality – an insular attitude turning away from faith worked out in community in favour of a closed capsule of private religion.

---

10 For further study, see "Bearing witness" in the section of *100 Stand-Alone Bible Studies* called "Walking in the light".

The thing is, you need both. Christianity starved of the heart's prayer and adoration, a social club-cum-welfare organization, misses the mark just as much.

In the sacred moment of confirmation, the recognition of these two aspects – personal commitment lived out as community engagement – comes together.

It's like a tree, hidden roots growing down into the depths balancing the aerial parts, maintaining a constant equilibrium of give and take, absorbing and emitting the nutrients that sustain life.

Mature faith accepts responsibility both for its hidden and mystical aspects (the life of prayer and thankfulness, daily walking in step with the risen Christ) and for its testimony (engagement with the body of believers and the wider world).

The sacred moment of confirmation builds the bridge between private faith and public witness. It is an opportunity to stand up and be counted, to nail one's colours to the mast, to say both "This is who I am" and "This is what I believe". In so doing, the new church member shares something of her-/himself and also something of Christ.

What is true of the other sacred moments also applies to confirmation: that this encounter with God starts at the centre, at the heart, from there to spread in widening ripples of influence to bear witness in every sphere of the Christian's life – personal, relational, professional, and civic.

When I, in my teens, attended the baptisms of school friends, as each dripping individual stepped from the baptistery, the congregation would sing, "Be thou faithful unto death, and I will give thee a crown of life." A sign that these sacred moments are glorious milestones, but the road leads onward; they are not a destination.

Questions

- Can you think of times in your life when faith impelled you to take a stand? Why did you make that choice? What happened?
- What do you think about the practice of church members sharing personal testimony in the context of public worship? How might this be built in to the worship of more formal styles of church?
- If you speak to, say, a Baptist about your "testimony", they may assume you mean your story – the narrative of your Christian experience. Quakers mean something quite different: the Quaker testimonies (Truth, Peace, Equality, Simplicity) are about living in such a way as to bear witness to certain eternal values. In what areas are you particularly working on achieving congruence between the faith you profess and the life you live, just now?

Prayer

You, O God, are beyond our comprehension, your mystery too deep for our minds to fathom. And yet you come to dwell in the human heart, and we call you Father. God of love, take up residence in our hearts, influence our choices, direct our lives. May your light shine in us and through us, bringing comfort, hope, and truth to a world that needs you so. Amen.

Marriage 1

BIBLE PASSAGES

Matthew 19:3-9, NRSVA

Some Pharisees came to him, and to test him they asked, "Is it lawful for a man to divorce his wife for any cause?'" He answered, "Have you not read that the one who made them at the beginning 'made them male and female', and said, 'For this reason a man shall leave his father and mother and be joined to his wife, and the two shall become one flesh'? So they are no longer two, but one flesh. Therefore what God has joined together, let no one separate." They said to him, "Why then did Moses command us to give a certificate of dismissal and to divorce her?" He said to them, "It was because you were so hard-hearted that Moses allowed you to divorce your wives, but at the beginning it was not so. And I say to you, whoever divorces his wife, except for unchastity, and marries another commits adultery."[11]

Hebrews 13:4, GNB

Marriage is to be honored by all, and husbands and wives must be faithful to each other. God will judge those who are immoral and those who commit adultery.

Commentary[12]

Marriage, like the other sacred moments of the church, implies a lifetime of faithfulness. The special day, the wedding vows, the joining of hands, and giving of rings are holy indeed – but they are only the beginning.

In our marriage vows, we commit ourselves completely to one another, for life. It is meant to be for ever. But things sometimes go wrong, don't they?

When we turn to the Bible for guidance, it's important to understand the context and meaning of its teaching.

In Old Testament times, divorce was allowed (men divorcing women or vice versa) for any of four reasons: adultery, and neglect of food, clothing, or love. The rabbis made detailed definitions of these grounds for divorce, but they were basically twofold – failure in duty to provide emotional or physical support.

Shortly before the life of Jesus, these four causes fell into abeyance, superseded by a catch-all "any-cause" basis for divorce, deriving from Deuteronomy 24:1,

---

11 See also Mark 10:2-12; 1 Corinthians 7:1-16; and Exodus 21:10-11.
12 The following online article is also highly recommended for considering this issue: http://www.instonebrewer.com/divorceremarriage/Articles/WhitefieldBriefing.htm

where divorce for "a cause of indecency" is allowed. Pharisees argued that though this originally meant adultery, in effect it could be anything. So divorce became very easy – and was for "any cause" at all. Burnt toast. Singing off-key. By the time of Jesus, "divorce" effectively meant "divorce for any cause".

So when Jesus was asked if he supported "divorce for any cause", and he said no, he didn't mean that he never supported divorce on any grounds whatsoever. He meant that he didn't support divorce with no good grounds.

Even though divorce in our modern society is so easy, for Christians looking to the Bible for guidance it is important to understand this.

The Bible does not require us to stay in a marriage characterized by neglect, abuse, or unfairness, certainly not in a violent marriage, and not where there has been adultery. But the Bible does see marriage as a serious commitment, and expects us to do our very best to make it a lifelong relationship of mutual faithfulness, kindness, and love.

Questions

- What do you think about prenuptial contracts, setting out division of assets and guardianship should the marriage fail?
- If you have been divorced, or experienced divorce in your family, what are your feelings about it? Do you think divorce is always a bad thing?
- What do you think about the idea of a Christian ceremony of parting, when a marriage ends in divorce? What positive aspects of such a ceremony can you identify? What would you put in it if you were planning it?

Prayer

Father, we pray for those known to us who are struggling with fractured and failing family relationships. Give us sensitivity and imagination in our dealings with them. Help us to listen, to support where we can, and to refrain from inflaming unhappiness by taking sides.

We pray for children scarred by quarrelling and broken homes, for children used to hurt, estranged partners or forced to choose between two beloved parents.

We pray for couples counsellors, for mediation services, for judges who decide on the division of assets and guardianship.

Give wisdom to those who desperately need it, patience and understanding to those maligned and hurt, comfort and a safe refuge to the little children. Teach us your ways, O Lord, of kindness and humility; impress them on our hearts and souls, and on our daily habits. For we ask it in Jesus' name. Amen.

Marriage 2[13]

BIBLE PASSAGE

Ephesians 5:22–25, 28–33, NRSVA

> Wives, be subject to your husbands as you are to the Lord. For the husband is
> the head of the wife just as Christ is the head of the church, the body of which
> he is the Saviour. Just as the church is subject to Christ, so also wives ought to
> be, in everything, to their husbands.
>
> Husbands, love your wives, just as Christ loved the church and gave himself up
> for her ... In the same way, husbands should love their wives as they do their own
> bodies. He who loves his wife loves himself. For no one ever hates his own body,
> but he nourishes and tenderly cares for it, just as Christ does for the church,
> because we are members of his body. "For this reason a man will leave his father
> and mother and be joined to his wife, and the two will become one flesh." This
> is a great mystery, and I am applying it to Christ and the church. Each of you,
> however, should love his wife as himself, and a wife should respect her husband.

Commentary

Our Bible passage is not easy reading for people in modern Western culture.
The struggle for gender equality, and against rape culture, has been lengthy and
turbulent. In such a context, what can this passage teach us?

As to the equality of the sexes, anyone who reads the New Testament in the
light of its contemporary culture cannot but be struck by how much it stands up
for women and insists they be treated not as chattels but as people. In our passage
from Ephesians, Paul delivers first the predictable teaching: "Wives, be subject to
your husbands as you are to the Lord." One can imagine this being well received.
He goes further: "For the husband is the head of the wife just as Christ is the head
of the church". One can imagine heads nodding – "Quite right!"

But, as he expounds on this, the implications become clear. To be someone's
head in the sense that Christ is head of the church means laying down your life for
her. "I am among you as one who serves,"[14] said Jesus of his lordship; and "For the
Son of Man came not to be served but to serve."[15]

---

13 For further study, see "His attitude to women" in the "Learning from the life of Jesus"
section, and "Esther" in the "Tell me about it!" section of *100 Stand-Alone Bible Studies*.
14 Luke 22:27, NIV.
15 Mark 10:45, NRSVA.

Paul's prescription for good marriage is mutual service characterized by gentleness, humility, and a willingness to accept responsibility. It is a recipe for domestic peace.

It has been argued that in a marriage, where difference of opinion seems irreconcilable, one of the couple must hold the casting vote – making leadership, or "headship", necessary. Paul's recommendation for mutual submission and willingness to take the lowest place points to a different way. An Ephesians 5 marriage gives each spouse the opportunity to strengthen discipleship in fostering gentle humility of attitude and a servant spirit.

Jesus' Golden Rule of doing unto others as you would have them do unto you[16] encourages the same approach. In the end a marriage is simply two people learning to love, living together with all their human frailty. Expectations, social conditioning, hormones, health issues, financial concerns, responsibility, family issues, bereavements, work-related issues, sexual attraction to others – within a marriage a couple may face all kinds of pressures, sometimes all at once. Each marriage is unique; it's unrealistic to expect a formula for consistent happiness, not least because people sometimes change. In the end, perhaps all one can conclude is that any marriage benefits from always practising courtesy and kindness, and all adversity can be softened by the compassion of a true friend.

Questions

- What do you feel about gender equality – in marriage, society, church, and the workplace? Do you feel comfortable with equality in leadership? Do you personally prefer a female or a male boss or church leader? Why?
- If you are married, what life lessons learned from your marriage would you like to share? If you are not married, what have you learned about life and marriage from the home in which you grew up?
- Because of increasing divorce and longer lives, many marriages now are between older couples. What do you think are the advantages and disadvantages of a marriage begun in mature years? Are there any different needs for a mature couple?

Prayer

O Lord, you have shown us how to live together in harmony. We see in the life of Jesus that love takes courage, leadership is expressed in humility, and peace is forged from forgiveness, acceptance, and understanding. May your Spirit shine so bright in our fellowship, our homes, and our daily lives that our witness is beautiful and draws people closer to you. May they see your light quietly shining in us. Amen.

---

16 Matthew 7:12.

Ordination 1

BIBLE PASSAGES

Mark 1:16–18,[17] GNB

As Jesus walked along the shore of Lake Galilee, he saw two fishermen, Simon and his brother Andrew, catching fish with a net. Jesus said to them, "Come with me, and I will teach you to catch people." At once they left their nets and went with him.

Mark 3:13–15, GNB

Then Jesus went up a hill and called to himself the men he wanted. They came to him, and he chose twelve, whom he named apostles. "I have chosen you to be with me," he told them. "I will also send you out to preach, and you will have authority to drive out demons."

Acts 1:21–26, GNB

[Replacing Judas Iscariot. Peter addresses a large gathering of the faithful]
"So then, someone must join us as a witness to the resurrection of the Lord Jesus. He must be one of the men who were in our group during the whole time that the Lord Jesus traveled about with us, beginning from the time John preached his message of baptism until the day Jesus was taken up from us to heaven."
So they proposed two men: Joseph, who was called Barsabbas (also known as Justus), and Matthias. Then they prayed, "Lord, you know the thoughts of everyone, so show us which of these two you have chosen to serve as an apostle in the place of Judas, who left to go to the place where he belongs." Then they drew lots to choose between the two men, and the one chosen was Matthias, who was added to the group of eleven apostles.

Commentary

The sacred moment of ordination to church leadership comes after a lengthy selection process followed by years of formation for ministry – a solemn occasion indeed. Candidates for ministry undergo thorough psychological and medical checks, police checks, rigorous vetting of their theological reading habits, and questioning about their outlook and attitudes, family commitments, and service to the church community. A minister of the church is trusted and respected within the faith community, but also beyond it as its representative. Revelations of child abuse and other moral failings have made our selection procedures ever more cautious.

17 See also verses 19–20.

It seems a world away from the church in its infancy, men leaving their nets to follow Jesus, choosing leaders by drawing lots – though among Amish[18] groups today the choice of church leaders by drawing lots is still followed; to discourage those chosen from pride, and to emphasize trust in God's guidance.

The sacred moment of ordination involves anointing and laying on of hands, according to biblical tradition.[19] Prayer with fasting is also mentioned in connection with ordination.[20] What is absent from the biblical narrative, and prominent in the modern church, is training. Perhaps they lived with a greater consensus of thought, and grew up in a more unified culture, than we do in the modern world. Though they travelled more than we sometimes think, social communities were more stable and rooted. Maybe their vetting procedure did not have to be institutionalized because they really knew one another from long association.

Questions

- Write down, to share with the group, a list of ten characteristics you look for in a church leader, in order of priority. Share the top three in the group, then go on to share the rest. What were your reasons, both for identifying the characteristics and for the order of priority?

- How is the leading of the Holy Spirit expressed through our selection and training process? If someone feels called by God to ministry but the church turns that person down, how can we support them through their disappointment, and how might their sense of call best be channelled? What case could you make for doing church quite differently, dismantling the structures and traditions and going back to informal groupings meeting in the homes of the faithful? Would that be liberating, or would we slowly reassemble formal structures over time?

- Share your memories of church leaders who have inspired and blessed you. What did you especially admire in them? How have they changed your own faith practice?

Prayer

Holy Spirit of God, we ask you to bless all those who bear the responsibility of church leadership. May their lives bear the hallmarks of your presence. Uphold them in weariness or discouragement, inspire them, keep their feet in the path of eternal life; for we ask this in Jesus' holy name. Amen.

---

18 An Anabaptist group originating from Switzerland but now based in the US. Known for extreme simplicity and withdrawal from the world, the Amish travel by horse and buggy, work with their hands, dress in old-fashioned, simple clothes, and emphasize family values.
19 Numbers 8:10–11; 1 Timothy 5:22; Acts 6:6; Acts 13:3; etc.
20 E.g. Acts 14:23.

Ordination 2

BIBLE PASSAGES

Psalm 8:2–4, KJV

Out of the mouth of babes and sucklings hast thou ordained strength because of thine enemies, that thou mightest still the enemy and the avenger.
When I consider thy heavens, the work of thy fingers, the moon and the stars, which thou hast ordained; what is man, that thou art mindful of him? and the son of man, that thou visitest him?

Isaiah 26:12, KJV

Lord, thou wilt ordain peace for us: for thou also hast wrought all our works in us.

Jeremiah 1:5, KJV

Before I formed thee in the belly I knew thee; and before thou camest forth out of the womb I sanctified thee, and I ordained thee a prophet unto the nations.

John 15:16, KJV

Ye have not chosen me, but I have chosen you, and ordained you, that ye should go and bring forth fruit, and that your fruit should remain: that whatsoever ye shall ask of the Father in my name, he may give it you.

Acts 13:48, KJV

And when the Gentiles heard this, they were glad, and glorified the word of the Lord: and as many as were ordained to eternal life believed.

Commentary

The word "ordain" comes from the same Latin root as the words "ordinary" and "order" – they are all to do with appointing, disposing, setting in order, by and with authority: "So shall it be."

"Ordinary" (in the usual sense, not the liturgical) means "in the usual way or course of events".

There is a sense of authority and peace about both words. They imply a structure, a pattern, in which each of us has a place.

Our Bible passages are all taken from the King James Bible because in more modern translations the word "ordained" is often lost from the text. The old wording helps us to grasp the sense of life as having purpose and design. Looking through such a lens, we see that there is no division between "ordained people" and "ordinary people" – those words both come from the same root, and all created beings have their allocated and specific role ordained by God; even the stars.

Though there is value in formal recognition by an organization, it is always preceded by the call of God that arises in a person's soul. The church won't be ordaining you any time soon if you feel no calling. The ordination is the outward and visible sign of the inward and invisible grace of God's anointing; it's not a career.

We cannot divide people up into two groups – those who are called and those who aren't. As Richard Bach said,[21] "Here is the test to find whether your mission on Earth is finished: if you're alive, it isn't."

The question is not "Are you an ordained person or not?" but "To what has God ordained you?"

Frederick Buechner[22] put it like this: "The place God calls you to is the place where your deep gladness and the world's deep hunger meet." This is the work to which you are ordained. This is the work concerning which Christ will one day say, "Well done, good and faithful servant."[23] Its wonder is that it's like the spring of living water arising naturally from the ground of your being – it's what you were made to do. The church may or may not have a special ceremony to ratify what God is asking of your life. Some of us will never have a certificate to hang on the wall; our vocations remain in the wild. Even so, like the stars, you are ordained. What is your calling, your gift?

Questions

- Sometimes it's easier to recognize unique gifting in others than in ourselves. Take a few minutes to write down, for each person in the group (or, if you are by yourself, each person in your family), what you think is his or her unique contribution. Where do they shine?

- Do you think you are doing what you were born to do? Is there anything that you feel called or drawn to study or undertake, but you haven't had the chance or the courage? If you feel you are on the right path, what could support that at the present time? What is the next step for you?

- What do you think of the idea of a church ceremony for ordination for all people – a special occasion where, each person having discerned their gift and calling, they receive laying on of hands and ordination to that work? How could the discernment process be organized to protect the inspiration of the occasion from becoming trivial guesswork?

---

21 Richard Bach, *The Adventures of a Reluctant Messiah*, published by Arrow Books in 1998.
22 Frederick Buechner, *Wishful Thinking: A Seeker's ABC*, published by Mowbray in1994.
23 Matthew 25:21, KJV.

Prayer

O Lord my God, you have called me and ordained me. I am not here by accident. I have a job to do and a responsibility to fulfil. Speak to me; call me by name. Let me not miss the special calling you have for my life. Let me not die without completing the work you ordained me for in this world. May I be faithful; in Jesus' name. Amen.

Anointing the Sick

BIBLE PASSAGES

James 5:14-16, NIVUK

Is anyone among you ill? Let them call the elders of the church to pray over them and anoint them with oil in the name of the Lord. And the prayer offered in faith will make the sick person well; the Lord will raise them up. If they have sinned, they will be forgiven. Therefore confess your sins to each other and pray for each other so that you may be healed.

Mark 6:13, NIVUK

They drove out many demons and anointed with oil many people who were ill and healed them.

2 Corinthians 12:8-9, NIVUK

Three times I pleaded with the Lord to take it away from me. But he said to me, "My grace is sufficient for you, for my power is made perfect in weakness." Therefore I will boast all the more gladly about my weaknesses, so that Christ's power may rest on me.

Matthew 26:39, NIVUK

Going a little farther, he fell with his face to the ground and prayed, "My Father, if it is possible, may this cup be taken from me. Yet not as I will, but as you will."

Commentary

The principal Bible foundation for the church's tradition of the anointing of the sick is our passage from James. This offers the clear expectation and intention of recovery: "the prayer offered in faith will make the sick person well; the Lord will raise them up."

Both in the Bible and in all the hundreds of years since it was compiled, many witnesses have borne testimony to sick people being healed by the power of the Holy Spirit in the name of Jesus. Yes, it works.

But to say so and leave it there would tell only half the story, because everyone who has been involved in healing ministry can also tell of many instances where the faithful prayed for the sick person but saw no recovery. Sometimes, subsidiary ailments or troubles clear up, but the main problem persists. This is not necessarily because the prayer was ill-formed or the sick person (or those who prayed) had insufficient faith.

John Wimber, that great US preacher who pioneered work in signs and wonders, and saw people healed in thousands, eventually died from cancer – as did his English friend David Watson, another man with a powerful Holy Spirit ministry.

Why the healing we hope for does not always happen, we don't understand. What we know for sure is that sometimes it does, that prayer helps every situation, that God can make even suffering an occasion of blessing, that God loves us and is with us in all circumstances of life, and that anointing the sick for healing is scriptural – so we do it.

Our study passages remind us *both* that God's power is shown among us in healing *and* that sometimes (as the Mark passage about Jesus in Gethsemane shows) the way of faith for us as individuals is not to be lifted out of adversity but to travel through it, trusting in God no matter what.

We bear in mind that in Jesus lies our salvation – a word that essentially means "healing"; he is the salve for our wounded souls. Christian ministry addresses physical conditions, and the work of the church has always included social and medical care; yet we are clear on the root of it, which is the Holy Spirit of Jesus at work in our souls. We turn to him to be made whole.

Questions

- Do you have any experience of God's healing? What happened? Does your church practise any specific kind of healing ministry? Describe it. How helpful do people find it?

- The awkward thing about prayer for healing is that sometimes nothing seems to change. This can create disappointment, a sense of inadequacy, or a feeling that God doesn't care about this particular person. Imagine you are planning a service with an element of healing ministry. How would you word the description and the prayers, so as both to encourage faith in divine healing and keep faith intact when miracles don't happen?

- There are many kinds of healing – spiritual, emotional, relational, and physical. There is also social healing – bringing peace to the wounds of the world. What types of healing does your church do best, and where are there gaps at the moment?

Prayer

Beloved Jesus, healer of man and nature, in your death on the cross you healed the divide between humanity and heaven; you healed the rift in the heart of creation. Heal us, Jesus, we pray – of our hidden wounds and secret sins, of our poisonous thoughts and pathological attitudes. Heal us and set us free. Anoint us with your free Spirit, give to us the joy of your salvation, so that we may be your agents of healing in a suffering and broken world. Amen.

Extreme Unction[24]

BIBLE PASSAGES

Romans 8:35–39, NIVUK

Who shall separate us from the love of Christ? Shall trouble or hardship or persecution or famine or nakedness or danger or sword? As it is written: "For your sake we face death all day long; we are considered as sheep to be slaughtered." No, in all these things we are more than conquerors through him who loved us. For I am convinced that neither death nor life, neither angels nor demons, neither the present nor the future, nor any powers, neither height nor depth, nor anything else in all creation, will be able to separate us from the love of God that is in Christ Jesus our Lord.

Acts 7:55–56, TLB

Stephen, full of the Holy Spirit, gazed steadily upward into heaven and saw the glory of God and Jesus standing at God's right hand. And he told them, "Look, I see the heavens opened and Jesus the Messiah standing beside God, at his right hand!"

Hebrews 12:1–2a, TLB

Since we have such a huge crowd of men of faith watching us from the grandstands, let us strip off anything that slows us down or holds us back, and especially those sins that wrap themselves so tightly around our feet and trip us up; and let us run with patience the particular race that God has set before us.

Keep your eyes on Jesus, our leader and instructor.

Commentary

The sacred moment called Extreme Unction is the anointing of the sick who, because of frailty, old age, or the nature of their illness, are likely to die. In the Catholic Church, the Anointing of the Sick and Extreme Unction are the same. The priest is called to anoint the sick when it seems possible that they may die. If it is certain that they will die soon, Extreme Unction (the Anointing of the Sick) is part of the Last Rites, along with the sacred moments of Reconciliation (confession of, and absolution from, sin) and the Eucharist.

24 For further study, see also "A Certain Hope: Ordinary Time 2" in the section of *100 Stand-Alone Bible Studies* called "Tracing the circle of the church's year".

In the Catholic Church, therefore, Extreme Unction (the Anointing of the Sick) is not so much intended to cure the sick person – though Catholics certainly believe in miracles – but more focused on healing the soul of all infirmity in preparation for leaving this world and entering eternal life.

I have separated Extreme Unction from the Anointing of the Sick in this book because in many congregations Anointing of the Sick is likely to be undertaken for any illness, so will not be synonymous with Extreme Unction (anointing people for the great healing of death rather than for simply getting better).

In the Bible, the Scriptures associated with anointing sick people focus on, and expect, recovery. Healing means physical healing, not death. Even so, our faith tradition is broad enough to encompass a vision of death as ultimate healing, and to see the place for anointing in preparation for the transition to our eternal home. There is room for us to include both regular prayer for healing, with anointing, for friends who are sick; and prayers for the dying, with anointing for healing from all clinging infirmity as they prepare to enter the presence of God.

Questions

- What has been your experience of death and dying? Have you seen people die? Was this a positive experience or upsetting? If you were asked to spend time with people who are dying, would you find that frightening or would you be quite comfortable with it? What are your feelings about death and dying in general?

- And what about your own death? Is this something to which you have given much thought, or do you avoid thinking about it? If you could choose how to die, what sort of death would you prefer? Might you opt for sudden death, or would you like time to say goodbye and finish off what you are doing here?

- Imagine your life was ending, and you were comfortable and peaceful in a hospice bed, free from pain. If you were offered the opportunity of prayers for the dying, would you like that or not? What would you like included, and who would you like to be present?

Prayer

Our times are in your hands, Father. Our days are your gift. It is in you we find healing and hope; it is by your presence and your Spirit we are made whole. Help us to walk every day looking steadfastly to Jesus. Help us to remain faithful to you whatever happens. And, when the day comes for us to leave this earth and turn again home, may death find us faithful and ready – true believers. For we ask it in Jesus' name. Amen.

25 For further study, see the section in *100 Stand-Alone Bible Studies* on "Walking in the light"
– about the character of a disciple.

Conversion 1

BIBLE PASSAGES

Ezekiel 36:25-27, NIVUK

I will sprinkle clean water on you, and you will be clean; I will cleanse you from all your impurities and from all your idols. I will give you a new heart and put a new spirit in you; I will remove from you your heart of stone and give you a heart of flesh. And I will put my Spirit in you and move you to follow my decrees and be careful to keep my laws.

Acts 3:19-21, NRSVA

Repent therefore, and turn to God so that your sins may be wiped out, so that times of refreshing may come from the presence of the Lord, and that he may send the Messiah appointed for you, that is, Jesus, who must remain in heaven until the time of universal restoration that God announced long ago through his holy prophets.

Isaiah 44:22, NIVUK

I have swept away your offences like a cloud,
    your sins like the morning mist.
Return to me,
    for I have redeemed you.

2 Chronicles 7:14, NIVUK

If my people, who are called by my name, will humble themselves and pray and seek my face and turn from their wicked ways, then I will hear from heaven, and I will forgive their sin and will heal their land.

Commentary

The question "When did you become a Christian?" can be surprisingly hard to answer. There are some, like Starr Daily, a violent criminal in solitary confinement, to whom God came sovereignly in the small bleak space of a prison cell, changing everything, bringing the beginning of love and hope. There are some like St Paul, to whom Christ appeared in a vision so dramatic and spectacular that it effected a complete turnaround. There are some visited by God or Jesus in their dreams – still, today, not just long ago – resulting in a whole new direction of faith.

For most people not brought up in a Christian home, conversion to faith in

Jesus starts through relationship. A person cannot help noticing the gentle and decent character of a new friend, their quietly persistent joy, their refusal to speak ill of others, the quality of their kindness. As the friendship continues, questions are asked and answered, curiosity develops, and the seeker starts out on the trail that leads to faith. Please note, this is a very different story from what is sometimes called "friendship evangelism", where religious people lure strangers into becoming friends with an undeclared agenda of converting them. That's not witness; it's a dodgy variety of salesmanship. Being drawn to faith through observing the life of a believer is a natural and honest form of evangelism.

But for many, many Christian people it is almost impossible to pinpoint a moment of conversion. Brought up in a Christian home, attending church in childhood, experiencing Christian school assemblies, the seeds of faith are sown early and germinate casually, gradually spreading and increasing.

Even then there can be surprises. When I worked as a school chaplain and taught Religious Education, I was once explaining to a class of twelve-year-olds the difference between opinions and facts – that faith statements belong to the class of "opinions" although they are regarded as facts. We went through the creed, picking out the faith statements (e.g. "He ascended into heaven") and comparing them with the facts ("He suffered under Pontius Pilate"). I explained that Jesus is one of the best-attested figures of the ancient world. When and where he lived is beyond reasonable doubt. A child put up her hand with a question: did I mean – was I saying – that Jesus actually existed? Twelve years old and in a Methodist school, and she had never so far grasped that Jesus – unlike Father Christmas or Jack Frost – was no mere legend. Helping people move beyond this surprise to the even bigger one that, because of the resurrection and ascension, Jesus is available to meet them in person whenever they are ready, is one of the most exciting privileges of evangelism.

Questions

- What do you believe about God, and about Jesus? Does the concept of "having a personal relationship with Jesus" describe what you feel and know – or do you feel uncertain about, or repelled by, the idea? Try to put into words the nature of your own spiritual perspective.

- Take a few minutes to jot down on a piece of paper, for sharing with the group, the people you have known (or who have influenced you from a distance) who have helped shape your spiritual outlook. Describe the difference they made to you.

- Take a moment to sketch out on a piece of paper the journey you made to faith. Where do you think it began? What were the milestones that led you to where you are now?

Prayer

O God, we can know you and love you, sense you near us, talk to you – and yet we will never fully understand you. Your immensity, your wonder, your power, your wisdom extend to depths of mystery our minds simply cannot fathom. Give us grace in every day of our lives to trust you, to get to know you better by travelling with you. Open our eyes and our hearts to the reality of personally knowing you. For we ask it in Jesus' name. Amen.

Conversion 2

BIBLE PASSAGES

Ephesians 4:22–24, GNB

So get rid of your old self, which made you live as you used to – the old self that was being destroyed by its deceitful desires. Your hearts and minds must be made completely new, and you must put on the new self, which is created in God's likeness and reveals itself in the true life that is upright and holy.

Deuteronomy 6:4–5, KJV[26]

Hear, O Israel: The Lord our God is one Lord: and thou shalt love the Lord thy God with all thine heart, and with all thy soul, and with all thy might.

Psalm 139:7–12, GNB[27]

Where could I go to escape from you?
   Where could I get away from your presence?
If I went up to heaven, you would be there;
   if I lay down in the world of the dead, you would be there.
If I flew away beyond the east
   or lived in the farthest place in the west,
you would be there to lead me,
   you would be there to help me.
I could ask the darkness to hide me
   or the light around me to turn into night,
but even darkness is not dark for you,
   and the night is as bright as the day.
Darkness and light are the same to you.

Commentary

Conversion to Christian faith is not instantaneous. It is a process of transformative discovery. There are other words for it in Christian vocabulary. It is also called "repentance", which means being sorry for wrongdoing and making a new start, and also means turning round to face in a new direction.

Another word for conversion is the Greek *metanoia*. Disconcertingly, this can refer to the whole experience of psychotic breakdown followed by healing

---

26 For further study on this text, see also the study "Putting God first" in *100 Stand-Alone Bible Studies*, in the section "Insights from the Law and the Prophets".
27 Looking up the whole psalm is recommended.

reconstruction of the personality. In the realm of faith, it means a complete change of heart, a new beginning. This is never a surface thing; it goes deep, it's profound. Earthworks of mammoth proportions.

So though undoubtedly there are people who come to faith and experience a change of heart in an instant, even for them the process of conversion cannot be accomplished all at once.

Salvation is already held out to us. God's love is given unconditionally. Whoever we are and whatever we've done, his arms are open wide for us – we can see this made terribly real when we gaze upon Jesus nailed to the cross, arms open wide, helpless, loving us that much. Accepting this love – saying yes – reciprocating by opening our hearts to him, this can be done in a moment. But the joy and the work of conversion are discovering that it is a multilayered experience. We may cry in glad affirmation, "Jesus is Lord!" without grasping all at once the loving humility, the courage and patience, the many times of falling down and starting again, that our joyous affirmation will require of us if it is to be real.

Questions

- Are there some aspects of Christian faith that you find it very hard to swallow even though you think they are important? Describe these – and also any parts of the faith that for a long time you couldn't come to terms with but now have.

- How important do you think feelings are in conversion of the heart? Should a person feel different when they come to faith? At once? Eventually? Whenever? Do you think it should be possible to tell if someone is a Christian? How can you tell? What are the signs you are looking for?

- The household of faith is made up of hundreds of thousands of individuals, all unique. There are as many spiritual viewpoints as there are people. What do you regard as the non-negotiable basics that all faithful people must believe if they are to be Christians, and what are the tenets of belief over which we can agree to differ, or take our time in working at understanding?

Prayer

Dear Father God, you made me and you know me better than I know myself. You see through my pretences, you love me despite my shortcomings and insecurities, you have a future for my life and a job for me to do. Thank you so much for calling me, for taking me on board, for including me. Help me live up to that calling as I walk through daily life at your side. I know I let you down sometimes, and I am so very sorry. Even so, by your grace, may I be filled with your Holy Spirit, and keep faith with Jesus all the way through to the end of my life. Amen.

Sanctification 1

BIBLE PASSAGES

Matthew 7:21–27, NIVUK

"Not everyone who says to me, 'Lord, Lord,' will enter the kingdom of heaven, but only the one who does the will of my Father who is in heaven. Many will say to me on that day, 'Lord, Lord, did we not prophesy in your name and in your name drive out demons and in your name perform many miracles?' Then I will tell them plainly, 'I never knew you. Away from me, you evildoers!'

"Therefore everyone who hears these words of mine and puts them into practice is like a wise man who built his house on the rock. The rain came down, the streams rose, and the winds blew and beat against that house; yet it did not fall, because it had its foundation on the rock."

1 Peter 2:1–3, RSV

Put away all malice and all guile and insincerity and envy and all slander. Like newborn babes, long for the pure spiritual milk, that by it you may grow up to salvation; for you have tasted the kindness of the Lord.

Ephesians 4:14–15, NIVUK

Then we will no longer be infants, tossed back and forth by the waves, and blown here and there by every wind of teaching and by the cunning and craftiness of people in their deceitful scheming. Instead, speaking the truth in love, we will grow to become in every respect the mature body of him who is the head, that is, Christ.

Colossians 1:9–12, NIVUK

We continually ask God to fill you with the knowledge of his will through all the wisdom and understanding that the Spirit gives, so that you may live a life worthy of the Lord and please him in every way: bearing fruit in every good work, growing in the knowledge of God, being strengthened with all power according to his glorious might so that you may have great endurance and patience, and giving joyful thanks to the Father, who has qualified you to share in the inheritance of his holy people in the kingdom of light.

1 John 3:2–3, NIVUK

Dear friends, now we are children of God, and what we will be has not yet been made known. But we know that when Christ appears, we shall be like him, for we shall see him as he is. All who have this hope in him purify themselves, just as he is pure.

Commentary

When somebody says, "Oh, her – yes, she's *very* holy!" the impression is created of self-conscious piety, a person oozing disapproval, around whom one cannot relax. Very often when people are around me and my family, they make a point of saying they are not going to tell a particular joke or use a swear word in our presence. They imagine that if we are people of faith we will uphold standards that feel unnatural to them, and be altogether unfamiliar with rude words. We let them go on thinking it.

But holiness is not a strained performance, not an affectation. Sanctification is not the tedious business of daily turning into more and more of a prig.

Our Bible passages speak of sanctification as both practical and honest. It is like building a house that won't fall down, on a solid and trustworthy foundation. Not a house of cards, or something that looks good and puts on airs; something made to stand up not only to the rigours of daily life but also to the buffeting of extreme weather – the tempests, the tornados.

Building a workaday faith to stand the test of time has to start with being real. God understands that we can't do the whole journey in one day. It takes time and effort to become who he wants us to be, a process of continual refining and maturing. It takes prayer and patience – but no pretending.

Questions

- Our passages emphasize the importance of sincerity. At the same time, we know love is top of Jesus' priority list. What can you share about the delicate art of speaking truth with love? How can we be honest without hurting people? How do we go about developing a good "truth sense" – a nose for what is real?

- Our Colossians passage speaks of living a life worthy of the Lord and pleasing him in every way. What does that entail? How have your ideas about a life pleasing to God developed over time? Share with the group about somebody you have known who struck you as very close to God.

- What aspects of your personal development as a Christian disciple are you working on at the moment? Are there any where you have tried and failed repeatedly and feel unsure about how to do better?

Prayer

By your grace, and with the help of your Holy Spirit, loving God, enable us to build a faith fit to stand the test of time – that will never weary or wear out. Help us to stay close to you, to be honest with ourselves and others, to be the kind of people others can rely on. Remind us every day to keep our eyes firmly on Jesus, to remember what he has taught us and how he showed us to live, so that bit by bit – hardly even noticing it – we will pick up his habits and grow to be more like him. Amen.

Sanctification 2

BIBLE PASSAGES

Philippians 2:12–16, NIVUK

Therefore, my dear friends, as you have always obeyed – not only in my presence, but now much more in my absence – continue to work out your salvation with fear and trembling, for it is God who works in you to will and to act in order to fulfil his good purpose.

Do everything without grumbling or arguing, so that you may become blameless and pure, "children of God without fault in a warped and crooked generation."[28] Then you will shine among them like stars in the sky as you hold firmly to the word of life.

Deuteronomy 7:6,[29] NIVUK

For you are a people holy to the Lord your God. The Lord your God has chosen you out of all the peoples on the face of the earth to be his people, his treasured possession.

2 Corinthians 6:14–18, KJV

Be ye not unequally yoked together with unbelievers: for what fellowship hath righteousness with unrighteousness? and what communion hath light with darkness?

And what concord hath Christ with Belial? or what part hath he that believeth with an infidel?

And what agreement hath the temple of God with idols? for ye are the temple of the living God; as God hath said, I will dwell in them, and walk in them; and I will be their God, and they shall be my people.

Wherefore come out from among them, and be ye separate, saith the Lord, and touch not the unclean thing; and I will receive you.

And will be a Father unto you, and ye shall be my sons and daughters, saith the Lord Almighty.

Commentary

There's a balance to be struck here. Christianity is an incarnational faith. Right at the heart of it is the true story of God coming to live with us in Jesus, not as a prince but as an ordinary working man. The concept of getting down among the

---

28 Quoting Deuteronomy 32:5.
29 For further study, see the whole of Deuteronomy 7 – how might we apply this today, in the light of the teaching of Jesus?

sweat and toil and basic ordinariness of human life is central. It's not an ivory-tower religion; it's a hands-on faith. Jesus was called Emmanuel – "God-with-us", and we are to imitate him.

Yet, though we are to be in the world,[30] we are not to be of the world.[31] As Jesus said to Pilate, "My kingdom is not of this world,"[32] and we are called to bring his kingdom in, here on earth. How does that work, then? How can we be simultaneously engaged and separate?

The theme of sight and insight is very strong in the Gospels (especially Mark and John), and the secret of transformation seems to be connected with how we see things.[33] As Paul puts it, "Be not conformed to this world, but be ... transformed by the renewing of your mind."[34] How we think, how we look at life, is the key to being involved in society without being corrupted.

The fellowship of other believers is also important. We are to be built together into a living temple[35] – we don't have to go it alone.

Questions

- Some Christians quite literally leave their jobs, friends, and families to join a Christian community – perhaps a religious order of monks or nuns – or to work in a retreat centre, or join a live-in "intentional" community. How do you feel about this way of life? How might it bless wider society? Does it appeal to you? Why or why not?

- In what ways do you believe Christians can best go about working for the prayer "Thy kingdom come" to be realized? Where do you see God at work through his people in human society? Are there any special areas of need in your neighbourhood waiting to be addressed by God's love in us? Are there any places or people we should avoid?

- In what circumstances do you find it most difficult to keep your equilibrium as a Christian? What helps, and what makes it worse?

Prayer

Thank you, O great and mysterious God, for coming close to us in Jesus. Thank you for coming to be with us so that for a few short years we could hug you, bring you a drink, share supper with you, see you laugh, hear your voice.

---

30 As John 3:16 beautifully affirms.
31 John 17:16.
32 John 18:36.
33 See the study "Transformation 1" in the section on "Watchwords of the faith" in this book.
34 Romans 12:2, KJV.
35 Ephesians 2:21.

Thank you for sharing our vulnerability and our suffering – and, by dying, for healing us. Help us to be your presence in the world today; may we hold your light high for the lost and the lonely to see, so the comfort of your presence goes on seeking and saving the lost. Be with us, and may we always stay close to you. Amen.

Aridity 1

BIBLE PASSAGES

Psalm 84:5–7, NRSVA

Happy are those whose strength is in you,
> in whose heart are the highways to Zion.
As they go through the valley of Baca
> they make it a place of springs;
the early rain also covers it with pools.
> They go from strength to strength;
the God of gods will be seen in Zion.

Exodus 17:1–7, NRSVA

From the wilderness of Sin the whole congregation of the Israelites journeyed by stages, as the Lord commanded. They camped at Rephidim, but there was no water for the people to drink. The people quarrelled with Moses, and said, "Give us water to drink." Moses said to them, "Why do you quarrel with me? Why do you test the Lord?" But the people thirsted there for water; and the people complained against Moses and said, "Why did you bring us out of Egypt, to kill us and our children and livestock with thirst?" So Moses cried out to the Lord, "What shall I do with this people? They are almost ready to stone me." The Lord said to Moses, "Go on ahead of the people, and take some of the elders of Israel with you; take in your hand the staff with which you struck the Nile, and go. I will be standing there in front of you on the rock at Horeb. Strike the rock, and water will come out of it, so that the people may drink." Moses did so, in the sight of the elders of Israel. He called the place Massah[36] and Meribah[37], because the Israelites quarrelled and tested the Lord, saying, "Is the Lord among us or not?"

Please also have open in your Bible the story about Jesus tempted in the wilderness in Matthew's Gospel (not Luke): chapter 4:1–11, any translation.

Commentary

Aridity is a certain feature in the way of faith. You can be sure you will encounter it. Sometimes it goes on for years.

---

36 *Massah* means "test".
37 *Meribah* means "quarrel".

Our Bible passage from Exodus offers a perfect template of the experience of aridity. A long, arduous journey and no destination in sight. Lack of resources. Faltering of faith. Disillusionment with leaders. Breakdown in community relationships. And the archetypal question: "Is the Lord among us or not?"

This is replicated in the geography of our spiritual journey. We hit patches where we feel empty and tired, everything seems pointless, vision is lost. Our companions and leaders no longer inspire us, relationships sour, and we wonder whether the whole God story is simply made up; or, if it's true, whether we were ever personally in it.

This incident at Massah surfaces again in the New Testament, in the temptation stories. Jesus responds to the devil with quotations from Deuteronomy. In Matthew's narrative, Jesus' temptations recall the temptations of the people of God in the wilderness. The second temptation[38] is turned aside with a quotation from Deuteronomy 6:16: "You shall not tempt the Lord your God, as you tempted him in Massah."

Matthew shows us Israel perfected in Christ,[39] and offers a new template for managing times of aridity, a rock-solid trust in God that does not fail in hard times.

Our passage from Psalm 84 puts it well: happy are those who, going through the valley of Baca,[40] make it a place of springs. This pinpoints the skill of spiritual survival as the ability to find the small sources of refreshment when the way is rocky. If *Baca* means "weeping" and the blessed find springs there (contrasting types of water), the implication is that they have the gift of discovering the hidden blessing in aridity and adversity, and thus turning the experience on its head.

Questions

- What has your experience of spiritual aridity been? Would you say you are in a time of aridity now? Can you say a little about why you think you are or are not?

- Sometimes whole faith communities go through times of aridity, when nothing seems to flourish or grow, and inspiration evaporates. What have you noticed about times of aridity and times of refreshment in churches you have attended? How did you feel? How did you respond?

- In times of personal aridity, what has helped and sustained you?

---

38 The first recalls Deuteronomy 8:3, referencing the manna in the desert, and the third recalls Deuteronomy 6:13, with application to the golden calf.

39 See Matthew 5:17.

40 The valley of Baca is literally the "valley of weeping", i.e. Life – this Vale of Tears – with its hardships and woes.

Prayer

Help us, O God who travels with us and watches over us, to learn patience. Help us to trust you and to take the long view. So strengthen and establish our fellowship with Jesus that we do not give up. Give us the art of finding those small things that cheer us up in times of discouragement, the hidden blessings welling up along even the most daunting and rocky stretches of the journey. Keep us with you, pilgrim God; keep us faithful. For we ask it in Jesus' name. Amen.

Aridity 2

BIBLE PASSAGES

Luke 7:18–23, TLB

The disciples of John the Baptist soon heard of all that Jesus was doing. When they told John about it, he sent two of his disciples to Jesus to ask him, "Are you really the Messiah? Or shall we keep on looking for him?"

The two disciples found Jesus while he was curing many sick people of their various diseases – healing the lame and the blind and casting out evil spirits. When they asked him John's question, this was his reply: "Go back to John and tell him all you have seen and heard here today: how those who were blind can see. The lame are walking without a limp. The lepers are completely healed. The deaf can hear again. The dead come back to life. And the poor are hearing the Good News. And tell him, 'Blessed is the one who does not lose his faith in me.'"[41]

1 Kings 19:4–9, TLB

[Elijah] went on alone into the wilderness, traveling all day, and sat down under a broom bush and prayed that he might die.

"I've had enough," he told the Lord. "Take away my life. I've got to die sometime, and it might as well be now."

Then he lay down and slept beneath the broom bush. But as he was sleeping, an Angel touched him and told him to get up and eat! He looked around and saw some bread baking on hot stones and a jar of water! So he ate and drank and lay down again.

Then the Angel of the Lord came again and touched him and said, "Get up and eat some more, for there is a long journey ahead of you."

So he got up and ate and drank, and the food gave him enough strength to travel forty days and forty nights to Mount Horeb, the mountain of God, where he lived in a cave.

But the Lord said to him, "What are you doing here, Elijah?"

Commentary

Isolation, disappointment, rejection, tiredness, hunger, and failure are triggers for plunging disciples into a period of aridity.

Prison reduces John the Baptist, that prophetic soul of immense spiritual stature, to vulnerability. This wild desert-dweller, trapped like a caged animal in his

---

41 Literally, "Blessed is he who keeps from stumbling over me."

cell, feels hope ebbing away. Like all prisoners under similar regimes, he must live with uncertainty, not knowing what his fate will be but having every good reason to be afraid. No angel comes to bust him out of the cell. He may be tortured. He may be executed. He has made enemies. He cannot get away. He is at their mercy.

Elijah is in a similar predicament – not in prison but on the run – worn out, frightened, and alone.

Aridity comes and goes whatever you do and whoever you are. But as you wait for times of aridity (and maybe depression[42] too) to pass, it's worth learning from the sufferings of these men to make a checklist: get some rest and return to your problems with a fresh mind; seek out cheerful companions who share your faith – people who like you and make you feel good; have something nourishing and sustaining to eat (not *just* chocolate); remind yourself of the things you did well and got right; nourish your soul with positive, uplifting books, movies, and songs.

John sent word to Jesus, and Jesus sent a message of encouragement back. Elijah prayed and God sent an angel with a snack. In arid times, send a message to Jesus and expect a response; look for God coming to find you, sometimes in unexpected disguises.

Questions

- Can you identify triggers for aridity or depression in your own life? How might you address or avoid those things? Are there ways to nip them in the bud – stop it before it starts?

- Write a list of ten things that pick you up and make you feel happy, to share with the group.

- When someone else feels down and discouraged, how might you help? See if you can identify sources of encouragement in our Bible passages. Make sure you discuss your suggestions, because what some find uplifting others find merely annoying; different perspectives within the group will be helpful.

Prayer

O Lord, our hope and life and light, you never fail or forsake us. Give us humility and common sense to support our faith with simple and practical precautions; strengthen our instinct to turn to you when things get tough. We are your children and you are our Father. We do not know the way very well and we easily get lost and confused. Please lead us and guide us; please shine your light to show us the next step. May your pure light within us take us all the way home. Amen.

---

42 I mean the simple kind of depression – feeling blue – that affects most of us sometimes and some of us a lot. If you think you or a friend are seriously, clinically depressed, these simple strategies won't help; you should see a doctor.

Perseverance 1

BIBLE PASSAGES

Isaiah 40:31, RSV

They who wait for the Lord shall renew their strength,
    they shall mount up with wings like eagles,
they shall run and not be weary,
    they shall walk and not faint.

Revelation 2:2–5, RSV

"I know your works, your toil and your patient endurance, and how you cannot bear evil men but have tested those who call themselves apostles but are not, and found them to be false; I know you are enduring patiently and bearing up for my name's sake, and you have not grown weary. But I have this against you, that you have abandoned the love you had at first. Remember then from what you have fallen, repent and do the works you did at first. If not, I will come to you and remove your lampstand from its place, unless you repent."

Mark 13:32–37, NRSVA

"Beware, keep alert; for you do not know when the time will come. It is like a man going on a journey, when he leaves home and puts his slaves in charge, each with his work, and commands the doorkeeper to be on the watch. Therefore, keep awake – for you do not know when the master of the house will come, in the evening, or at midnight, or at cockcrow, or at dawn, or else he may find you asleep when he comes suddenly. And what I say to you I say to all: Keep awake."

Commentary

Anyone who hopes to follow and develop a practice of Christian spirituality over several decades has to become familiar with the cheerful art of perseverance.

Human beings are creatures of mind and body as well as spirit, and the wise disciple knows how to engage all three of those aspects in the service of staying faithful. In order to be positive in outlook, resilient, and patient, with enough stamina to keep the inner flame burning, simple physical strategies of high-quality nutrition, enough rest and leisure as well as work are all important. The mind must be engaged too. Church can be intensely boring if there is no intellectual stimulus. To stay faithful, keep reading, keep exploring, keep discussing, discover a nose for adventure.

Habit is essential for perseverance. It has been said, "You will never change your life unless you change something you do daily. The secret of success is in your daily routine."[43] Habits have an energy of their own, a momentum, that can keep the disciple moving forward even in times of deep discouragement. The routines of prayer, worship, Bible study, fellowship, courtesy and kindness, humility and listening – these shape a person's character so that they don't know what or how else to be. Enthusiasm is no longer necessary.

In our passage from Revelation, we come across the rebuke, "I have this against you, that you have abandoned the love you had at first". It's helpful to understand this is not about feelings. Nobody can keep white-hot fervour going from their teens to their deathbed. It's about perseverance: "repent and do the works you did at first". It doesn't mean you must never let that toothy smile slip; it means you stay on the path of simplicity, prayer, and kindness – you keep the faith.

Questions

- Who has helped you persevere in your faith? Who has encouraged and cheered you, kept you on track when you felt like giving up? Who has shown you an example of perseverance?

- What habits of prayer or Bible study have been especially helpful in seeing you through times when you felt less inspired? Can you recommend any study notes or Christian writers whose work encourages you?

- What tips can you share about the simple physical things that you rely on for a pick-me-up when you cannot stay positive? Are you a hot-bath person, or does chocolate or a country walk always work for you?

Prayer

Father, you know me and love me. You know I am no saint: I get tired and cross, I lose hope and get bored and disappointed. Please forgive me for the many times I have let you down through my ordinary human frailty. Please know that I do love you, I do want to serve you, I do want you to be pleased with me and proud of me. I humbly ask you to clear the cluttering debris away from the fountain of life at the core of my being. Take not your Holy Spirit from me, O Lord; keep me following, keep me faithful, keep me close to you. In Jesus' name. Amen.

---

43 John C. Maxwell, *The 15 Invaluable Laws of Growth: Live Them and Reach Your Potential*, published by Center Street in 2012.

Perseverance 2

BIBLE PASSAGES

Galatians 6:7–10, RSV

Do not be deceived; God is not mocked, for whatever a man sows, that he will also reap. For he who sows to his own flesh will from the flesh reap corruption; but he who sows to the Spirit will from the Spirit reap eternal life. And let us not grow weary in well-doing, for in due season we shall reap, if we do not lose heart. So then, as we have opportunity, let us do good to all men, and especially to those who are of the household of faith.

Luke 18:1–8, NRSVA

Then Jesus told them a parable about their need to pray always and not to lose heart. He said, "In a certain city there was a judge who neither feared God nor had respect for people. In that city there was a widow who kept coming to him and saying, 'Grant me justice against my opponent.' For a while he refused; but later he said to himself, 'Though I have no fear of God and no respect for anyone, yet because this widow keeps bothering me, I will grant her justice, so that she may not wear me out by continually coming.'" And the Lord said, 'Listen to what the unjust judge says. And will not God grant justice to his chosen ones who cry to him day and night? Will he delay long in helping them? I tell you, he will quickly grant justice to them. And yet, when the Son of Man comes, will he find faith on earth?"

1 Corinthians 13:7–8, NIVUK

[Love] always protects, always trusts, always hopes, always perseveres.
     Love never fails. But where there are prophecies, they will cease; where there are tongues, they will be stilled; where there is knowledge, it will pass away.

Lamentations 3:22–23, RSV

The steadfast love of the Lord never ceases,
     his mercies never come to an end;
they are new every morning;
     great is thy faithfulness.

Luke 9:62, KJV

No man, having put his hand to the plough, and looking back, is fit for the kingdom of God.

Commentary

In Christian tradition, consistency, loyalty, and the courage to persevere are highly prized. The letter to the Hebrews speaks of "Jesus Christ, the same yesterday, today and forever".[44] The Old Testament tells of God whose steadfast love never ceases. We aspire to the same unwavering, unfailing stability.

Sometimes perseverance itself becomes the goal, the admired accomplishment, and we forget to ask, persevere in what? We end up with a bullish obduracy, an inflexibility in which we take a mistaken pride, confusing it with faithfulness.

Christian perseverance does not mean never changing our mind, or resisting the new perspective of maturity. A friend of mine refused to train as a preacher in case the insights of Christian scholarship might require him to relinquish the somewhat basic and naïve approach to the Bible he held. He was right: that would have happened; but it would have been development, not betrayal.

Sometimes – if a marriage breaks down, for example – we have to learn how to let go, when we'd imagined we would only ever have to know how to hang on. Perseverance is a wonderful thing, but so is the grace to move on when the occasion demands it.

Questions

- Looking at our passages, pick out those activities or attitudes where the Bible is encouraging us to persevere. In what do you believe we should always persevere, as Christians? Where might we need to learn to let go of something we thought we should always hang on to, in our habits of mind and personal discipleship?
- Thinking now of your church community, can you identify some things that began as a good idea but hardened into tradition that has lost its usefulness? And are there some things that have fallen into disuse where you wish the church instead had persevered?
- Thinking of how your faith as a Christian affects your personal relationships – for example with your family of origin, friends, children, stepfamily, partner and ex-partners – can you think of times when you persevered and times when you decided to let go? With hindsight, which choices were the right decisions? Where are the regrets? What can you learn about perseverance from these experiences?

Prayer

Faithful God, make us like you; help us to persevere. Help us establish characteristics of commitment, responsibility, and reliability, so that others can depend on us and we do not let you down as often as we sometimes have done. But give us also the

44 Hebrews 13:8, any translation.

grace to bend with the wind, and the wisdom to know when to let go. May our perseverance always be focused more on loving than on being in the right. For we ask it in Jesus' name. Amen.

Renewal 1

BIBLE PASSAGES

Psalm 51:8–12, RSV

Fill me with joy and gladness;
    let the bones which thou hast broken rejoice.
Hide thy face from my sins,
    and blot out all my iniquities.
Create in me a clean heart, O God,
    and put a new and right spirit within me.
Cast me not away from thy presence,
    and take not thy holy Spirit from me.
Restore to me the joy of thy salvation,
    and uphold me with a willing spirit.

Ezekiel 37:1–6, 11–13, NRSVA

The hand of the Lord came upon me, and he brought me out by the spirit of the Lord and set me down in the middle of a valley; it was full of bones. He led me all round them; there were very many lying in the valley, and they were very dry. He said to me, "Mortal, can these bones live?" I answered, "O Lord God, you know." Then he said to me, "Prophesy to these bones, and say to them: O dry bones, hear the word of the Lord. Thus says the Lord God to these bones: I will cause breath to enter you, and you shall live. I will lay sinews on you, and will cause flesh to come upon you, and cover you with skin, and put breath in you, and you shall live; and you shall know that I am the Lord"...

"Mortal, these bones are the whole house of Israel. They say, 'Our bones are dried up, and our hope is lost; we are cut off completely.' Therefore prophesy, and say to them, Thus says the Lord God: I am going to open your graves, and bring you up from your graves, O my people; and I will bring you back to the land of Israel. And you shall know that I am the Lord..."

Commentary

One time we desperately need renewal, and know we do, is when we have done something wrong. Our passage from Psalm 51 is thought to have been written by King David after he admitted to himself (and to Nathan the prophet[45]) the

---

45 2 Samuel 12:1–15, any translation.

shameful nature of his taking advantage of Uriah's wife, Bathsheba.[46] The key distinction between the condemnation of the enemy and the conviction of God's Holy Spirit is that condemnation drives us inwards and leads to despair, whereas the conviction of the Spirit sets us free, leading us out of sin into fresh resolve and renewed purpose.

David did sin quite spectacularly on that occasion, but most sin is not as dramatic. Our passage from Ezekiel offers a graphic image of spiritual death – the slow atrophy of faith communities who increasingly rely on rules and rituals, on human authority and the form of tradition – "the way we do things here". I can well imagine the prophet standing in a pulpit (or behind all the electronic paraphernalia of a sound system), looking out over a congregation in deadlock over pews versus chairs, or which hymnbooks to use, or what to wear on Sunday, or who could be allowed to play the organ or arrange the flowers or speak at the microphone – and God asking, "Well? What d'you think? Can these dry bones live?" Now as then, the prophet would have to answer, "Only you can possibly say, O Lord. What do I know?"

Questions

- If someone asked you to organize a programme of renewal for your church, where would you start? Where has your church begun to feel tired, grow stale?
- If Jesus appeared in front of you right now, and offered to bring about renewal in up to three areas of your spiritual life, what would you ask him to do?
- When Pope John XXIII said of Brother Roger's work in Burgundy, "Ah, Taizé – that little springtime!", he put his finger on the pulse of renewal – something fresh and unself-conscious, natural and glad. Where have you experienced renewal in Christian life and worship? Where do you find it in your life now? If it is missing, how might it be found again?

Prayer

Revive us, O Lord, by the power of your Holy Spirit. Rouse us to life and hope and renewed vigour in our faith and prayer and love. Speak to us. Show us what to do, what to choose, how to follow Jesus. Amid all the paralysis of fear and despair afflicting the world in which we live, shine your light upon the next step and the next and the next for us. Keep us in your way, dearest Lord, faithful and following, with our eyes fixed on you. Amen.

---

46 2 Samuel 11, any translation.

Renewal 2

BIBLE PASSAGES[47]

Psalm 126, KJV

When the Lord turned again the captivity of Zion, we were like them that dream.
Then was our mouth filled with laughter, and our tongue with singing: then said
  they among the heathen, The Lord hath done great things for them.
The Lord hath done great things for us; whereof we are glad.
Turn again our captivity, O Lord, as the streams in the south.
They that sow in tears shall reap in joy.
He that goeth forth and weepeth, bearing precious seed, shall doubtless come
again
  with rejoicing, bringing his sheaves with him.

John 4:13–14, NRSVA

Jesus said to her, "Everyone who drinks of this water will be thirsty again,
but those who drink of the water that I will give them will never be thirsty.
The water that I will give will become in them a spring of water gushing up to
eternal life."

1 Kings 17:8–16, RSV

Then the word of the Lord came to him, "Arise, go to Zarephath, which belongs
to Sidon, and dwell there. Behold, I have commanded a widow there to feed
you." So he arose and went to Zarephath; and when he came to the gate of the
city, behold, a widow was there gathering sticks; and he called to her and said,
"Bring me a little water in a vessel, that I may drink." And as she was going to
bring it, he called to her and said, "Bring me a morsel of bread in your hand."
And she said, "As the Lord your God lives, I have nothing baked, only a handful
of meal in a jar, and a little oil in a cruse; and now, I am gathering a couple of
sticks, that I may go in and prepare it for myself and my son, that we may eat it,
and die." And Elijah said to her, "Fear not; go and do as you have said; but first
make me a little cake of it and bring it to me, and afterward make for yourself
and your son. For thus says the Lord, the God of Israel, 'The jar of meal shall
not be spent, and the cruse of oil shall not fail, until the day that the Lord sends
rain upon the earth.'" And she went and did as Elijah said; and she, and he, and
her household ate for many days. The jar of meal was not spent, neither did the
cruse of oil fail, according to the word of the Lord which he spoke by Elijah.

---

47 See also Joel 2:25–29; Job 42:10–17; and 2 Kings 5:1–19; any translation.

Commentary

When we speak of renewal in a Christian context – or revival – the conversation is generally about deeper religious fervour: zeal, commitment, powerful experience of the Holy Spirit, and sometimes signs and wonders.

Our Bible passages sound so humble and earthy by comparison: release from prison; sowing and harvesting; living water; a widow's starvation rations. And in our footnoted references, restoration after agricultural disaster, slow recovery from comprehensive ruin, and wondrous healing from sickness.

What these stories include, which discussion of renewal often does not, is a holistic view of humanity – body/mind/spirit, individual/community/planet. This integrated outlook is especially important if our faith is to extend its circle of concern beyond the consumerist West. A well-fed person in a comfortable home in a dominant country can afford to consider renewal isolated from life into a spiritual category. Those who live on the edge of survival often cultivate deeper faith because God is their only hope. Abandoned by humanity, they rely on miracles.

The Bible stories of renewal invite us to look at the whole person, and humanity in the wider context of creation. This not only offers hope for the destitute, but will unexpectedly deepen our spiritual practice and bring us closer to the living God.

Questions

- Looking first at our passage from Psalm 126, can you think of a time in your own life, or somebody else's, when you saw the power of God bring release from captivity – whether from a physical prison, a relationship, an addiction, or a state of mind? And can you think of an instance in your life when you trusted in God through a time of deep unhappiness, but out of that experience came a harvest of joy?

- Looking now at our verses from John 4: how do you respond to this description of the Holy Spirit as like a fountain of life welling up inside you? Does it feel like that to you? Or do you feel more like the woman – baffled, confused, and thinking "Sir, give me some of that water; it would make life so much easier"? What is your honest response to this passage?

- Moving now to the 1 Kings story about the widow, notice that the Lord did not provide through Elijah a large pension, a domestic servant, and a palace to live in. She gave what she could, and the Lord blessed her sacrificial generosity with a miraculous gift of renewal. Imagine you were her. What difference would that gift make to her life?

Prayer

O God, source of hope, renewer of life, you support us and provide for us. You care what happens to us, you reach down and comfort us as we go through life's traumas and adversities. Father, we don't always understand; suffering and sorrow harrow and bewilder us. But we can see this much anyway: you are with us, you care about us, and you want our lives to be blessed. Help us so to live in your flow of grace that we make the very best of the life we have, both for ourselves and for all those whose circumstances mingle with our own. Amen.

Covenant

God and his people
God and creation
God and you
Our relationship to each other

God and his people

BIBLE PASSAGE

Romans 9:4–5, NRSVA

They are Israelites, and to them belong the adoption, the glory, the covenants, the giving of the law, the worship, and the promises; to them belong the patriarchs, and from them, according to the flesh, comes the Messiah, who is over all, God blessed for ever.

Commentary

You have only one tiny little passage set out above, but do not fear – you have by no means been short-changed. In this study, it will be helpful if everyone has a Bible, and the numerous references to covenant in the Bible can be looked up and read out around the group.

There are seven covenants made between God and humanity in the Bible. The reason I say "humanity" rather than "his people" is that these covenants start way before the people of God were organized into a faith community.

The first covenant is right at the beginning, with Adam. This has two parts. The first belongs to Adam's days of innocence in Eden, and is known as the Edenic Covenant (Genesis 1:26–30 and 2:16–17). It outlines human responsibility towards God in creation. The second part (Genesis 3:16–19) is the redrawing of boundaries after the fall, and includes the curse proceeding from disobedience.

The second covenant is with Noah (Genesis 9), that God will never again destroy humanity by flood.

The third covenant is with Abraham (Genesis 12:1–3, 6–7; 13:14–17; 15; 17:1–14; 22:15–18), involving promises about Abraham's line of descent, making great his name, and establishing the people of God.

The fourth covenant (Deuteronomy 30:1–10) is known as the Palestinian or "Land" covenant, about the terms of establishment of the people of God in the Promised Land.

The fifth covenant is with Moses (Deuteronomy 11, etc.), setting the conditions for blessing on obedience to the law of Moses (see Exodus 20).

The sixth covenant is with King David (2 Samuel 7:8–16), building on the promises in the covenant with Abraham, promising that David's lineage will never permanently pass away, and that eventually a king of David's line will once more be enthroned. We see this promise as looking forward to Jesus (Luke 1:32–33).

The seventh and final covenant in the Bible is the new covenant (prefigured in Jeremiah 31), effected by the sacrificial death of Jesus for the forgiveness of sins. This new covenant brings things pleasingly back full circle to the whole of humanity, just as the first covenant with Adam was – and so Jesus is sometimes called "the second Adam", because he put right what went wrong at the fall. We will look at the new covenant in the study after next – "God and you".

So the issues covered by the seven covenants with God are our relationship with creation, the stability of the natural world, the establishment of a faith family, the provision of somewhere to call home, a moral code governing human society, the emergence of the Prince of Peace, and the redemption of humanity in Christ's salvation. Together these covenants provide all that is necessary for human well-being. They offer the framework for God's *shalom* in human living.

Something you will notice about these covenants is that in every case God sets the terms. Human beings have the chance to fall in line or face comprehensive curse and devastation. It's important to realize this doesn't imply that God is a heartless dictator. To understand properly, we have to remember the name of God – I AM THAT I AM. God is the ground of our being, the source of all life. From God proceeds the nature of truth, including that mundane aspect of truth we call simply "reality" – the way things are. So when God sets the conditions of covenant, he is not choosing one of a number of alternative realities to impose on us – he's making clear that this is how life is; this is how life works. He's pointing out to us the way of blessing and well-being, the road to *shalom*. He's helping us. In his covenant relationship with humanity, God not only takes us under his wing, he also holds out to us the dignity and respect of being allowed to accept or refuse. And I guess there will always be somebody who thinks they know better, thinks they can fly in the face of reality and try something different; and that somebody will occasionally be me. And that's what forgiveness is for.

Questions

- The first covenant with Adam, and the second covenant with Noah, is to do with our setting in the natural world and our responsibility as stewards of creation. How can you fulfil your share of that responsibility to cherish and protect the earth and its creatures, in the real circumstances of your daily life?
- The third covenant with Abraham establishes the faith family, and the fourth provides a home for the people of God. In what ways have home and family been important in your life? In what ways might we help refugees who have been driven from their homes by war and natural disaster? How can we express this provision of God's love by helping homeless people in our own neighbourhood?

- The fifth covenant is about shaping a moral code to create a harmonious society. What areas of morality do you feel we should prioritize in improving our own society today? Where have we gone adrift from God's promise of blessing? And what aspects of life are we getting right?

Prayer

Thank you, God almighty, God transcendent, God beyond the stars, for considering in detail the needs of human happiness. Thank you for setting the conditions for justice and peace and the well-being of all creation. Thank you for making the framework of blessing that will allow us to dwell in safety, dignity, and security. We ask one thing more: that you will enlarge our understanding to see how this works, so that we may integrate into our lives your recipe for human happiness. Amen.

God and creation

BIBLE PASSAGES

Genesis 9:8–17,[48] NRSVA

God said to Noah and to his sons with him, "As for me, I am establishing my covenant with you and your descendants after you, and with every living creature that is with you, the birds, the domestic animals, and every animal of the earth with you, as many as came out of the ark. I establish my covenant with you, that never again shall all flesh be cut off by the waters of a flood, and never again shall there be a flood to destroy the earth." God said, "This is the sign of the covenant that I make between me and you and every living creature that is with you, for all future generations: I have set my bow in the clouds, and it shall be a sign of the covenant between me and the earth. When I bring clouds over the earth and the bow is seen in the clouds, I will remember my covenant that is between me and you and every living creature of all flesh; and the waters shall never again become a flood to destroy all flesh. When the bow is in the clouds, I will see it and remember the everlasting covenant between God and every living creature of all flesh that is on the earth." God said to Noah, "This is the sign of the covenant that I have established between me and all flesh that is on the earth."

Jeremiah 33:20–21,[49] NIVUK

This is what the Lord says: "If you can break my covenant with the day and my covenant with the night, so that day and night no longer come at their appointed time, then my covenant with David my servant – and my covenant with the Levites who are priests ministering before me – can be broken and David will no longer have a descendant to reign on his throne."

Commentary

The Age of Enlightenment began during the mid-seventeenth century, and continued through the eighteenth. It changed our thinking right through to the present day, including our scientific thinking and understanding about the spirituality of other species than our own. The word "animal" means "that which has a soul", but Enlightenment thinking discounted sentience in any other species than our own.

---

48 See also *100 Stand-Alone Bible Studies*, the study called "Keeping faith with a faithful God" in the section "Insights from the Law and The Prophets".
49 Also verses 25–26.

All Western thinking has been substantially influenced by the great changes of the Age of Enlightenment, including theological thought. A stance developed that all creation is no more than a resource for humans to exploit, that only humans have souls, and that spirituality is limited to God himself and us.

But the Bible does not support this view. Scripture sees all species as responsive to, and in relationship with, God.[50] In the second creation story, God makes Adam from mud, and he remains a lifeless form until God puffs breath into him, whereupon he becomes a *nephesh*, a living being with a soul. As the Hebrew word *ruach* means "spirit" as well as "breath" (or "wind"), the implication is that what gives life is the Spirit of God, hence all that lives is spiritual. This is borne out by the way Scripture speaks about creation, and the fact that members of other species also merit the term *nephesh*.

To say only the human species is ensouled is unbiblical. Nowhere is this made more clear than in the account of the covenant in Genesis 9, made between God and all creation. It would be unthinkable for God who is Spirit to enter a covenant with an inanimate ("un-souled") item – it would be like a human marrying a computer. The covenant relationship makes it clear that all creation is ensouled. This is not a whimsical story or a figure of speech, and anyone who considers him-/herself to be a biblical Christian should take it seriously.

Questions

- What do you think is the spiritual status of animals, birds, plants, and other species – insects, fungi, etc.? How have you reached this view?
- Spend a while thinking, as a group, of ways in which we depend on other species to provide our food, clothing, and the materials for our homes, tools, toiletries, etc.
- What measures should be put in place by human society to show respect and reverence for the presence of God in creation? Explore together how we might go about pursuing this symbiotic relationship with gentleness, taking responsibility for compassion in our God-given dominion over other creatures.

Prayer

Teach us, Creator God, to hold all life in reverence. When we take a plant or animal for food, may we do so soberly and with gratitude. May we walk lightly on the earth and ensure our stewardship works for all the species that share the land with us. May we reverence the water, the air, the land itself, because all creation is in covenant with you, the living God.

---

50 For further study, some supporting Scripture passages: Numbers 22:21–38; Jonah 1:17; Psalm 19; Psalm 36:6; Psalm 50:10–12; Psalm 104; Psalm 148; Daniel 3:52–90 (not all translations have this: try the New American Bible [Revised Edition]).

God and you

BIBLE PASSAGES[51]

Ephesians 2:11–22, RSV

Therefore remember that at one time you Gentiles in the flesh, called the uncircumcision by what is called the circumcision, which is made in the flesh by hands – remember that you were at that time separated from Christ, alienated from the commonwealth of Israel, and strangers to the covenants of promise, having no hope and without God in the world. But now in Christ Jesus you who once were far off have been brought near in the blood of Christ. For he is our peace, who has made us both one, and has broken down the dividing wall of hostility, by abolishing in his flesh the law of commandments and ordinances, that he might create in himself one new man in place of the two, so making peace, and might reconcile us both to God in one body through the cross, thereby bringing the hostility to an end. And he came and preached peace to you who were far off and peace to those who were near; for through him we both have access in one Spirit to the Father. So then you are no longer strangers and sojourners, but you are fellow citizens with the saints and members of the household of God, built upon the foundation of the apostles and prophets, Christ Jesus himself being the cornerstone, in whom the whole structure is joined together and grows into a holy temple in the Lord; in whom you also are built into it for a dwelling place of God in the Spirit.

Mark 14:23–24, NLT

And he took a cup of wine and gave thanks to God for it. He gave it to them, and they all drank from it. And he said to them, "This is my blood, which confirms the covenant between God and his people. It is poured out as a sacrifice for many."[52]

Luke 22:20, NIVUK

"This cup is the new covenant in my blood, which is poured out for you."

Matthew 26:28, NIVUK

"This is my blood of the covenant, which is poured out for many for the forgiveness of sins."

---

51 Also look up Jeremiah 31:31–32 and Hebrews 8.

52 When Mark says "for many", he doesn't mean "for a large number but not all of you". The phrase could be translated as "the many"; it means everyone. "The mass", you could say – and that's what the Eucharist has been called.

Commentary

For our well-being as individuals, our covenant relationship with God is of tremendous importance. Human life is ruined by cynicism, despair, isolation, and greed. These dislocate us from any moral compass and rob life of its flavour.

Knowing ourselves to be in covenant relationship with God changes everything. We have a reason to live, a cause to serve. We are not left comfortless in difficult circumstances. Our lives are characterized by trust and faithfulness. Our natural instincts are channelled constructively, trained and disciplined in limitations imposed by kindness and mercy. Even if there were no God and we only imagined a deity, the results of our concocted religion would have done us a good turn. But, as it is, we are surrounded by a great cloud of witnesses[53] to the Good News that God is real and loves us.

As well as strengthening our lives with belonging and purpose, this new covenant brought about by the sacrificial death of Jesus heals and restores us. It salves the sores and abscesses of sin afflicting our souls, and the wounds inflicted by the sin of others. So the covenant brings both structure and liberation for our lives. As Cranmer expressed it in the old morning collect from the Book of Common Prayer, God's service is perfect freedom and by this we are defended against the spiritual corrosion that is the real enemy of humankind.

Questions

• When you think about the idea of being in a covenant relationship with God, what does it feel like to you? Like a marriage, or being employed by a powerful boss, or being in the court of King Arthur – how do you imagine it?

• The Bible has many promises that God makes to his covenant people, and in difficult times the faithful have often clung to these. Which biblical promises have meant a lot to you?[54]

• What do you think being in a covenant relationship with God means for your life in practical terms? What are the benefits you have experienced and what are the responsibilities?

Prayer

> *O God, who art the author of peace and lover of concord, in*
> *knowledge of whom standeth our eternal life, whose service is perfect*

---

53 Hebrews 12:1, any translation.
54 In case your mind has gone blank, here are a few. Hebrews 13.5, Isaiah 43.1-2, Jeremiah 29:11; Matthew 11:28-29; Isaiah 46:4; John 10:27-28; 2 Corinthians 12:9.

freedom; defend us thy humble servants in all assaults of our enemies; that we, surely trusting in thy defence, may not fear the power of any adversaries; through the might of Jesus Christ our Lord. Amen.[55]

---

55 First collect from Morning Prayer, *Book of Common Prayer.*

Our relationship to each other

BIBLE PASSAGE

1 Peter 2:1–12, NIVUK

Therefore, rid yourselves of all malice and all deceit, hypocrisy, envy, and slander of every kind. Like newborn babies, crave pure spiritual milk, so that by it you may grow up in your salvation, now that you have tasted that the Lord is good.

As you come to him, the living Stone – rejected by humans but chosen by God and precious to him – you also, like living stones, are being built into a spiritual house to be a holy priesthood, offering spiritual sacrifices acceptable to God through Jesus Christ. For in Scripture it says:

"See, I lay a stone in Zion,
    a chosen and precious cornerstone,
and the one who trusts in him
    will never be put to shame."
Now to you who believe, this stone is precious. But to those who do not believe,
"The stone the builders rejected
    has become the cornerstone,"
    and,
"A stone that causes people to stumble
    and a rock that makes them fall."

They stumble because they disobey the message – which is also what they were destined for.

But you are a chosen people, a royal priesthood, a holy nation, God's special possession, that you may declare the praises of him who called you out of darkness into his wonderful light. Once you were not a people, but now you are the people of God; once you had not received mercy, but now you have received mercy.

Dear friends, I urge you, as foreigners and exiles, to abstain from sinful desires, which wage war against your soul. Live such good lives among the pagans that, though they accuse you of doing wrong, they may see your good deeds and glorify God on the day he visits us.

Commentary

A wise old friend of mine used to say that there are three stages to the descent into moral disintegration. She said, the first generation believes in God, and from their faith proceeds their morality. The second generation no longer believes in God but adheres to the inculcated traditions of morality. The third generation abandons the morality.

As our Bible passage puts it, "They stumble because they disobey the message." Our spiritual covenant with God always and inevitably has a social and moral dimension. Personal, intimate relationship with the divine creates a moral imperative, determining the kind of society we shape. This is what the Bible calls "the fear of the Lord".

The nature of our covenant relationship with God becomes apparent in our dealings with one another. God covenants that he will supply our needs,[56] that his grace will be sufficient,[57] that he will keep us through temptation,[58] save us from sin, give us eternal life – victory over death.[59] He promises that all things will work together for good for his people.[60] If God's Spirit dwells in us, then our life together will exhibit the moral force of this fountain of life; so we in turn will supply the needs of others, help them stand strong against temptation, forgive one another, work for the common good, lift up the fallen, and be agents of life not death.

Questions

- In your own life, how has your personal faith affected your relationships with the people who know you – family, friends, and colleagues? Has this always tended towards harmony, or are there times when it has brought discord?

- Thinking of your church and the people in it, how might they be identified as the covenant people of God? How does it show in their lives?

- Thinking of our national life, where can you see the influence of God's covenant people in wider society? And where is that influence absent and needed in our national life today?

Prayer

> *Captain of Israel's host and guide*
> *Of all who seek the land above,*
> *Beneath thy shadow we abide,*
> *The cloud of thy protecting love;*
> *Our strength, thy grace; our rule, thy word;*
> *Our end, the glory of the Lord.*

---

56 Philippians 4:19.
57 2 Corinthians 12:9.
58 1 Corinthians 10:13; Jude 24.
59 1 Corinthians 15:54–57.
60 Romans 8:28.

By thine unerring Spirit led,
We shall not in the desert stray;
We shall not full direction need,
Nor miss our providential way;
As far from danger as from fear
While love, almighty love, is near. Amen.

("Captain of Israel's Host and Guide", Charles Wesley)

Atonement

When we were still far off
The Lamb of God
The Light of the World
Justification
Making all things new

When we were still far off

BIBLE PASSAGES

Isaiah 1:18, NIVUK

"Come now, let us settle the matter," says the Lord. "Though your sins are like scarlet, they shall be as white as snow; though they are red as crimson, they shall be like wool."

Romans 5:6–11, NRSVA

For while we were still weak, at the right time Christ died for the ungodly. Indeed, rarely will anyone die for a righteous person – though perhaps for a good person someone might actually dare to die. But God proves his love for us in that while we still were sinners Christ died for us. Much more surely then, now that we have been justified by his blood, will we be saved through him from the wrath of God. For if while we were enemies, we were reconciled to God through the death of his Son, much more surely, having been reconciled, will we be saved by his life. But more than that, we even boast in God through our Lord Jesus Christ, through whom we have now received reconciliation.

Ephesians 2:12–13, TLB

Remember that in those days you were living utterly apart from Christ; you were enemies of God's children, and he had promised you no help. You were lost, without God, without hope.

But now you belong to Christ Jesus, and though you once were far away from God, now you have been brought very near to him because of what Jesus Christ has done for you with his blood.

Commentary

The principle behind the concept of the atonement is that wrongdoing upsets the balance of life, disturbing the God-given pattern, and something has to be done to redress it.

Through unfolding church history, various "theories of atonement", as they are called, have emerged. The Early Church Fathers saw Christ's death as a ransom,[61] redeeming fallen humanity from slavery to sin. So, though it was often not explicitly stated, that ransom was usually seen as paid to the devil who held humanity captive.

---

61 Because of Mark 10:45.

In the first century Irenaeus offered the recapitulation theory, in which Christ the second Adam undid, by his death on the Tree, the sin of the first Adam in taking the fruit of the tree.

In the eleventh century Anselm proposed the satisfaction (sometimes called "commercial") theory, in which Christ's death was in payment not to the devil but to God to satisfy his wrath and pay the penalty for offending him.

The Reformers of the sixteenth century advanced the moral example (or moral influence theory) first proposed by Peter Abelard in the eleventh century; that Christ died to soften our hearts towards God's great love for us, drawing us to repentance.

The governmental theory of the sixteenth century was that God made an example of Christ as the representative of humanity, so Jesus dies in token of the unacceptability of human sin in God's eyes.

Since then, other theologians have put forward variants on these ideas, with the addition of one different approach – the accident theory, suggesting that Christ's death was not to redress an imbalance, but simply an awful unnecessary tragedy. But this view does therefore not, strictly speaking, propose a theory of atonement.

All these theologians are agreed that the death of Christ on the cross was a pivotal moment, allowing those who were far from God to come home to his love. It was redeeming and transforming, saving and healing – for humankind and all creation. As such the cross can be seen as sitting at the heart of creation: "God was in Christ reconciling the world unto himself".[62]

Questions

- What are your own thoughts about the atonement? What is the nature of the victory Christ won on the cross? How do you believe it affects your life?

- Christians believe that, in the fall, the sin of Adam implicated all humanity and the natural world as well. Who do you think is affected by the redeeming death of Jesus? Just believers? Or does it make a difference to people who are not Christian, and to the realm of nature?

- What does the idea of being far from God mean to you? If God is everywhere, in what sense can we be far from him? Why do you think people sense God's presence more in one place than another?

Prayer

Thank you, Father, for bringing us home to yourself in Jesus. Thank you for not only forgiving us, but also paying the price of our sin, mending the placing where we have torn the web of creation, healing the wounds we have made in the *shalom*

---

62 2 Corinthians 5:19, KJV.

of your intention. Help us now to live as those who are transformed, renewed, and healed, bearing your love into the broken places of the world and showing everyone we meet what it means to be redeemed by Jesus. Amen.

The Lamb of God[63]

BIBLE PASSAGES

John 1:29, RSV

The next day [John the Baptist] saw Jesus coming toward him, and said, "Behold, the Lamb of God, who takes away the sin of the world!"

Revelation 12:10–11a, NIVUK

"Now have come the salvation and the power
and the kingdom of our God,
and the authority of his Messiah.
For the accuser of our brothers and sisters,
who accuses them before our God day and night,
has been hurled down.
They triumphed over him
by the blood of the Lamb
and by the word of their testimony."

Leviticus 5:6, NIVUK

As a penalty for the sin they have committed, they must bring to the Lord a female lamb or goat from the flock as a sin offering; and the priest shall make atonement for them for their sin.

Leviticus 5:17–19, NIVUK

"If anyone sins and does what is forbidden in any of the Lord's commands, even though they do not know it, they are guilty and will be held responsible. They are to bring to the priest as a guilt offering a ram from the flock, one without defect and of the proper value. In this way the priest will make atonement for them for the wrong they have committed unintentionally, and they will be forgiven. It is a guilt offering; they have been guilty of wrongdoing against the Lord."

Exodus 12:3, 6–7, 12–13,[64] NIVUK

Tell the whole community of Israel that ... each man is to take a lamb for his family, one for each household... all the members of the community of Israel must slaughter them at twilight. Then they are to take some of the blood and

---

63 See also "Abraham" in the section of *100 Stand-Alone Bible Studies* called "Tell me about it!"
64 I recommend you look at Exodus 12:1–30 in any translation.

put it on the sides and tops of the door-frames of the houses where they eat the lambs ... On that same night I will pass through Egypt and strike down every firstborn of both people and animals, and I will bring judgment on all the gods of Egypt. I am the Lord. The blood will be a sign for you on the houses where you are, and when I see the blood, I will pass over you.

Hebrews 10:14,[65] NIVUK

For by one sacrifice he has made perfect for ever those who are being made holy.

Commentary

The idea of Jesus being the Lamb of the World comes from the prophetic words of John the Baptist quoted in our Bible passage from John 1. He was referencing the Hebrew law about making atonement for guilt and sin. Leviticus requires those who have sinned (knowingly or not) to offer a lamb in atonement. The two types of sacrifice for sin (see our two passages from Leviticus above) were a guilt offering and a sin offering.

The letter to the Hebrews sees Jesus as both high priest and a once-for-all sacrifice, making atonement in his death on the cross for the guilt and sin of all humanity and rendering any further animal sacrifice unnecessary. He is the mediator, a priestly figure – both the one who is the sacrifice and the one who *offers* it, freely and willingly.

The offering of a lamb as a sacrifice for atonement of sin is different from the Passover lamb, whose blood was sprinkled on the doorposts and lintels of the Israelites so that the angel of death who came for the Egyptian firstborn would see it and pass by. However, this concept of being saved by the blood of the lamb, whether from sin and guilt or from death, is incorporated into our language and thinking about Jesus as the Lamb of God, whose willing sacrifice atones from sin and saves us from spiritual death.

Questions

- How helpful to you is this theological imagery about the atonement? Do you find the idea of the sacrificial lamb, whose shed blood saves us, easy to relate to or somewhat inaccessible? What feelings does it inspire? Does it make you feel grateful and relieved, or happy and free, or does the whole thing feel rather repugnant and barbaric?
- Read also the passage about the scapegoat in Leviticus 16:6–10. Though we no longer sacrifice animals to atone for sin, can you think of examples in modern society of people being in effect scapegoats, or people whose careers or lives

---

65 I recommend you look at Hebrews 10:1–14 in any translation.

or happiness have been sacrificed for what was not their doing only but the responsibility of the whole of society?

- We read in the New Testament[66]: "Greater love has no one than this: to lay down one's life for one's friends." Of course, these words apply to Jesus and his saving death for us, but can you also think of everyday instances, whether in the context of home and family or in in the wider sphere of national life, where these words apply?

Prayer

Thank you, Jesus, for dying for me, for setting me free from the deathly power of sin. Help me now to live for you, my life an open channel for the redeeming power of your love and saving grace. Amen.

---

66 John 15:13, NIVUK.

The Light of the World

BIBLE PASSAGES[67]

Isaiah 45:6b–7, RSV

I am the Lord, and there is no other. I form light and create darkness, I make weal and create woe, I am the Lord, who do all these things.

Isaiah 9:2, RSV

The people who walked in darkness
    have seen a great light;
those who dwelt in a land of deep darkness,
    on them has light shined.

Matthew 4:12–17, RSV

Now when [Jesus] heard that John had been arrested, he withdrew into Galilee; and leaving Nazareth he went and dwelt in Capernaum by the sea, in the territory of Zebulun and Naphtali, that what was spoken by the prophet Isaiah might be fulfilled:

"The land of Zebulun and the land of Naphtali,
    toward the sea, across the Jordan,
Galilee of the Gentiles –
    the people who sat in darkness
have seen a great light,
    and for those who sat in the region and shadow of death
light has dawned."

From that time Jesus began to preach, saying, "Repent, for the kingdom of heaven is at hand."

Commentary

Zoroastrianism is now a minority faith; few know of it. In the years when the Scriptures were formed, it was huge, a pervasive and substantial cultural influence hard for us to appreciate at this distance. Zoroaster and Abraham emerged in neighbouring countries at about the same time, to become founders of world

---

67 See also the section called "Themes from the four Gospels" in *100 Stand-Alone Bible Studies*, the study called "The light of the world" in the section on John's Gospel.

religions. Zoroaster believed life to be a raging battle for supremacy between the forces of light and those of darkness, with legions of angels and all humanity fighting on either side. Abraham believed all life – prosperity and adversity – to be the gift and doing of one God. The religions these men developed were in dialogue with one another; you can read Abraham's point of view countering Zoroaster's in Isaiah's discourses to the Zoroastrian Cyrus of Persia.[68] Matthew's Gospel (his wise men are Zoroastrian) was probably written for and from a heavily Jewish congregation with a strongly Zoroastrian Gentile component.[69]

The New Testament proposes the at-one-ment of division between God and humanity, between Jew and Gentile, the healing of all division in Jesus. In him is the fulfilment of the law that only took the Jewish people so far. With Jesus, morning star, Light of the World, arises the dawn that resolves forever the Zoroastrian battles between the forces of light and dark. In Jesus all things hold together and find their fulfilment, reconnected with their origin, the one true God. We can see this in our Bible passages, as Jesus cites Isaiah's prophecy in calling people to repentance.

Questions[70]

- Do you personally relate better to the Zoroastrian concept of life and society as a struggle between the forces of light and darkness, or to the Jewish concept of all life's experiences being at God's disposal and command? Both emphases are present in Scripture and both are fulfilled in Jesus.

- The psychoanalyst Carl Jung saw healing as the integration of all aspects of our being, including our "shadow" side, the darker aspects of our personality. Can you envisage ways in which the atonement Jesus brings might integrate and rehabilitate our more challenging characteristics, rather than severing or disconnecting from them?

- In what ways can the concept of Jesus as Light of the World speak to us of restoring union with God?

---

68 See Isaiah 45 – look for the parts that say, "I am the Lord and there is no other", and mention making crooked paths straight, bringing order out of chaos, healing disease, all signs of victory of the Light in Zoroastrianism. Note the refusal of the spiritual dichotomy between light and darkness, God reigning supreme over both. Also Isaiah 44:28. Read further about Cyrus in 2 Chronicles 36:22 and in the book of Ezra – 1:1, 1:2, 1:7, 1:8, 3:7, 4:3, 4:5, 5:13, 5:14, 5:17, 6:3, 6:14.

69 See the section called "Themes from the four Gospels" in *100 Stand-Alone Bible Studies*, the study called "The Zoroastrians" in the section on Matthew's Gospel.

70 The *Star Wars* movies explore Light versus Dark themes brilliantly, and Jim Henson and Frank Oz's 1982 film *The Dark Crystal* offers a wonderful fantasy exploration of embracing the Jungian shadow to achieve healing and integration.

Prayer

O God, our light, our healing, and our hope, you were in Jesus showing us the way. While he was in the world he shone the light for us to see and to follow. And now we, in faithfulness to him, are to be the light of the world bringing healing and hope to others. Help us to hold our light high. Help us to use our light not to dazzle others but to reveal the path of goodness. By your grace may all that we are be gradually drawn into your light, until nothing is left unintegrated, nothing within us at war. May we be at one with you, made whole in your love. Amen.

Justification

BIBLE PASSAGES

Romans 5:1–2, NRSVA

> Therefore, since we are justified by faith, we have peace with God through our Lord Jesus Christ, through whom we have obtained access to this grace in which we stand; and we boast in our hope of sharing the glory of God.

Galatians 2:15–21, NRSVA

> We ourselves are Jews by birth and not Gentile sinners; yet we know that a person is justified not by the works of the law but through faith in Jesus Christ. And we have come to believe in Christ Jesus, so that we might be justified by faith in Christ, and not by doing the works of the law, because no one will be justified by the works of the law. But if, in our effort to be justified in Christ, we ourselves have been found to be sinners, is Christ then a servant of sin? Certainly not! But if I build up again the very things that I once tore down, then I demonstrate that I am a transgressor. For through the law I died to the law, so that I might live to God. I have been crucified with Christ; and it is no longer I who live, but it is Christ who lives in me. And the life I now live in the flesh I live by faith in the Son of God, who loved me and gave himself for me. I do not nullify the grace of God; for if justification comes through the law, then Christ died for nothing.

Galatians 3:11–14, NRSVA

> Now it is evident that no one is justified before God by the law; for "The one who is righteous will live by faith." But the law does not rest on faith; on the contrary, "Whoever does the works of the law will live by them." Christ redeemed us from the curse of the law by becoming a curse for us – for it is written, "Cursed is everyone who hangs on a tree" – in order that in Christ Jesus the blessing of Abraham might come to the Gentiles, so that we might receive the promise of the Spirit through faith.

Commentary

We learn that we are saved by grace, and justified through faith in Jesus – but what does "justification" mean?

The explanation we often give to children is that justification means it's "just as if I'd never sinned". We were guilty. We were sinful. But the saving death of Jesus has put that right.

As with the sacred moments the church celebrates, however, this can be done in an instant, but it is also a process.

From the printing world comes another insight into justification. A page of text is usually left-aligned, but if you justify the text you space it so that both edges are straight. Similarly, when we are justified by faith in Jesus, the process involves realigning us according to God's pattern – no more ragged edges; we are brought into alignment with his love and grace. So the change is not just in terms of benefits received. If we think of justification in legal terms – the judge who pronounces us "not guilty" because Jesus has borne away our sins – we run the risk of imagining that Jesus will pay the price and we can carry on exactly as before. This is not so. The image of the justified text helps us here, because we can see that though the editor is the one who effects the change, nonetheless the text still does have to be differently configured. It can't be both left-aligned and justified. That would be impossible.

And so it is with us. Christ has paid the price, offered us full and free salvation. He has justified us. And the evidence is all in our changed lives.

Questions

- What difference does faith in Jesus make to your life? What changes has it brought? What do you do or think that rests entirely on believing in Jesus?
- The UK is a Christian country, with an established church. The evangelical church has a very strong representation in the US. What is there about the national life of those two countries that bears witness to this Christian belief?
- Some people find the Christian doctrines about atonement and justification very puzzling – wondering how the death of Jesus can make a difference to someone 2,000 years later. What would you say to them?

Prayer

Father God, how grateful we are for the saving death of Jesus. Thank you for your grace seen in him. Thank you for your love received in him. Thank you for the Holy Spirit you have poured into our hearts because of him. Help us to be trustworthy citizens of your kingdom. In our daily lives, in our words and decisions and attitudes, may we be your faithful witnesses and honest servants. Amen.

Making all things new

BIBLE PASSAGES

Leviticus 16:29–34, NRSVA

This shall be a statute to you for ever: In the seventh month, on the tenth day of the month, you shall deny yourselves, and shall do no work, neither the citizen nor the alien who resides among you. For on this day atonement shall be made for you, to cleanse you; from all your sins you shall be clean before the Lord. It is a sabbath of complete rest to you, and you shall deny yourselves; it is a statute for ever. The priest who is anointed and consecrated as priest in his father's place shall make atonement, wearing the linen vestments, the holy vestments. He shall make atonement for the sanctuary, and he shall make atonement for the tent of meeting and for the altar, and he shall make atonement for the priests and for all the people of the assembly. This shall be an everlasting statute for you, to make atonement for the people of Israel once in the year for all their sins. And Moses did as the Lord had commanded him.

1 Peter 1:13–16, NIVUK

Therefore, with minds that are alert and fully sober, set your hope on the grace to be brought to you when Jesus Christ is revealed at his coming. As obedient children, do not conform to the evil desires you had when you lived in ignorance. But just as he who called you is holy, so be holy in all you do; for it is written: "Be holy, because I am holy."

Ephesians 4:22–24, NIVUK

You were taught, with regard to your former way of life, to put off your old self, which is being corrupted by its deceitful desires; to be made new in the attitude of your minds; and to put on the new self, created to be like God in true righteousness and holiness.

Commentary

The Christian theology of atonement is rooted in Judaism, going back to the days of Moses. Our first Bible passage chronicles the origin of the Jewish Day of Atonement.

In popular Jewish tradition, at Rosh Hashanah (the Jewish New Year) God writes into the Book of Life what will happen to a person during the year. But he waits for Yom Kippur – the Day of Atonement, ten days later – to seal the verdict.

It's a way of saying that what happens to us comes from the hand of God, but is also determined by our response. Between Rosh Hashanah and Yom Kippur come the Days of Awe, a time for deep reflection and amendment of life, acknowledging and putting right any wrongdoings against God or one's neighbour. Then at Yom Kippur, known as the Sabbath of Sabbaths, the holiest day of the Jewish year, the faithful confess and seek forgiveness for their sins.

It is a time of *teshuvah* – a Hebrew word with the root meaning of "returning". This implies both repentance (turning around) and getting back to what we were always meant to be. The four steps of *teshuvah* are: sincere regret for wrongdoing; complete severance from wrongdoing; confession of sin; commitment to a changed life.

So the Day of Atonement is a time of wiping the slate clean and making a brand new start with God. This has been an annual observance of the Jewish faith from the time of Moses to the present day.

When, in the book of Revelation, Christ enthroned in heaven declares "Behold, I make all things new",[71] or when Paul writes "When anyone is in Christ there is a new creation; the old has passed away, the new has begun",[72] there would have been resonances for the early church community with observance of the Day of Atonement. In Jewish tradition, self-reflection, repentance, and returning are all implicit in the miracle of being made new. Transformation comes from God as a gift of grace, but it requires our co-operation.

Questions

- In the Christian faith, emphasis is placed on Christ's once-for-all sacrifice cleansing our sin, and on being born again as a one-off event. What do you feel we could learn from the Jewish practice of an annual Day of Atonement offering a spiritual reboot and spring clean?

- What similarities and what differences do you see between the reflective period of the Days of Awe in the Jewish tradition and the reflective time of Lent in the Christian tradition?

- The practice of confession to a priest in the Catholic Church (and confession to the community in some Anabaptist churches) has no counterpart in most other mainstream churches. How can we make our confession and repentance real if we have no inbuilt opportunity to practise it within our church congregations?

---

71 Revelation 21:5, KJV.
72 2 Corinthians 5:17, my paraphrase.

Prayer

Thank you, Father, for special times of renewing and returning, the seasons of hope that have found us. Help us to keep a discipline of honesty and authenticity, never going through the motions but always opening our hearts fully to your Spirit. Give us humility and gentleness in our attitudes towards one another, so that seeking and granting forgiveness feels natural among us, not unfamiliar or strained. May we walk in the way of Jesus in heartfelt simplicity, made new every morning by the upwelling gift of your Spirit in our innermost being. Amen.

Watchwords of the faith

Grace 1

BIBLE PASSAGES

2 Corinthians 12:7–10, NRSVA

To keep me from being too elated, a thorn was given to me in the flesh, a messenger of Satan to torment me, to keep me from being too elated. Three times I appealed to the Lord about this, that it would leave me, but he said to me, "My grace is sufficient for you, for power is made perfect in weakness." So, I will boast all the more gladly of my weaknesses, so that the power of Christ may dwell in me. Therefore I am content with weaknesses, insults, hardships, persecutions, and calamities for the sake of Christ; for whenever I am weak, then I am strong.

Ephesians 2:4–10, NRSVA

God, who is rich in mercy, out of the great love with which he loved us even when we were dead through our trespasses, made us alive together with Christ – by grace you have been saved – and raised us up with him and seated us with him in the heavenly places in Christ Jesus, so that in the ages to come he might show the immeasurable riches of his grace in kindness towards us in Christ Jesus. For by grace you have been saved through faith, and this is not your own doing; it is the gift of God – not the result of works, so that no one may boast. For we are what he has made us, created in Christ Jesus for good works, which God prepared beforehand to be our way of life.

Commentary

Mastery and grace are the two feet on which we walk the way of faith. Mastery is necessary – we are actually supposed to advance, learning to be patient and humble, compassionate, wise, and kind. But mastery is reached only through repeated failure; we each have our own unique and personal style and approach, but what every master has in common is a history of messing things up and being willing to keep on trying, to get up and start again, to continue with what seems not only unpalatable but impossible. And for that we need grace.

The grace of God is the reaching out to us of God's unconditional love. It fuels our endeavour. It tilts the odds in our favour. It quite literally – in the cross of Jesus – makes a way through for us.

So grace is made visible in human weakness; it has the particular loveliness of transforming our faults and failings into testimony, into a map of progression from which our sisters and brothers can draw encouragement.

This means that even the worst person you can conjure up in your imagination is still a rich field of potential for the outworking of God's unconditional love in grace. No matter what you have done or how ashamed and guilty you feel, no matter how wretched you feel when you see the task before you and know it is beyond you, grace is the presence of God to do it with you, coming alongside you. What seems too much for you probably is exactly that, but are you going to say it is too much for God?

Grace is also seen at work in community; it's not a solitary thing. We help each other along; where one is unkind another is forgiving; where one is pigheaded another is patient – and so we travel to heaven in good company, through our interactions and relationships making grace appear.

Questions

- Can you think of a time in your life when you saw the love of God at work not because you were strong and good, but because you messed up and got things wrong?

- Can you think of an example from among your church or friends or family where grace was made visible in the way people treated one another?

- In your own life right now, into what situation would you really welcome an inpouring of God's grace? Remember that God does the unexpected – by all means be clear about the outcome for which you hope, but be ready for the difficulty to be resolved in ways you had not imagined.

Prayer

God of power and love, we rely on your patience and understanding; we rest upon your kindness and acceptance. May the healing and renewal of your grace so work in us that we become the instruments of your grace towards our sisters and brothers who are struggling and feeling alone. Thank you for your gentleness with us, and help us to be gentle with each other. Amen.

And a prayer of Brennan Manning for anyone who is struggling, to be repeated over and over: *Abba, I belong to you.*

Grace 2

BIBLE PASSAGES

John 1:14, 16, RSV

And the Word became flesh and dwelt among us, full of grace and truth; we have beheld his glory, glory as of the only Son from the Father ... And from his fullness have we all received, grace upon grace.

John 1:17, RSV

For the law was given through Moses; grace and truth came through Jesus Christ.

Psalm 45:2, RSV

You are the fairest of the sons of men; grace is poured upon your lips; therefore God has blessed you for ever.

Luke 2:40, NIVUK

And the child grew and became strong; he was filled with wisdom, and the grace of God was on him.

Zechariah 11:7, KJV

And I will feed the flock of slaughter, even you, O poor of the flock. And I took unto me two staves; the one I called Beauty [or grace], and the other I called Bands [or unity]; and I fed the flock.

Proverbs 3:21–23, NIVUK

My son, do not let wisdom and understanding out of your sight,
    preserve sound judgment and discretion;
they will be life for you,
    an ornament to grace your neck.

Proverbs 22:10–11, NIVUK

Drive out the mocker, and out goes strife;
    quarrels and insults are ended.
One who loves a pure heart and who speaks with grace
    will have the king for a friend.

Commentary

We know that grace is the unmerited favour of God – his unconditional love expressed towards us in mercy and kindness.

But there are other meanings associated with the word "grace", which can helpfully shed light on it for us.

We call the blessing over a meal "grace", because it's a thanksgiving, and the Latin word for "thanks" is *gratias*. This continues into the modern Romance languages: the Spanish for "thank you" is *gracias*, and the Italian is *grazie*. You can detect the same root in our English word "gratitude".

We also use the word "grace" for a particular type of beauty – that of a dancer, especially – usually in connection with attitude or movement or line, expressive of flow and finesse.

And in music, we have "grace notes": musical ornaments that are not essential to the melody or harmonies, but serve to make the composition more lovely, adding that little extra to finish it off. The musical version of "the icing on the cake". And the cherry on top.

The English word has a Latin root – *gratia* – and, in different contexts in the Latin, *gratia* can take a variety of meanings: thanks, gratitude, goodwill, favour, liking, esteem, charm, or something pleasant or pleasing.

Also associated is the word *gratis*, which means "free". A *persona non grata* is someone whose presence is not appreciated, who is not free to remain here.

If we put all these together, we form an understanding of grace in terms of something pleasant and welcome to us, gratitude in the heart, bothering with the little extras that make life beautiful, enhancing interactions, not striking a jarring note. If grace dwells with and within us, this loveliness will gradually come to characterize our attitudes and actions – we will become graceful people.

Even though we are called to a prophetic life, and must sometimes challenge and resist wrongdoing, the ways of grace must surely advance the cause of our message.

Questions

- Who epitomizes for you the quality of grace? Describe what you see in them that is so graceful.
- In what areas of your life would you like to see grace develop? How might you go about working on that? If it would help to have a working partner on the project, who would you choose?
- A favourite blessing begins "May the grace of our Lord Jesus Christ". Where do you see grace in the life of Jesus?

Prayer

Because of your loving-kindness, may our lives breathe the fragrance of your grace. When people look at us, may they see the courtesy and sensitivity of your love, the natural humility of your generosity; may they see Jesus in us. Amen.

Salvation 1

BIBLE PASSAGES

Psalm 27:1, NIVUK

The Lord is my light and my salvation –
whom shall I fear?
The Lord is the stronghold of my life –
of whom shall I be afraid?

Psalm 51:12, NIVUK

Restore to me the joy of your salvation
and grant me a willing spirit, to sustain me.

Isaiah 26:18, NIVUK

We were with child, we writhed in labour,
but we gave birth to wind.
We have not brought salvation to the earth,
and the people of the world have not come to life.

Isaiah 45:17, NIVUK

But Israel will be saved by the Lord
with an everlasting salvation;
you will never be put to shame or disgraced,
to ages everlasting.

Isaiah 61:10, NIVUK

I delight greatly in the Lord; my soul rejoices in my God. For he has clothed me
with garments of salvation and arrayed me in a robe of his righteousness, as
a bridegroom adorns his head like a priest, and as a bride adorns herself with
her jewels.

Acts 4:12, NIVUK

Salvation is found in no one else, for there is no other name under heaven given
to mankind by which we must be saved.

James 1:21, NIVUK

Therefore, get rid of all moral filth and the evil that is so prevalent, and humbly
accept the word planted in you, which can save you.

Revelation 12:10, NIVUK

"Now have come the salvation and the power and the kingdom of our God, and the authority of his Messiah. For the accuser of our brothers and sisters, who accuses them before our God day and night, has been hurled down."

Commentary

From time to time, when typing this, I "saved" the document, to make sure it would not be lost for ever.

Back in the 1970s, in the days of Youth Praise, and Jesus Freaks in California, there arose an evangelistic vogue for asking people, "Are you saved?" Button badges proclaiming "God loves you" and "Jesus saves" were popular. In due course those who had nothing in particular to offer, and subsisted intellectually on mocking others, derived a sense of superiority by jokes like "Jesus saves Green Shield stamps" (another ubiquitous 1970s phenomenon).

So right there, different definitions of "save" emerge. To conserve or hoard up is one possibility; to protect from loss or destruction is another. The bemused targets of what we called witnessing sometimes asked, "Saved from what?" I think our answer was usually, "Hell". These were rarely productive conversations.

So, how does Jesus save us? From what or from whom? What does he conserve and what does he protect? What would happen otherwise?

As we look through our biblical texts, or search a concordance for the term "salvation", we quickly see that the word abounds in the Old Testament, before the coming of Jesus. It has to do with political rescue, vindication against the slurs and oppression of enemies, release from shame – being able to hold one's head high again. It often relates to physical circumstances such as imprisonment or famine. The Bible envisages a God who cares about the detail of our lives, and whose rescue and help are practical interventions.

In the New Testament, we find the proposal that salvation can be found in Jesus alone – and this means the larger dimension of complete spiritual renewal that offers us moral freedom from the strongholds of sin and the bondage of corruption. In his death on the cross he sets free our captive souls; this is real, but it is also a mystery.

When we put the Testaments together we find a rich understanding of what salvation can mean – the personal and political, the moral and spiritual, the cosmic and universal. And that salvation manifests as freedom, gladness, joy, hope, and life.

Questions

- Think about the question "Are you saved?" What does it mean to you? What would you say? Is it easy or difficult to answer? How helpful is it for evangelistic outreach? Some might answer, "None of your business!" Would that be true? Is our salvation a private matter or is it to do with community?

- Our Acts passage tells us the power to save is found in Jesus alone, yet our James passage challenges us to clean up our act so salvation can take root in us. In what sense is our salvation a partnership with God, and in what sense is it God's initiative of grace alone?

- What difference has the experience of salvation in Christ made to your experience of life?

Prayer

Jesus, my rock, my hope, my strength – my salvation is in you. Establish your Spirit in me, both inwardly in my heart and outwardly in my life, so that everything I say and do bears witness to the saving power of your love. Amen.

Salvation 2

BIBLE PASSAGES

Psalm 107:20, NRSVA

He sent out his word and healed them,
and delivered them from destruction.

Isaiah 53:4–6, NIVUK

Surely he took up our pain
and bore our suffering,
yet we considered him punished by God,
stricken by him, and afflicted.
But he was pierced for our transgressions,
he was crushed for our iniquities;
the punishment that brought us peace was on him,
and by his wounds we are healed.
We all, like sheep, have gone astray,
each of us has turned to our own way;
and the Lord has laid on him
the iniquity of us all.

Isaiah 58:8, NIVUK

Then your light will break forth like the dawn,
and your healing will quickly appear;
then your righteousness will go before you,
and the glory of the Lord will be your rear guard.

Jeremiah 8:22, NRSVA

Is there no balm in Gilead?
Is there no physician there?
Why then has the health of my poor people
not been restored?

Jeremiah 17:14, NIVUK

Heal me, Lord, and I shall be healed;
save me and I shall be saved,
for you are the one I praise.

Luke 19:9, NIVUK

Jesus said to [Zaccheus], "Today salvation has come to this house, because this man, too, is a son of Abraham."

Commentary

In our previous study, we thought about different slants of meaning in the word "salvation" – how it could be about keeping safe from loss or destruction, or about rescue.

There's another meaning tucked inside the word. A "salve" is a soothing ointment we put on sore, diseased, or broken places, to bring healing. Our verse from Jeremiah 8 was the inspiration for the African American Spiritual:

There is a balm in Gilead
To make the wounded whole
There's power enough in heaven
To cure the sin-sick soul.

As we read about salvation in the Bible, we find a persistent emphasis on God's healing of individuals and communities suffering from spiritual sickness for which they could find no other cure.[73] Salvation is the coming of God's *shalom* – peace and wholeness.

This has sometimes led to the suggestion that people who are chronically unwell or disabled have done something wrong – are to blame for their condition, or at fault when prayers for healing do not bring hoped-for improvement. Such attitudes are unhelpful and misguided; yet it remains true that much (possibly all) illness and all healing include an emotional and spiritual aspect. Discuss your thoughts about this relationship between healing and salvation in your group.

Questions

- Think of some examples – whether of public figures or individuals personally known to you – of people who have done wrong, but it is unclear to you whether they are morally accountable or actually just ill. Can we think of all wrongdoing as a kind of illness, or are sin and sickness two quite separate things?

- You sometimes hear people say in despair that our whole society is sick. What do you think we need to put in place for the salvation – the healing – of our society? What attitudes and environments tend towards health – or illness?

---

73 See the story of the Gerasene demoniac in Luke 8:26–39, or the paralyzed man let down through the roof in Luke 5:17–39, or the man by the Pool of Bethesda in John 5:1–15, or the reference to the healing of Mary of Magdala in Luke 8:2.

- Can you think of times when you personally did wrong because you were tired or unwell? It could be possible that self-care is an aspect of our salvation; being gentle with ourselves is part of our responsibility to ensure we are the best possible version of ourselves. In what ways do (or could) you personally care for yourself in order to serve God faithfully?

Prayer

Lord, I am not worthy that you should come under my roof; but only say the word, and your servant will be healed. Breathe your Spirit into me and I shall be restored. Touch my life, that I may live. Enter my heart, that I may be transformed. In Jesus' name – Amen.

Love 1

BIBLE PASSAGES

1 Corinthians 13:4–8a, RSV

Love is patient and kind; love is not jealous or boastful; it is not arrogant or rude. Love does not insist on its own way; it is not irritable or resentful; it does not rejoice at wrong, but rejoices in the right. Love bears all things, believes all things, hopes all things, endures all things.

Love never ends ...

1 Corinthians 16:13–14, RSV

Be watchful, stand firm in your faith, be courageous, be strong. Let all that you do be done in love.

1 John 4:7–8, 11–12, RSV

Beloved, let us love one another; for love is of God, and he who loves is born of God and knows God. He who does not love does not know God; for God is love ...

Beloved, if God so loved us, we also ought to love one another. No man has ever seen God; if we love one another, God abides in us and his love is perfected in us.

John 13:35, NRSVA

"By this everyone will know that you are my disciples, if you have love for one another."

Commentary

There is no doubt in the mind of any Christian that love is central to our faith practice. Even people raised as atheists, or who don't realize Jesus was a real historical individual, are clear that to be properly Christian involves being unselfish and kind. Every single Christian knows it, and every single Christian struggles with it, because it's not easy to do.

Advice on advancing in the way of love varies, and you'll have your own helpful experience to share. But some of the advice – like being accepting of others and willing to consider their point of view – is, to my mind, part of the *practice* of love not part of the *how to* of getting there. So I'm suggesting four key things to help you, if you want to take this seriously and advance in the way of love:

- #1 Habit. A lot of relational nastiness happens when we're caught off guard. When we're tired, distracted, hungry, or unwell, somebody says something that catches us on the raw, and we react without thinking. If you have a habit of swearing, snapping, sarcasm, or rudeness, it'll show then – in the reaction before thought kicks in. If we layer up gentleness of thought and speech by building a daily habit, when we're caught off guard we'll have the momentum of that to bridge the gap between reaction and thought. I think it was habit that got Jesus through the horrendous ordeal of Holy Week. By thirty-three years old, he'd been obeying his Abba so long that it had become reflexive; he had laid down no other foundation for response.

- #2 Simplicity. An impediment to love is clutter to manage – too many relationships, commitments, and belongings to think about, complicated and ambitious plans. The less stuff you try to wodge in, the more care and attention you can lavish on what's there. Love means paying proper attention and spending time. This can only happen if you insist on doing things simply.

- #3 Solitude. In the hurly-burly of interaction, we tend to forget ourselves, get carried away. It's not at the start of conversations that people start bitching about others or an argument develops, it's as time gets late. Make a habit of leaving early and having space to reflect and consider. Give yourself wide margins to your interactions.

- #4 Diet. When the body is toxic we feel drained and become depressed or irritable. Some foods destabilize mood – the peaks and troughs caused by sugar are well known. Chemical-rich and nutrient-poor food affects mood. Anyone serious about becoming calm, kind, and loving does well to learn about high-quality diet and practise it. This also applies to mental diet – books and magazines, intake of social media, consumption of films and TV, as regards both amount and content, will influence our characters, assumptions, and responses. Good diet helps the practice of love immensely.

Questions

- When do you find it difficult to be loving? When are you inclined to drop the ball? What helps in remedying that?

- When do you find it easiest to be loving? What brings out the best in you? What can you do to encourage this circumstance in your life?

- I've given you four key things to help advance your practice of love. What other tips have helped you along the way?

Prayer

Abba, you are love itself; your whole being is love. Help us in our struggle to follow Jesus and practise the way of love he came here to show us. Help us to be practical and serious in tackling this. Spirit of love, blow on the spark of love in our hearts until it becomes a steady flame. Amen.

Love 2

BIBLE PASSAGES

Colossians 3:12–15, NIVUK

Therefore, as God's chosen people, holy and dearly loved, clothe yourselves with compassion, kindness, humility, gentleness and patience. Bear with each other and forgive one another if any of you has a grievance against someone. Forgive as the Lord forgave you. And over all these virtues put on love, which binds them all together in perfect unity.

Let the peace of Christ rule in your hearts, since as members of one body you were called to peace. And be thankful.

Ephesians 6:4, NRSVA

Fathers, do not provoke your children to anger, but bring them up in the discipline and instruction of the Lord.

Galatians 5:13–15, 25–26, NIVUK

You, my brothers and sisters, were called to be free. But do not use your freedom to indulge the flesh; rather, serve one another humbly in love. For the entire law is fulfilled in keeping this one command: "Love your neighbour as yourself." If you bite and devour each other, watch out or you will be destroyed by each other …

Since we live by the Spirit, let us keep in step with the Spirit. Let us not become conceited, provoking and envying each other.

Ephesians 4:26, NIVUK

"In your anger do not sin"[74]: do not let the sun go down while you are still angry, and do not give the devil a foothold.

Proverbs 15:1, 18, NIVUK

A gentle answer turns away wrath,
    but a harsh word stirs up anger.
A hot-tempered person stirs up conflict,
    but the one who is patient calms a quarrel.

---

74 Psalm 4:4.

Commentary

The ancient Greeks identified four kinds of love.[75] In our first study on love, we thought about the kind of love they called *agape*, not natural attraction but intentional loving-kindness because we believe that's the right way to be.

But even where people are naturally drawn to each other and become friends or lovers, the way of love can be rocky and have some big potholes; and families are often riven by jealousy and strife.

So this study is to help Christian management of natural loves – between friends, lovers, or family members. The suggestions of the first study carry over, and here are three further ideas:

- #1 Boundaries. "Good fences make good neighbours", the saying goes. Courtesy and respect are crucial to successful relationship – the way we speak to one another, being punctual, not betraying secrets, avoiding humiliating or abusing each other by thoughtlessness. In families (even for our pets), allowing privacy and respecting property is important – even if space permits only the place someone sleeps and their shelf or box of belongings. Where relationships are in complete breakdown, sometimes only distance will stop things worsening; parting can sometimes be the most loving gift you can manage to offer – but do it kindly.

- #2 Mutuality. Loving is more than transactional, and we aren't in it for what we can get, but our relationships sour if there is no two-way flow, if everything is on one person's terms and the other is there only to acquiesce. Bluntly, both people need to be getting something out of this if it's going to work.

- #3 Unqualified apology. In every long-term relationship, conflict inevitably occurs. When things stutter or break down, it's important to address what's gone wrong and put it right; apologizing alone does not suffice. But for minor or accidental transgressions, and as an essential component of resolving bigger issues, the unqualified apology helps a lot. It means saying not, "I'm sorry I was late but the traffic was bad / you aren't always ready / I had work to finish off ..." – just, "I'm so sorry I was late."

Questions

- Right now in your life, is there a relationship struggling or failing? What's gone wrong? What do you think might help to put things right from your point of view? Can you hazard a guess at what might help put things right from the other person's point of view?

- Can you think of a time when your relationship with someone dear to you temporarily ran into trouble? What was needed to put things right?

---

75 C. S. Lewis wrote about this in his book *The Four Loves*, published by Geoffrey Bles in 1960.

- Thinking of your own relationships or what you have observed in someone else's life, what do you think makes good friendships or marriages successful?

Prayer

Father God, we place into your hands the people we live with and love. Make us wise and sensitive in our interactions with them. Show us how to be authentic but still considerate. May the presence of Jesus, which everywhere brought healing and peace, illuminate our ordinary loves. Amen.

Holiness 1

BIBLE PASSAGES

Exodus 3:1–5, RSV

Now Moses was keeping the flock of his father-in-law, Jethro, the priest of Midian; and he led his flock to the west side of the wilderness, and came to Horeb, the mountain of God. And the angel of the Lord appeared to him in a flame of fire out of the midst of a bush; and he looked, and lo, the bush was burning, yet it was not consumed. And Moses said, "I will turn aside and see this great sight, why the bush is not burnt." When the Lord saw that he turned aside to see, God called to him out of the bush, "Moses, Moses!" And he said, "Here am I." Then he said, "Do not come near; put off your shoes from your feet, for the place on which you are standing is holy ground." And he said, "I am the God of your father, the God of Abraham, the God of Isaac, and the God of Jacob." And Moses hid his face, for he was afraid to look at God.

Genesis 28:10–12, 16–17, RSV

Jacob left Beer-sheba, and went toward Haran. And he came to a certain place, and stayed there that night, because the sun had set. Taking one of the stones of the place, he put it under his head and lay down in that place to sleep. And he dreamed that there was a ladder set up on the earth, and the top of it reached to heaven; and behold, the angels of God were ascending and descending on it! ...

... Then Jacob awoke from his sleep and said, "Surely the Lord is in this place; and I did not know it." And he was afraid, and said, "How awesome is this place! This is none other than the house of God, and this is the gate of heaven."

Exodus 40:9–10, 34, RSV[76]

Then you shall take the anointing oil, and anoint the tabernacle and all that is in it, and consecrate it and all its furniture; and it shall become holy. You shall also anoint the altar of burnt offering and all its utensils, and consecrate the altar; and the altar shall be most holy. ...

... Then the cloud covered the tent of meeting, and the glory of the Lord filled the tabernacle.

---

76 I recommend you read Exodus chapter 35 to the end, about the making of the tabernacle.

Acts 7:48–50, RSV

Yet the Most High does not dwell in houses made with hands; as the prophet says,

"Heaven is my throne,
  and earth my footstool.
What house will you build for me,
  says the Lord,
or what is the place of my rest?
  Did not my hand make all these things?"

Commentary

These passages from the Bible speak most interestingly about the presence of the Lord in things and places. Celtic Christians (and the pre-Christian Celts before them) spoke of "thin places" – where mystery seemed tangible and the presence of the holy was strong.

A Christian centre near where I live offers various bedrooms for retreats. One they have called "The prophet's room", because so many people have felt close to God there, and experienced powerful dreams as they slept. It has become a favourite place for those seeking God to spend time.

But, since the death of Jesus when the veil of the tabernacle was torn in two, and since the time of Pentecost when God's Spirit was poured out on all people so that the whole ministry of God belonged to all his household (rather than being contained within the specialized ministry of prophets and priests), we are more inclined to look askance at the localization of God's presence into "thin places" and holy relics or sacred artefacts.

Questions

- In some Christian denominations, relics, icons and altar vessels are considered especially holy. Some Christians will reserve every crumb of the consecrated Communion bread to be consumed by the faithful – others sprinkle theirs for the birds. What are your experiences and feelings about this?
- Have you felt the presence of God very strongly in particular places? What happened, and how did you feel? What are your thoughts about pilgrimage sites such as Santiago de Compostela, or Taizé, or Iona?
- In your life, are there items or places of especial value to you – a wedding ring, the church where you married, a special Bible, something that belonged to your mother, a lock of your child's infant hair? How would you feel if they were lost or destroyed? Explore your feelings about this.

Prayer

Sometimes we sense your presence so vividly; sometimes we are awed by your mystery and power. Other times you seem so faint and far away that we wonder if we imagined you. Help us, you who are always with us, to keep walking in faith, trusting in your presence. Help us make every place into holy ground just by being there with you. Amen.

Holiness 2

BIBLE PASSAGES

Hebrews 12:10b–14, NIVUK

God disciplines us for our good, in order that we may share in his holiness.
No discipline seems pleasant at the time, but painful. Later on, however,
it produces a harvest of righteousness and peace for those who have been
trained by it.

Therefore, strengthen your feeble arms and weak knees. "Make level paths
for your feet," so that the lame may not be disabled, but rather healed. Make
every effort to live in peace with everyone and to be holy; without holiness no
one will see the Lord.

1 Peter 1:13–16, NIVUK

Therefore, with minds that are alert and fully sober, set your hope on the
grace to be brought to you when Jesus Christ is revealed at his coming. As
obedient children, do not conform to the evil desires you had when you lived
in ignorance. But just as he who called you is holy, so be holy in all you do; for
it is written: "Be holy, because I am holy."

Isaiah 1:16–17, NIVUK

Wash and make yourselves clean.
    Take your evil deeds out of my sight; stop doing wrong.
Learn to do right; seek justice. Defend the oppressed.
    Take up the cause of the fatherless; plead the case of the widow.

Amos 5:21–24, NRSVA

I hate, I despise your festivals,
    and I take no delight in your solemn assemblies.
Even though you offer me your burnt-
    offerings and grain-offerings,
I will not accept them;
    and the offerings of well-being of your fatted animals
I will not look upon.
    Take away from me the noise of your songs;
I will not listen to the melody of your harps.
    But let justice roll down like waters,
and righteousness like an ever-flowing stream.

Commentary

In our first study on holiness, we considered our *experience* of holiness, our sense of the numinous, and our encounter with God.

Now we are thinking about holiness within us, embodied by us, a lived discipline for every day.

Charles Wesley began the Holy Club in Oxford in the 1720s, a small group meeting for prayer and Bible study. His brother John came along to the group, and out of these simple, informal beginnings grew the Methodist Church – from which the Holiness movement developed.[77]

John Wesley's faith was rooted in the Bible, and expressed in personal and social holiness. He described holiness as "the renewal of the whole image of God". This was not a matter of personal piety only – saying prayers, reading the Bible, dressing modestly, behaving with dignity and decorum – but included, as an essential internal dimension to faith, working for social justice and societal change.

The abolition of slavery, the relief of the poor, fair trade, "the transformation of the economic and political order, the establishment of Pentecostal commun(al)ism and the abolition of war"[78] were part and parcel of Wesley's vision of what holiness meant.

We can trace the same socio-political vision running through the Law and the Prophets, and in the teaching of Jesus in the Gospels.

For Wesley, as for Amos, Isaiah, and Jesus, there was no question of keeping politics and religion separate, or of contenting oneself with private devotion while turning one's back of a suffering world and despoiled creation. Their vision was of the kingdom of God embracing justice and peace for all humanity and the well-being of all creation. To give one's life to this cause, not as a religious duty but empowered by a fierce flame of love, is what holiness is.

Questions

- The concept of holiness can be daunting. It works best when attempted together, with each taking responsibility for small aspects of a big project. How can your household realistically and sustainably contribute to justice and peace and the well-being of creation? How can your church contribute? How can you personally fit in?

- Holiness is often defined as being "set apart for God". In what ways does our faith set us apart from, and how does it draw us closer to, our fellow human beings?

---

77 A nineteenth-century Methodist group asserting that the development of Christian perfection – a holy life – completed the work of salvation begun on coming to faith.
78 Theodore W. Jennings, *Good News to the Poor: John Wesley's Evangelical Economics*, published by Abingdon Press in 1990.

- Holiness requires commitment to social justice, but it is not only that. What does the practice of personal holiness mean for you, behind closed doors, when the rest of the world has gone away?

Prayer

Holy God, holy and wise, holy and immortal, holy and strong – have mercy upon us. Abba, we belong to you. By your great love that cares for the whole world but also for each of us personally, lead and guide us, pick us up and carry us; do whatever it takes to keep us in your way of perfect love. Amen.

Meekness and submission 1

BIBLE PASSAGES

Matthew 5:5, RSV

Blessed are the meek, for they shall inherit the earth.

Luke 22:27, GNB[79]

I am among you as one who serves.

Matthew 21:4–6, KJV[80]

All this was done, that it might be fulfilled which was spoken by the prophet, saying,
Tell ye the daughter of Sion, Behold, thy King cometh unto thee, meek, and
sitting upon an ass, and a colt the foal of an ass. And the disciples went, and did
as Jesus commanded them.

Matthew 21:12–13, KJV[81]

And Jesus went into the temple of God, and cast out all them that sold and
bought in the temple, and overthrew the tables of the moneychangers, and the
seats of them that sold doves, and said unto them, It is written, My house shall
be called the house of prayer; but ye have made it a den of thieves.

John 2:13–17, GNB

It was almost time for the Passover Festival, so Jesus went to Jerusalem. There
in the Temple he found people selling cattle, sheep, and pigeons, and also the
moneychangers sitting at their tables. So he made a whip from cords and drove
all the animals out of the Temple, both the sheep and the cattle; he overturned
the tables of the moneychangers and scattered their coins; and he ordered
those who sold the pigeons, "Take them out of here! Stop making my Father's
house a marketplace!" His disciples remembered that the scripture says, "My
devotion to your house, O God, burns in me like a fire."

---

79 It would be helpful to look up the whole passage, Luke 22:24–27 – Jesus speaks in response
to his disciples arguing over which of them is the greatest.

80 This is the occasion when Jesus sent his disciples to borrow a donkey for him to ride into
Jerusalem – Palm Sunday. You might like to read the whole passage in Matthew 21:1–9.

81 In Matthew's Gospel, this follows on from the entry into Jerusalem at the beginning of Holy
Week, the days leading up to the crucifixion, whereas John sets the same incident right at
the beginning of Jesus' ministry, following on from his first miracle at the wedding in Cana –
clearing the way of the Lord, as Isaiah prophesied (see Isaiah 40:3).

John 13:12–16, NRSVA

After he had washed their feet, had put on his robe, and had returned to the table, he said to them, "Do you know what I have done to you? You call me Teacher and Lord – and you are right, for that is what I am. So if I, your Lord and Teacher, have washed your feet, you also ought to wash one another's feet. For I have set you an example, that you also should do as I have done to you. Very truly, I tell you, servants are not greater than their master, nor are messengers greater than the one who sent them."

Commentary

These might not seem like the most obvious passages to pick for a study on meekness, but it's important for us to understand what we mean when we describe Jesus as meek – and even more important to grasp what his idea of meekness is.

Because here's the thing: Jesus neither intends nor wants you to be a doormat. One of the reasons the church has been a Petri dish for the bacterial growth of child abuse for so many years is our misunderstanding of Christian meekness. We have understood it to mean being malleable and trusting, uncomplaining and subservient to those over us in hierarchical authority – put simply, letting others treat us as they please and putting up with their outrageous behaviour. That's not meek, it's timid. "For the Spirit God gave us does not make us timid, but gives us power, love and self-discipline" (2 Timothy 1:7, NIVUK).

Jesus was bold, confident, strong, assertive – fully in control of the situations that included him. He was also in control of himself, respecting other people and their boundaries – for example he often asked sick people what they wanted of him rather than rushing in with assumptions about healing; he gave them the dignity of making decisions as part of their healing. His followers are called not to limp subservience but to the more difficult task of living up to the power within us while remembering to include the restraint required of gentleness and respect, being mindful of boundaries and willing to take on lowly and unglamorous roles and tasks.

Questions

- In raising our children, how can we give them assertive confidence to withstand bullies and predators, while teaching them to respect others and encouraging appropriate social restraint (such as politeness, or sitting quietly in church!)?
- In your own life, where are you inclined to be too timid and allow others to overstep your boundaries, and where could you do well to increase your contribution of humble service?
- Describe some examples you have seen of Christian meekness in action, and consider them together.

Prayer

Servant King, mighty Prophet, crucified Lord of all, give me the courage and self-discipline to follow in your way. Give me courage to challenge bullies and speak truth to power, but with it the willingness to make the tea and do the washing up. Help me to strike the right balance of humble service and prophetic life. Amen.

Meekness and submission 2

BIBLE PASSAGES[82]

Ephesians 5:1, 21, NIVUK

Follow God's example, therefore, as dearly loved children and live a life of love, just as Christ loved us and gave himself up for us as a fragrant offering and sacrifice to God ... Submit to one another out of reverence for Christ.

Romans 12:10b, NIVUK

Honour one another above yourselves.

Matthew 5:38–41, NIVUK

You have heard that it was said, "Eye for eye, and tooth for tooth." But I tell you, do not resist an evil person. If anyone slaps you on the right cheek, turn to them the other cheek also. And if anyone wants to sue you and take your shirt, hand over your coat as well. If anyone forces you to go one mile, go with them two miles.

Luke 10:38–42, NIVUK

As Jesus and his disciples were on their way, he came to a village where a woman named Martha opened her home to him. She had a sister called Mary, who sat at the Lord's feet listening to what he said. But Martha was distracted by all the preparations that had to be made. She came to him and asked, "Lord, don't you care that my sister has left me to do the work by myself? Tell her to help me!"

"Martha, Martha," the Lord answered, "you are worried and upset about many things, but few things are needed – or indeed only one. Mary has chosen what is better, and it will not be taken away from her."

Mark 3:31–35, NIVUK

Jesus' mother and brothers arrived. Standing outside, they sent someone in to call him. A crowd was sitting round him, and they told him, "Your mother and brothers are outside looking for you."

"Who are my mother and my brothers?" he asked.

Then he looked at those seated in a circle round him and said, "Here are my mother and my brothers! Whoever does God's will is my brother and sister and mother."

---

82 See also all of Ephesians 5 and the study in this book called "Marriage 2" on page 37.

Commentary

Biblical teaching on submission offers two different approaches or aspects. The first, which comes most readily to mind, is the consistent biblical recommendation to live at peace with the structures of patriarchal society – children honouring and obeying parents, wives gently submitting to husbands, slaves gladly and without resentment working for those who own them. Both the Old Testament and the teaching of Paul (by background a Pharisee) encourage us in that direction.

It is important to note that the Old Testament (both the prophets and the law) urge mercy and restraint – leaving margins for the gleaners, giving back the cloak a poor man offered as a pledge, taking care of the fatherless and widows, etc.

When Paul in his letters writes about children obeying their parents, he also encourages parents to refrain from goading or provoking their children. When he writes of wives submitting to their husbands, he also challenges husbands to lead with humility and self-sacrifice, following the example of Jesus.

This is the conventional mode: of patriarchal society, but gently and graciously applied.

Jesus himself offers a startlingly different approach. The non-resistance he advocates is subversive and assertive: the Roman soldier had the right to require you to carry his pack a mile, but would get into trouble if you took it two. A right-handed man struck his inferior on the right cheek back-handed – offering him the other cheek obliged him to strike with an open hand, the blow of an equal.

When Martha asked Mary to resume the female role of household service, Jesus defended her choice to sit among the men and learn theology with them. When his family arrived (to take him into custody as a madman) and asked to see him, he resisted the social expectations to prioritize their right of access. Consistently, Jesus redefined submission as obedience to God, not to any human being or any social custom.

Questions

- What social rules of respect, authority, and submission did you grow up with? Who was in charge, in your household, when you were a child? Were you happy with that, or did you make changes once you grew up?

- Does a community need authority figures? Do you think it is important to have leaders who must be obeyed and rules to stick to – or is it just as good (or better?) always to consult and negotiate? What pros and cons can you imagine?

- Imagine you have been drawn in to a conversation where you find the other person's views objectionable, even obnoxious. You remember the Romans 12 injunction to honour others above yourself, but want to stand up for what you believe as well. How might you go about that?

Prayer

You, Jesus, are our Lord and Master – only you. By your free Spirit, may we stand tall, stand in our own space with dignity and confidence; yet, by the humility and self-sacrifice of your cross, remind us of the cost of following you. May we be as self-controlled and gentle as we are confident and free. Amen.

Kenosis 1

BIBLE PASSAGES

Philippians 2:3–11, GNB

Don't do anything from selfish ambition or from a cheap desire to boast, but be humble toward one another, always considering others better than yourselves. And look out for one another's interests, not just for your own. The attitude you should have is the one that Christ Jesus had:

He always had the nature of God,
>   but he did not think that by force he should try to remain[83] equal with God.
Instead of this, of his own free will he gave up all he had,
>   and took the nature of a servant.
He became like a human being
>   and appeared in human likeness.
He was humble and walked the path of obedience all the way to death –
>   his death on the cross.
For this reason God raised him to the highest place above
>   and gave him the name that is greater than any other name.
And so, in honor of the name of Jesus,
>   all beings in heaven, on earth, and in the world below will fall on their knees,
and all will openly proclaim that Jesus Christ is Lord,
>   to the glory of God the Father.

Luke 22:24–27, NIVUK

A dispute also arose among them as to which of them was considered to be greatest. Jesus said to them, "The kings of the Gentiles lord it over them; and those who exercise authority over them call themselves Benefactors. But you are not to be like that. Instead, the greatest among you should be like the youngest, and the one who rules like the one who serves. For who is greater, the one who is at the table or the one who serves? Is it not the one who is at the table? But I am among you as one who serves."

John 12:12–15, NET

The next day the large crowd that had come to the feast heard that Jesus was coming to Jerusalem. So they took branches of palm trees and went out to

---

83 "Remain" or "become".

meet him. They began to shout, "Hosanna! Blessed is the one who comes in the name of the Lord! Blessed is the king of Israel!" Jesus found a young donkey and sat on it, just as it is written, "Do not be afraid, people of Zion; look, your king is coming, seated on a donkey's colt!"

Commentary

The Nicene Creed, agreed upon in 325 AD, has this to say about Jesus:

> *For us and for our salvation*
> *he came down from heaven:*
> *by the power of the Holy Spirit*
> *he became incarnate from the Virgin Mary,*
> *and was made man.*

Christians believe the mystery of the incarnation is that the eternal, almighty omniscient, omnipresent God was fully present in Jesus, who was also fully human. It's easy to say that and to write it down, but impossible to comprehend intellectually – and that's what we mean when we say it's a mystery.

Theologians have puzzled and argued through the centuries since about the exact nature of the *kenosis* this involves. *Kenosis* is a Greek word meaning "self-emptying". Our Bible passage from Philippians has the crucial verse (verse 7): "he gave up all he had". The NIV translates this as "made himself nothing"; the Authorized Version has "made himself of no reputation", and the NRSVA has "emptied himself".

The arguments are about the specifics of what Jesus retained of his divine attributes, and what he gave up in being fully human. But for our purposes, in reading the Bible not as an intellectual exercise but to show us how to live, the important thing to grasp is that he did this; he gave up advantage, power, and majesty to be an ordinary person living with all the rest of us. Further, though he had the power and grace and wisdom to be a great teacher, he turned aside from status to embrace humility. Our passage from John shows his response to the people's desire to make him a political leader: he chose a humble donkey not a war horse, deliberately fulfilling a scripture affirming that he was the coming king but clarifying that his leadership was not a political statement – rather, the kingdom of heaven drawing near. Jesus' understanding and teaching of the messiah as a suffering servant[84] revolutionized the outlook and expectation of his fellow Jews, who had been hoping for another king like David to usher in a new golden age for Israel.

---

84 You may find Isaiah's Servant Songs helpful as background study: Isaiah 42:1-9; 49:1-13; 50:4-11; and 52:13 – 53:12. The last one is of particular relevance here.

Questions

- In what ways are humility and servanthood expressed in your church tradition?
- What examples of humility have you seen in home and family life?
- Theologians argue about whether *kenosis* meant Jesus was all-knowing and all-powerful, or whether his humanity meant he had to learn and develop like everyone else – only gradually growing into the understanding of himself as messiah. What do you think?

Prayer

Father God, the humility of Jesus challenges us, and putting it into practice is very hard to do. Give us grace not only to love humility in others, but to practise it ourselves, so that slowly we may become more like the Master we serve. Amen.

Kenosis 2

BIBLE PASSAGES

Matthew 11:16–19, NIVUK

"To what can I compare this generation? They are like children sitting in the market-places and calling out to others:

'We played the pipe for you, and you did not dance;
we sang a dirge, and you did not mourn.'

For John came neither eating nor drinking, and they say, 'He has a demon.' The Son of Man came eating and drinking, and they say, 'Here is a glutton and a drunkard, a friend of tax collectors and sinners.' But wisdom is proved right by her deeds."

Luke 7:36–39, then 44–47, NIVUK

When one of the Pharisees invited Jesus to have dinner with him, he went to the Pharisee's house and reclined at the table. A woman in that town who lived a sinful life learned that Jesus was eating at the Pharisee's house, so she came there with an alabaster jar of perfume. As she stood behind him at his feet weeping, she began to wet his feet with her tears. Then she wiped them with her hair, kissed them and poured perfume on them.

When the Pharisee who had invited him saw this, he said to himself, "If this man were a prophet, he would know who is touching him and what kind of woman she is – that she is a sinner."

... [Jesus] turned towards the woman and said to Simon, "Do you see this woman? I came into your house. You did not give me any water for my feet, but she wet my feet with her tears and wiped them with her hair. You did not give me a kiss, but this woman, from the time I entered, has not stopped kissing my feet. You did not put oil on my head, but she has poured perfume on my feet. Therefore, I tell you, her many sins have been forgiven – as her great love has shown. But whoever has been forgiven little loves little."

Commentary

As a teenager, I went to church every week, but preferred the peaceful service of Evensong over the larger Parish Communion in the morning. One weekend my sister challenged me on this, saying I should be going to morning church. "I will be going to church," I explained, "but I like the evening service better." She replied: "That's all the more reason why you should go to the morning service."

This, in a nutshell, epitomizes the widespread misconception of what *kenosis* means in the context of Christian discipleship. Self-denial, being "a living sacrifice", developed early into asceticism – deliberately choosing what is uncomfortable, unpleasant, or uncongenial; and calling this holiness.

In our readings we see that, for Jesus, becoming fully human meant immersing himself fully in the human experience – enjoying a party, a nice meal, a glass of wine; opening himself to the richness of intimacy and human affection, allowing himself to be caressed and loved tenderly, anointed with perfume, washed with tears, wiped dry with a woman's hair. The *kenosis* of Jesus was not in the same room as asceticism. His humility and servant spirit were brave unto death, but he fully lived and fully loved – Jesus did not hate his own humanity.

We might imagine *kenosis* not as self-loathing or self-punishment, but simply as getting out of the way of the flow of grace; not obstructing the goodness of God by the insistence of ego. Jesus said, you cannot serve God and Mammon, and this is literally so. God is all about creating and giving, Mammon is about destroying and consuming, and *kenosis* in Christian discipleship is about loving, giving, and forgiving; not grabbing, hoarding, and resenting. *Kenosis* is not about loss and psychological starvation; if we all love and give, everyone is blessed – even ourselves.

Questions

- How does the concept of *kenosis* – self-emptying, giving up ego – make you feel? Liberated? Threatened? What possibilities do you see in it? Are there also dangers?

- In your own life, how do you think you might strike a balance between enjoying the delights of being human and accepting the limits of wise restraint? How might this apply to what you eat, what you buy, and how you conduct yourself towards others in your personal relationships?

- John the Baptist lived a radically plain and simple life in the desert. Jesus was far more involved with people, going to their parties and eating in their homes. What aspects of such spiritual expression do you feel are just a matter of temperament and what is a matter of calling? How do you experience this in your own life?

Prayer

Help us, Creator God, to make the most of the time you have given us on this earth. May we not die without knowing what it is to be fully human, fully alive.

Thank you that Jesus showed us both what you, the one true God, are really like, and also the best of what humanity can be. Amen.

Passion 1

BIBLE PASSAGE

Luke 22:39–51, NRSVA

He came out and went, as was his custom, to the Mount of Olives; and the disciples followed him. When he reached the place, he said to them, "Pray that you may not come into the time of trial." Then he withdrew from them about a stone's throw, knelt down, and prayed, "Father, if you are willing, remove this cup from me; yet, not my will but yours be done." Then an angel from heaven appeared to him and gave him strength. In his anguish he prayed more earnestly, and his sweat became like great drops of blood falling down on the ground.

When he got up from prayer, he came to the disciples and found them sleeping because of grief, and he said to them, "Why are you sleeping? Get up and pray that you may not come into the time of trial."

While he was still speaking, suddenly a crowd came, and the one called Judas, one of the twelve, was leading them. He approached Jesus to kiss him; but Jesus said to him, "Judas, is it with a kiss that you are betraying the Son of Man?" When those who were around him saw what was coming, they asked, "Lord, should we strike with the sword?" Then one of them struck the slave of the high priest and cut off his right ear. But Jesus said, "No more of this!" And he touched his ear and healed him.

Commentary

If you've read any Victorian novels, you might have come across the phrase, "She fell into a passion". Nowadays we might say, "She had a tantrum/meltdown". Back then, the word "passion" meant incontinent emotion – rage or distress so great that the person experiencing it could not contain it. I detect a whiff of contempt around "fell into a passion", as though it would happen only to an immature person not fully in control of herself (and, yes, it usually is a "she"); as though a more dignified soul would rise above his circumstances with better grace.

In modern-day job interviews, candidates are sometimes asked to say what they are passionate about – what are the things they care about deeply? So "passion", one way or another, has come to mean the experience of deep emotion, of caring intensely. We also associate it with sexual love: nowadays, if you pick up a novel promising passion, it won't mean tantrums.

As we travel through Lent to Easter, we begin Holy Week with Palm Sunday, when we remember Jesus riding into Jerusalem on the donkey with all the people shouting "Hosanna!" It sometimes seems odd that this comes the week after Passion Sunday, when we commemorate the passion of Jesus – the agonies he endured in the week that culminated in his death: betrayal by his friend, arrest and rough treatment, mockery, scourging, torture. We look steadily at his fear and abandonment, his physical agony, his loneliness. We also make the connection between Jesus's pain and his love – that he went through all that he did because he cared so deeply, both for us and for God. In the Garden of Gethsemane he collapsed in fear and dread at the prospect of what was to come. He accepted it because it was what he came here to do. The passion – the agony he experienced – was because of the passion in his heart, the unquenchable flame of his love.

Questions

- What do you care passionately about in life? Can you make a short list of three to five things? Have these things changed over time or did you always care passionately about these? What did you care about passionately when you were a child?

- Is there anything you care about passionately enough to die for it? Your family? Your faith? Your country? Your home or belongings or pets? Would that depend on what kind of death was involved?

- Is passion sometimes unhelpful? When in personal relationships is it kinder to stand back than to rush in? When have you had to make such a decision?

Prayer

> *When I survey the wondrous cross*
> *On which the Prince of glory died,*
> *My richest gain I count but loss,*
> *And pour contempt on all my pride.*
>
> *Were the whole realm of nature mine,*
> *That were an offering far too small.*
> *Love so amazing, so divine,*
> *Demands my soul, my life, my all.*
> **(Isaac Watts, 1707)**

Passion 2

BIBLE PASSAGES[85]

Mark 15:1b, 4–5, RSV

They bound Jesus and led him away and delivered him to Pilate ... And Pilate again asked him, "Have you no answer to make? See how many charges they bring against you." But Jesus made no further answer ...

Mark 15:15–20, RSV

So Pilate, wishing to satisfy the crowd, released for them Barabbas; and having scourged Jesus, he delivered him to be crucified.

And the soldiers led him away inside the palace (that is, the praetorium); and they called together the whole battalion. And they clothed him in a purple cloak, and plaiting a crown of thorns they put it on him. And they began to salute him, "Hail, King of the Jews!" And they struck his head with a reed, and spat upon him, and they knelt down in homage to him. And when they had mocked him, they stripped him of the purple cloak, and put his own clothes on him. And they led him out to crucify him.

Mark 15:27–32, RSV

And with him they crucified two robbers, one on his right and one on his left. And those who passed by derided him, wagging their heads, and saying, "Aha! You who would destroy the temple and build it in three days, save yourself, and come down from the cross!" So also the chief priests mocked him to one another with the scribes, saying, "He saved others; he cannot save himself. Let the Christ, the King of Israel, come down now from the cross, that we may see and believe." Those who were crucified with him also reviled him.

Commentary

In the first of our studies on passion, we looked at its meaning of deep and powerful feeling. It can come as something of a shock to discover that the root of the word feels intuitively like the exact opposite: "passion" comes from the Latin *passionem* (nominative *passio*), from which we get our word "passive". The past participle is *pati-*, where "patient" comes from, whether that be in the sense of waiting quietly without intervention, or being on the receiving end of medical attention.

---

85 You might like to look at the full text of Mark 15 to help explore our questions.

There's another English word connected to this – "suffer" (from the Latin *sufferre*, i.e. *sub-* "from below" and *ferre* "to bear"). We use it to mean "endure pain", but it also means "allow"; as when Jesus said, "Suffer the little children to come unto me, and forbid them not" (Mark 10:14, KJV).

This sheds a different light on the passion of Jesus – that horrendous week when he had to undergo such bitter suffering as makes us shudder. The full meaning of his passion includes not only his love and his agony, but also his relinquishment of power and control. When passers-by taunted him on the cross, they thought they were mocking him as a charlatan – that he had no power to save himself. But Jesus, who raised Lazarus[86] from the dead and stilled the storm[87] and whose power and glory flashing forth caused the soldiers to fall at his feet,[88] could indeed have saved himself. In his passion, he surrenders himself to the worst humanity can do.[89] Here he plumbs the depths of human experience, surrendering himself to absolute vulnerability. There is a significant relationship between the manger and the cross; in the first Jesus experiences the helplessness of birth and infancy, reliant on the provision of others; in the second he surrenders to the experience of suffering and dying, having given himself up to the choices and decisions of others.

Questions

- In our Bible passages, what words or phrases do you notice that speak of passivity and vulnerability, of Jesus being subject to the power of others?

- What similarities and differences can you find between the manger and the cross? What aspects of human experience did Jesus enter into at the beginning and end of his life? When you think about these two scenarios, how can you relate them to the present-day world in which you live? Where do we, in our day-to-day lives, meet the Jesus of the manger and the cross? In practical terms, how can we respond to him with love? How is this modern encounter with him bound up with our salvation?

- Thinking about the events of Holy Week – the fickle crowd, the Last Supper, the collapse in dread in Gethsemane, Judas's betrayal, the arrest, the mockery, torture, and agonizing death – where can you find connections with experiences you have witnessed or personally undergone in your own life?

---

86 John 11:38–44.
87 Mark 4:35–41.
88 John 10:1–8.
89 See the studies on *"Kenosis"* in this book, pages 135–39.

Prayer

Jesus, Emmanuel, God-with-us, thank you for the courage of your love. Thank you for being willing to go all the way down to the very depths of human experience, to come and find us in our loneliness and fear, in the grief of our betrayals and the desolation of torture. In the agony of your passion we find the hard jewel of your compassion; love that walks beside us wherever we are. Amen.

Obedience 1

BIBLE PASSAGE

Deuteronomy 30:11–20, NIVUK

Now what I am commanding you today is not too difficult for you or beyond your reach. It is not up in heaven, so that you have to ask, "Who will ascend into heaven to get it and proclaim it to us so that we may obey it?" Nor is it beyond the sea, so that you have to ask, "Who will cross the sea to get it and proclaim it to us so that we may obey it?" No, the word is very near you; it is in your mouth and in your heart so that you may obey it.

See, I set before you today life and prosperity, death and destruction. For I command you today to love the Lord your God, to walk in obedience to him, and to keep his commands, decrees and laws; then you will live and increase, and the Lord your God will bless you in the land you are entering to possess.

But if your heart turns away and you are not obedient, and if you are drawn away to bow down to other gods and worship them, I declare to you this day that you will certainly be destroyed. You will not live long in the land you are crossing the Jordan to enter and possess.

This day I call the heavens and the earth as witnesses against you that I have set before you life and death, blessings and curses. Now choose life, so that you and your children may live and that you may love the Lord your God, listen to his voice, and hold fast to him. For the Lord is your life, and he will give you many years in the land he swore to give to your fathers, Abraham, Isaac and Jacob.

Commentary

I'm sure it won't surprise you if I say the Bible is stacked full of verses about obeying God. In many cases, as in our Deuteronomy passage, these are "if … then" commands – if you obey, success and well-being will attend you; if you disobey, calamity will befall you.

In considering these commands, it's important to take a wide and long view, and avoid superstition.

When my daughter was only two, she was playing happily in the front garden, whirling round and round. An old man passing by our gate stopped and told her: "If you keep on doing that you'll fall over."

She cheerfully ignored him, kept spinning, got dizzy, and fell down. Then she ran indoors, silent and afraid, under the impression (I think) that the old man had put a spell on her or uttered some supernatural omen. Though – obviously – he hadn't meant his warning as a threat, she didn't have the life experience to realize it.

Similarly, when God tells us to live like this and we will prosper, depart from this and we will suffer and die, he's not harassing us with threats or imposing arbitrary rules because he's a childish despot addicted to power.

God is I AM THAT I AM – his nature establishes reality. If we follow his way life will go well for us because *that's the way things are*. It doesn't mean our path will always be smooth and easy, but that we will be equipped to meet the challenges we encounter.

Having God's law in our hearts and lives isn't a matter of learning a list of rules by rote and sticking to them inflexibly. It's aligning our whole lives with his whole self, growing into mature understanding through knowing the Scriptures, steeping our souls in prayer, and paying careful attention to every insight, every scientific fact, true wisdom from any and every quarter. All truth is God's truth.

Questions

- To obey God intelligently we have to understand what he wants of us. Alongside your personal study of the Bible, whom do you trust to guide and advise you?
- What does obeying God mean in practical terms in your own life?
- Some very prosperous and successful people are greedy, corrupt, promiscuous, and violent. How are we to understand the Bible promises that we will do well and be protected if we walk in God's way?

Prayer

> *Give me understanding, so that I may keep your law*
>   *and obey it with all my heart.*
> *Your word is a lamp for my feet,*
>   *a light on my path.*
> *Accept, Lord, the willing praise of my mouth,*
>   *and teach me your laws.*
> *Your statutes are my heritage for ever;*
>   *they are the joy of my heart.*
> *My heart is set on keeping your decrees*
>   *to the very end.*
> **(Psalm 119:34, 105, 108, 111–112, NIVUK)**

Amen.

Obedience 2

BIBLE PASSAGES[90]

1 Chronicles 29:23, RSV

Then Solomon sat on the throne of the Lord as king instead of David his father; and he prospered, and all Israel obeyed him.

Matthew 8:9, RSV

"I am a man under authority, with soldiers under me; and I say to one, 'Go,' and he goes, and to another, 'Come,' and he comes, and to my slave, 'Do this,' and he does it."

Acts 5:27–29, RSV

And when they had brought them, they set them before the council. And the high priest questioned them, saying, "We strictly charged you not to teach in this name, yet here you have filled Jerusalem with your teaching and you intend to bring this man's blood upon us." But Peter and the apostles answered, "We must obey God rather than men."

Romans 6:16, RSV

Do you not know that if you yield yourselves to any one as obedient slaves, you are slaves of the one whom you obey, either of sin, which leads to death, or of obedience, which leads to righteousness?

Romans 13:1–2, RSV

Let every person be subject to the governing authorities. For there is no authority except from God, and those that exist have been instituted by God. Therefore he who resists the authorities resists what God has appointed, and those who resist will incur judgment.

Ephesians 6:1, 5a, RSV

Children, obey your parents in the Lord, for this is right ... Slaves, be obedient to those who are your earthly masters ...

Matthew 8:27, RSV

And the men marvelled, saying, "What sort of man is this, that even winds and sea obey him?"

---

90 Look also at Daniel 3 – the story of the burning, fiery furnace.

Commentary[91]

In understanding scriptural teaching on obedience, it's necessary to look at the whole Bible, grasp the principles it teaches, and apply them advisedly. The Bible sees authority in terms of order and accountability, established and upheld to serve justice and protect the vulnerable. The people are accountable to their leader, who is in turn accountable to God. Notice that in our passage from 1 Chronicles, Solomon is described as sitting on *God's* throne – not his or David's.

The centurion who asked Jesus to heal his servant (our passage Matthew 8:9) understood this perfectly, grasping that it was not because of *his personal* authority but because of the authority structure *to which he was accountable* that he was owed obedience.

So, in general the Bible is in favour of authority structures, as they work for social well-being. They are seen as approved by God. But the biblical story is also bristling with examples of individuals called to speak truth to power, to stand up against authority at immense personal cost, in circumstances where the established authority loses its way and steps out of the accountability structure that validates and sanctifies it. This means all of us are called to understand the principles underlying social justice and holy righteousness. None of us should be blindly obedient. Normally we are accountable through the structures of society – our parents, teachers, civic and religious authorities – but it is to God not them that we ultimately owe fealty. We remain personally accountable to him for our choices and actions, if those in authority over us leave his way. At that point our allegiance is still to him, but no longer to them.

The last of our passages shows the perfect example of authority – Jesus, so completely aligned with the will of God that even the forces of nature come under his command.

Questions

- In our society, in what ways do you think our leaders faithfully uphold biblical principle, and where might they fall short or have strayed? How can we as citizens work within the authority structures of society to uphold the ways of God?

- Over what issues would you be prepared to engage in civil disobedience as a matter of principle?

- Old-fashioned methods of raising children exacted obedience, punishing disobedience by isolation, spanking, and withholding food or love. Modern methods favour explanation and gentle restraint, allowing discussion and

---

91 For extension study, see *100 Stand-Alone Bible Studies*, the section on "Learning from the life of Jesus", the study called "His attitude to authority"; and in the section on "Insights from the Law and Prophets", the study called "Putting God first".

dissent, believing that children are doing their best and require clear boundaries and consistent guidance. What are your views?

Prayer

God our Father, we thank you for your gentleness with us. So often we have chosen easier and more attractive options than the way you asked of us. Thank you for forgiving us and continuing to call us your own. Help us to walk in your way with insight and intelligence, not because we are afraid of you but because you invite us into goodness, wisdom, and truth. Amen.

Kairos and *chronos* 1

BIBLE PASSAGES

Mark 8:27–29, NIVUK

Jesus and his disciples went on to the villages around Caesarea Philippi. On the way he asked them, "Who do people say I am?"

They replied, "Some say John the Baptist; others say Elijah; and still others, one of the prophets."

"But what about you?" he asked. "Who do you say I am?"

Luke 19:41–44, NIVUK

As he approached Jerusalem and saw the city, he wept over it and said, "If you, even you, had only known on this day what would bring you peace – but now it is hidden from your eyes. The days will come upon you when your enemies will build an embankment against you and encircle you and hem you in on every side. They will dash you to the ground, you and the children within your walls. They will not leave one stone on another, because you did not recognise the time of God's coming to you."

Mark 1:15, NIVUK

"The time has come," he said. "The kingdom of God has come near. Repent and believe the good news!"

2 Corinthians 6:1–2, NIVUK

As God's fellow workers we urge you not to receive God's grace in vain. For he says,
"In the time of my favour I heard you,
and in the day of salvation I helped you."
I tell you, now is the time of God's favour, now is the day of salvation.

Luke 4:17–21, NIVUK

Unrolling [the scroll, Jesus] found the place where it is written:
"The Spirit of the Lord is on me, because he has anointed me to proclaim good news to the poor. He has sent me to proclaim freedom for the prisoners and recovery of sight for the blind, to set the oppressed free, to proclaim the year of the Lord's favour."
Then he rolled up the scroll, gave it back to the attendant and sat down.
The eyes of everyone in the synagogue were fastened on him. He began by saying to them, "Today this scripture is fulfilled in your hearing."

Commentary

The *kairos* is an important biblical concept. There are two Greek words for the two different types of time – *kairos* and *chronos*. The word "chronological" comes from *chronos*, referring to the linear flow of events as we might order them on a timeline. A wag once said that life is just one darned thing after another[92]: that's *chronos*.

Kairos is the other kind of time. It means both "time" and "action", and is something like an actor's cue or the starting gun of a race; what is sometimes called "God's *now* moment" – the time to act.

With regard to my own searching and questioning, a dear friend[93] once wrote to me, "Watch for the *kairos*." The ancient Chinese sage Lao Tsu said, "In action, watch the timing."[94]

The art of the effective is not so much about Herculean effort as about being the right person in the right place doing the right thing at the right time. This is, essentially, the nature of the prophetic life. The key to it is paying attention to what God is saying and doing, and being ready to respond.

Questions

- Shakespeare said: "There is a tide in the affairs of men, which, taken at the flood, leads on to fortune; omitted, all the voyage of their life is bound in shallows and in miseries. On such a full sea are we now afloat, and we must take the current when it serves, or lose our ventures."[95] Can you think of *kairos* moments in history that were triumphantly taken – or regrettably allowed to pass?

- Can you think of a moment in your life when you knew this was the right moment to act – and you were ready with your leap of faith? And can you think of a time when you weren't ready, and the moment passed by, and maybe that made a lasting difference?

- What do you think we might do to make ourselves ready to respond when the *kairos* moment suddenly shines clear and life says *"Now!"*?

Prayer

O Ancient of Days, our times are in your hand, and every opportunity, everymoment, is your gift. Help us to value every passing day, and help us to

---

92 "Life is just one damn thing after another," attributed to Elbert Hubbard; in *Items of Interest*, Vol. 33 (1911), page 8.
93 Father Thomas Cullinan OSB.
94 Tao Te Ching, chapter 8.
95 *Julius Caesar*, Act 4, Scene 3, lines 218–224.

inhabit our time so vividly and consciously that we remain sensitive to what you are saying, what you are doing. Grant that we may not miss the *kairos* when it comes, but live attuned to your voice and your presence, ready in every moment for the whispered "Now!" Amen.

Kairos and *chronos* 2

BIBLE PASSAGE

Ecclesiastes 3:1–15, NIVUK

There is a time for everything,
and a season for every activity under the heavens:

a time to be born and a time to die,
a time to plant and a time to uproot,

a time to kill and a time to heal,
a time to tear down and a time to build,

a time to weep and a time to laugh,
a time to mourn and a time to dance,

a time to scatter stones and a time to gather them,
a time to embrace and a time to refrain from embracing,
a time to search and a time to give up,
a time to keep and a time to throw away,
a time to tear and a time to mend,
a time to be silent and a time to speak,

a time to love and a time to hate,
a time for war and a time for peace.

What do workers gain from their toil? I have seen the burden God has laid
on the human race. He has made everything beautiful in its time. He has
also set eternity in the human heart; yet no one can fathom what God has
done from beginning to end. I know that there is nothing better for people
than to be happy and to do good while they live. That each of them may eat
and drink, and find satisfaction in all their toil – this is the gift of God. I know
that everything God does will endure for ever; nothing can be added to it and
nothing taken from it. God does it so that people will fear him.[96]

96 This could be more helpfully rephrased: "God does all this, so we hold him in reverence."
Young's Literal Translation has (for verse 14): *I have known that all that God doth is to the age, to
it nothing is to be added, and from it nothing is to be withdrawn; and God hath wrought that they
do fear before Him*, which means, in effect, that God who made everything else also made our
reverence of him. What it *doesn't* mean is that God is putting on a display of power for the purpose
of impressing or frightening us.

Whatever is has already been,
and what will be has been before;
and God will call the past to account.

Commentary

The ordinary is underrated. If Kairos and Chronos were sisters, Kairos would be the glamorous, fascinating, charismatic one, tossing her glorious hair and (justifiably) promising great things. Chronos would have hung the laundry out in good time to dry and be standing with her apron on, quietly humming a song and doing the washing up. Kairos is good for a night out that you'll never forget, but Chronos is the one to marry.

In the church's liturgical year we follow the round from Advent through Christmas, Epiphany, Lent, Easter, Pentecost, and Trinity. Then came the "Sundays after Trinity", seeing us through to All Saints. A few decades ago adjustments were made, and the Sundays after Trinity (and a few other in-betweeners) became "Ordinary Time". How boring does that sound? But I love this hallowing of our ordinary time – where we are born and die, where we encounter all the dear and beautiful homeliness of the everyday, where we build the habits of reverence and peace that make our lives holy. And ordinary time, the *chronos* of our lives, is also the setting for the *kairos*, allowing it to stand out and shine.

Questions

- What would an ordinary day hold, for you?
- If war or natural disaster suddenly devastated your life, what are the ordinary, everyday things you would miss?
- How might we best work with the *chronos*, the ordinary flow of our days, to make ourselves ready for the *kairos* moments when they come?

Prayer

God of quietness and peace, God of small and homely things, God who made us to flourish in wholesome routines and habits of reverence, thank you so much for the round of days that shapes our lives. Thank you for the seasons that come and go – the snowdrops and the butterflies that have their time and are gone, the frost and fire, the unfurling of leaves, the tadpoles in the garden pond. There is so much joy and comfort in ordinary things, so much peace in quiet days and simple pleasures. Still our restlessness, God of our ordinary time, and teach us the skilful art of contentment. May every morning that we open our eyes find us grateful for the gift of a new day, and mindful that the time will come when there will be no more pearls to string, and the work will be ready for inspection. Amen.

Power 1

BIBLE PASSAGES

2 Timothy 1:7, KJV

For God hath not given us the spirit of fear; but of power, and of love, and of a sound mind.

Zechariah 4:6b, KJV

Not by might, nor by power, but by my spirit, saith the Lord of hosts.

2 Corinthians 4:6–7, KJV

For God, who commanded the light to shine out of darkness, hath shined in our hearts, to give the light of the knowledge of the glory of God in the face of Jesus Christ.

But we have this treasure in earthen vessels, that the excellency of the power may be of God, and not of us.

2 Corinthians 12:9–10, RSV

[The Lord] said to me, "My grace is sufficient for you, for my power is made perfect in weakness." I will all the more gladly boast of my weaknesses, that the power of Christ may rest upon me. For the sake of Christ, then, I am content with weaknesses, insults, hardships, persecutions, and calamities; for when I am weak, then I am strong.

Commentary

Our Bible passages bring out a very exciting aspect of God's power at work in our lives. Why it is exciting is that it imports the excellent news that you can be the world's most ineffectual and inadequate person and that won't be a problem; it might even help. Even if you can't think, speak, or move, that won't be an obstacle. Because (so says the Lord himself) "my power is made perfect in weakness."

In fact, when it comes to the power of God, our strengths and natural abilities, our talents and status and influence and wealth, can be a positive hindrance. As Jesus pointed out, his kingdom is not of this world. Building the kingdom of heaven on earth is not about creating an effective organization. It's not a numbers game and success doesn't come into it.

Being open, simple, and humble are the requirements. All you have to do is pay close attention to what God is doing so you can join in and not obstruct it. And even if you're in a coma and aren't paying conscious attention to anything, you can still be part of the power of God at work, because you aren't in a position to obstruct it.

The power of God makes use of our frailty and failings. There is no need for anxiety, shame, or fear; we need only put ourselves and our resources at his disposal.

Our passage from Timothy offers a small footnote to this relaxing news: the part about sound mind. "Let go and let God" is a cheerful maxim, but it's important as well to use such common sense and intelligence as we have. We owe it to our Lord to do our very best for him; to actually plan and make strategies and think things through, so as to maximize the resources we can put at his disposal. This isn't about just not bothering to try hard. But it is Good News indeed to discover that even if we feel we have little to contribute, that isn't important. We give what we can, what we have, and God makes up the rest.

Questions

- Can you think of a time when you saw something of God, or he spoke to you, through a little child or through somebody very poor or sick or old?
- What would you evaluate as the strengths in your life, which you could put at God's disposal? Be honest; false humility obscures truth. And what would you regard as your weaknesses? Try to imagine ways God could perhaps use those weaknesses to strengthen the goodness, kindness, and love of your brothers and sisters, and so help build the kingdom.
- Can you remember a time when you really messed things up, but something good came of it anyway? As you discuss these experiences in the group, try to discern the hand of God at work in these things that have happened.

Prayer

God of love, please use us to build your kingdom. Please do us the honour of letting us help in your great work of healing, hope, and love. Show us what we can do, and show us how not to hinder your work. Help us to see how even our insignificance and ordinariness can be useful to you, and can be channels of your grace. For we ask it in Jesus' name. Amen.

Power 2

BIBLE PASSAGE

Ephesians 6:10–20, NIVUK

Finally, be strong in the Lord and in his mighty power. Put on the full armour of God, so that you can take your stand against the devil's schemes. For our struggle is not against flesh and blood, but against the rulers, against the authorities, against the powers of this dark world and against the spiritual forces of evil in the heavenly realms. Therefore put on the full armour of God, so that when the day of evil comes, you may be able to stand your ground, and after you have done everything, to stand. Stand firm then, with the belt of truth buckled round your waist, with the breastplate of righteousness in place, and with your feet fitted with the readiness that comes from the gospel of peace. In addition to all this, take up the shield of faith, with which you can extinguish all the flaming arrows of the evil one. Take the helmet of salvation and the sword of the Spirit, which is the word of God.

And pray in the Spirit on all occasions with all kinds of prayers and requests. With this in mind, be alert and always keep on praying for all the Lord's people. Pray also for me, that whenever I speak, words may be given me so that I will fearlessly make known the mystery of the gospel, for which I am an ambassador in chains. Pray that I may declare it fearlessly, as I should.

Commentary

There are so many reasons to love this inspiring and luminous Bible passage, but what's especially helpful for us in thinking about the power of God is that it identifies and lists the different aspects of God's power available to us, using the imagery of armour to protect us and weapons to defend ourselves with.

Paul does make it very clear that this fight is not against each other. We are not meant to be taking sides or attacking people. Anywhere we are doing that, we are destroying ourselves and our battle is not the Lord's. Our fight is against spiritual forces of evil – that would be such things as greed, inequality, cruelty, child abuse, lies, war, and bullying; not people.

He identifies truth, righteousness, faith, and salvation as our instruments of power. Particularly interesting is where he says: "with your feet fitted with the readiness that comes from the gospel of peace". This means that the gospel of peace is to be our impetus, like the fuel in our tank, the thing that gets and keeps us moving. The gospel of peace – that is, peace as we encounter it in Jesus – comes from forgiveness and reconciliation, from trust in God, a clean heart, from living in God's will and choosing not what is personally advantageous but what is right.

He says the sword in our hand is to be the word of God. That can include the Scriptures, of course, for we surely encounter God's word in the Bible. But the word of God goes beyond that. Jesus himself is the living Word of God,[97] and there is also the "now" word of God in prophecy and the prophetic life – the movement of the Spirit in our hearts that directs and chastens us, impels and restrains us.

Paul also identifies prayer as part of this power at work in our lives. I'm choosing my words carefully, not saying "the power we wield", because in truth the idea is for us to make ourselves available for God to use us, not for us to use God. In prayer, we take up our calling to anchor the Light to the patch of earth where we find ourselves, to invoke and call upon the Holy Spirit, activating the channel that Jesus has created between humanity and heaven.

Questions

- In our battle against evil, what are the ways in which we can be sure to challenge and resist destructive forces without making the mistake of identifying the people who are doing wrong as our enemies? How can we stand firm with people against the sins that shame us all, rather than taking sides against those who represent viewpoints unacceptable to us?

- In our contemporary society, what would you pick out as the issues on which you feel called to stand firm? What does this mean for you in practical terms?

- Paul speaks of prayer and staying alert in the same breath – paying attention to what's going on and committing it to prayer. He links this to making known the mystery of the gospel. What ways can you identify of moving forward your commitment to pray for our world and God's people in it? If you are or have been in a prayer triplet,[98] what have been your experiences of this? Is it something this group could consider?

Prayer

Almighty God, our Sovereign Lord of Hosts, please channel your power through our lives. Sweep aside all that clogs and impedes your grace and love in us; heal all that disables the movement of the gospel of peace in us. Fill us with truth and faith, with righteousness and your living word. Help us to live as people willing to make a difference. Help us to stand our ground, steady and strong in your love. Amen.

---

97 See chapter 1 of John's Gospel.
98 Three friends meeting regularly to pray.

Miracles 1[99]

BIBLE PASSAGE

Mark 1:21–34, RSV

And they went into Capernaum; and immediately on the sabbath he entered the synagogue and taught. And they were astonished at his teaching, for he taught them as one who had authority, and not as the scribes. And immediately there was in their synagogue a man with an unclean spirit; and he cried out, "What have you to do with us, Jesus of Nazareth? Have you come to destroy us? I know who you are, the Holy One of God." But Jesus rebuked him, saying, "Be silent, and come out of him!" And the unclean spirit, convulsing him and crying with a loud voice, came out of him. And they were all amazed, so that they questioned among themselves, saying, "What is this? A new teaching! With authority he commands even the unclean spirits, and they obey him." And at once his fame spread everywhere throughout all the surrounding region of Galilee.

And immediately he left the synagogue, and entered the house of Simon and Andrew, with James and John. Now Simon's mother-in-law lay sick with a fever, and immediately they told him of her. And he came and took her by the hand and lifted her up, and the fever left her; and she served them.

That evening, at sundown, they brought to him all who were sick or possessed with demons. And the whole city was gathered together about the door. And he healed many who were sick with various diseases, and cast out many demons; and he would not permit the demons to speak, because they knew him.

Commentary

A spiritual teacher I much admire is given to saying every sunrise is a miracle; every flower, every newborn baby is a miracle. I know what he means, but it does muddy the water when people say such things. A miracle is not simply anything that moves you and excites wonder.

Nor is coincidence miraculous. If when walking down the road to the bus stop I pass six people who all have ginger hair, that would be odd enough to make me think – but I wouldn't call it miraculous.

That's not to say these things are empty of spiritual content. The world is God-breathed and all of it is spiritual, in a covenant relationship with God. The whole

---

99 We have three studies on miracles in this book. Here we are thinking about miracles in general. In the next study, "Miracles 2", we'll be thinking about different types of miracle. In the following section, in a study called "Spiritual Charisms", we'll consider the conditions required for miracles to happen.

of life proceeds from God; we must expect it to be full of wonder and meaning. Through coincidence, through the wonders of nature, life – and sometimes God – speaks to us. That's spiritual but not miraculous.

The classic definition of a miracle is an occurrence involving God's intervention suspending the laws of nature, intervening in a natural process.

Now, because this is a conversation not a Sunday-school class, and you are here to think your own thoughts and make up your own minds, I'm going to tell you I personally disagree with that definition of a miracle. I believe that when miracles happen, nature acts exactly in accordance with how nature would always act *given that set of circumstances*, which are so unusual that we never normally get the chance to see them. It is conceivable, though increasingly unlikely, that human beings could so develop spiritually that they could eventually observe, analyze, and understand the forces in play when a miracle occurs. But, to do that, miracles would have to happen more often and more predictably; and, for that to come about, human beings would have to radically alter their mindset on a grand scale.

Questions

- Despite a certain consensus, there's considerable variation in what people individually call "miraculous". What do you think is a miracle, and what is not? Where is the borderline between a straight-up miracle, and God present in or speaking through life circumstances that are astonishing and wonderful but not technically miraculous (e.g. some answers to prayer)?

- Have you ever had personal, direct experience of a miracle? What happened? If you haven't, or aren't sure, what is the nearest thing you have seen to the direct action or intervention of God in your life?

- In our Bible passage, we see Jesus hit the ground running in Capernaum at the beginning of his ministry. Notice how Mark uses the phrases "at once" and "immediately", and starts sentences with "And", to indicate the breathless pace at which everything went. In this section, Mark concentrates on healings and casting out demons. What are demons, in this context? Beings that get inside a person? The term used then for psychiatric and neurological illness? What do you think?

Prayer

God of love and power, we give you thanks for the ministry of Jesus. Thank you for the hope it brought to people who had no other chance to get well. Thank you for how it demonstrates your concern for our well-being. Thank you for what it shows us about the kingdom. As the sacred gospel still continues to unfold in our own lives, please help us to be part of what Jesus is doing today, through his body on earth now – us. Amen.

Miracles 2

BIBLE PASSAGES[100]

Luke 13:11–13, RSV

And there was a woman who had had a spirit of infirmity for eighteen years; she was bent over and could not fully straighten herself. And when Jesus saw her, he called her and said to her, "Woman, you are freed from your infirmity." And he laid his hands upon her, and immediately she was made straight, and she praised God.

Luke 8:43–44, RSV

And a woman who had had a flow of blood for twelve years and could not be healed by any one, came up behind him, and touched the fringe of his garment; and immediately her flow of blood ceased.

Mark 4:37–41, RSV

And a great storm of wind arose, and the waves beat into the boat, so that the boat was already filling. But he was in the stern, asleep on the cushion; and they woke him and said to him, "Teacher, do you not care if we perish?" And he awoke and rebuked the wind, and said to the sea, "Peace! Be still!" And the wind ceased, and there was a great calm. He said to them, "Why are you afraid? Have you no faith?" And they were filled with awe, and said to one another, "Who then is this, that even wind and sea obey him?"

2 Kings 5:14, RSV[101]

So he went down and dipped himself seven times in the Jordan, according to the word of the man of God; and his flesh was restored like the flesh of a little child, and he was clean.

Commentary

Having established in our last study what we consider to be miracles, let's look now at the different types. We usually divide miracles into four different categories: miracles of healing, miracles of nature, miracles of supply, and miracles involving subduing demonic powers.

---

100 Please also look at the healing of the Gerasene demoniac (Luke 8:26–39), and the healing of the   man at Beautiful Gate (Acts 3:1–16); any translation.
101 Please have your Bible open at this story, 2 Kings 5:1–14; any version.

Our passage from Mark 4 is a nature miracle. The healing of the Gerasene demoniac is a subduing of demonic powers. The feeding of the five thousand[102] would be an example of a miracle of supply.

I think it's also helpful to have in mind that miracles of healing subdivide into those that involve healing touch and/or command (as in our passage from Luke 13), those that happen just through touching the clothing or belongings of the minister of healing[103] (as in our passage from Luke 8), and those that happen in a completely different location from the minister of healing, such as the healing of Naaman (who had leprosy), in our extract from 2 Kings. It's worth reading the whole story. Of particular note here is the interesting detail that not only did his leprosy clear up completely, but his flesh after healing was much finer and more supple than you would normally expect in a middle-aged man – "like the flesh of a little child". The healing restored his whole body at a very profound level; it was not just a localized improvement.

It's important for us to consider that the Bible stories of miracles do not all centre on Jesus. The healing of Naaman involved the prophet Elisha, and there are many instances in the Old Testament of the prophets performing miracles. Jesus' disciples, even when quite raw recruits, also wrought miracles.[104]

Questions

- What examples from the Bible can you remember of the four types of miracle? What examples of these different types of miracle have you encountered or heard about in modern life?

- In the story of Naaman's healing, look at the part played by his wife's maidservant. Look also at the part of the small boy in the feeding of the five thousand. What did they do? To what extent did the miracles depend on their involvement? What can we learn from that about our own contribution to making miracles happen?

- Some Bible miracles involve raising the dead.[105] In your view, should we categorize raising the dead as a healing miracle or a nature miracle? What are your reasons?

Prayer

Amazing God, every day with you is a walk in wonderland. Because you hold

---

102 Mark 6:30–44.

103 See Luke 7:1–10, the healing of the Centurion's servant; any translation.

104 E.g. the sending out of the seventy-two in Luke 10:1–23.

105 E.g. the valley of dry bones in Ezekiel 37:1–14 and the widow of Nain's son in Luke 7:11–17; any version.

our lives in your hands, we can always be full of hope, knowing that you love us and you can do anything. Help us to trust you. Help us to believe in your mighty power. May even our difficult times be leavened by joy in what you can do. Amen.

Transformation 1[106]

BIBLE PASSAGES

1 John 3:2, GNB

My dear friends, we are now God's children, but it is not yet clear what we shall become. But we know that when Christ appears, we shall be like him, because we shall see him as he really is.

2 Corinthians 5:16–17, ESVUK

From now on, therefore, we regard no one according to the flesh. Even though we once regarded Christ according to the flesh, we regard him thus no longer. Therefore, if anyone is in Christ, he is a new creation. The old has passed away; behold, the new has come.

Genesis 28:16, KJV

Jacob awaked out of his sleep and he said: "Surely the Lord is in this place; and I knew it not."

Romans 12:2, KJV

And be not conformed to this world: but be ye transformed by the renewing of your mind, that ye may prove what is that good, and acceptable, and perfect, will of God.

Matthew 6:22–23, NRSVA

The eye is the lamp of the body. So, if your eye is healthy, your whole body will be full of light; but if your eye is unhealthy, your whole body will be full of darkness.

Commentary

Transformation is at the heart of the biblical story, whether it is the loss of innocence in the Adam and Eve story of the fall, the journeying of the people of God away from child sacrifice to animal sacrifice in the story of the binding of Isaac, or the moving on from scapegoats and sacrifices to the concept of grace as a simple gift freely given, only waiting to be embraced. The biblical experience of God is about a continual development and expansion of understanding, a gradual opening to the realization that the presence of God is for all places and all peoples. God is not a local god shining

---

106 The study on "Sanctification 2" in the section "The Way of a Disciple" is helpful extension material for this. Likewise the study "Faith and Sight 2" later in this section, and "Transfiguration: Sight and Insight" in the section of *100 Stand-Alone Bible Studies* called "Themes from the Four Gospels: Mark".

his light over a select and limited collection of people. He is there to surprise us in every encounter. So spiritual transformation is experienced culturally by the whole faith community in the unfolding journey the Bible charts. And of course we see transformation in the lives of individuals as they find faith – for example the conversion of Paul in Acts 9, who became blind in order that he might gain new insight!

According to the Bible, this transformation starts in the mind and is all about perception. It relies on vision. The kind of people we are depends on our attitudes, which in turn depend on how we see things. Though transformation is ultimately about character and holiness – what we do and say, our habits and decisions – it begins with looking deeply and discovering new insight. It springs from the willingness no longer to be conditioned by how our society sees things, but to have our eyes opened to the vision of Christ – who looks at life very differently from the world.

An important aspect of this is looking at Christ – gazing upon him in the prayer of adoration, and looking into his life as the Gospels narrate it and other believers bear witness to it.

Questions

- Can you think of a time when something happened that called into question all your assumptions and made you see everything differently? Perhaps a story or an incident on the news, or someone who acted differently from how you expected.

- Our passage from Romans says, *Be not conformed to this world: but be ye transformed by the renewing of your mind.* In what ways do you find yourself slowly conforming to the creeping influence of the world? What helps you renew your mind? Is this something Jesus just does for you, or is it also to do with your own choices of what you think about and get involved in?

- What are some of the ways you think Jesus sees life differently from our society – from "the World"?

Prayer

Open my eyes that I may see
Glimpses of truth Thou hast for me;
Place in my hands the wonderful key
That shall unclasp and set me free.
Silently now I wait for Thee,
Ready my God, Thy will to see;
Open my eyes, illumine me,
Spirit divine!
(Clara H. Scott, 1895)

Transformation 2

BIBLE PASSAGES

John 3:3, KJV

Except a man be born again, he cannot see the kingdom of God.

1 Corinthians 15:51–58, ESVUK

Behold! I tell you a mystery. We shall not all sleep, but we shall all be changed, in a moment, in the twinkling of an eye, at the last trumpet. For the trumpet will sound, and the dead will be raised imperishable, and we shall be changed. For this perishable body must put on the imperishable, and this mortal body must put on immortality. When the perishable puts on the imperishable, and the mortal puts on immortality, then shall come to pass the saying that is written:

"Death is swallowed up in victory."
"O death, where is your victory?
O death, where is your sting?"

The sting of death is sin, and the power of sin is the law. But thanks be to God, who gives us the victory through our Lord Jesus Christ.

Therefore, my beloved brothers, be steadfast, immovable, always abounding in the work of the Lord, knowing that in the Lord your labour is not in vain.

Proverbs 29:18, KJV

Where there is no vision, the people perish: but he that keepeth the law, happy is he.

Commentary

There are two aspects or directions to transformation. It's like when you drop a stone into a pond – the ripples spread both from the centre to the edge and back from the edge to the centre. The two aspects of transformation operate on different time frames. They are like the two types of growth in a tree (these create the rings in the trunk) – the fast summer growth giving flexibility, and the slow winter growth creating endurance. You need both.

One aspect of transformation travels from the centre to the periphery of your being. This is the vision, the insight we looked at in "Transformation 1". It pivots the orientation of the soul from the dullness of materialism, the realm of death, to the insight of the world of light. One moment you just don't get it, then suddenly you see. It changes everything. It is, in effect, a rebirth. It transforms you. And though you can get tired and discouraged once you have been born again, you cannot go back to being like you were before you hatched.

The second aspect of transformation is habit. This travels in the opposite direction – from the periphery of your soul in to the centre. If vision establishes the essential self, habit establishes what we call "second nature". Habit protects you from losing your way in times of stress and pressure. It has an energy, a momentum that builds. If the transformation of vision is instantaneous, coming in a flash of understanding that changes everything, habit is the routine proceeding from that insight, establishing and confirming it. The small daily choices, actions, and patterns of speech compound and develop, strengthening into a *modus operandi* that is extremely hard to shift.

If you put these two aspects together – insight and habit – you have a strong disciple; strengthened even against his or her own weakness and vulnerability.

Can you see how both aspects are present in our Bible passages? The vision, but also the law in our Proverbs verse, and in Corinthians: " …we shall all be changed, in a moment, in the twinkling of an eye… Therefore, my beloved brothers, be steadfast, immovable, always abounding in the work of the Lord." Paul is speaking of the transformation of all creation at the second coming, but it begins now in the transformation of our hearts and lives.

Questions

- In what ways have you tried to establish habits that express and confirm your personal beliefs?
- Can you identify areas in your life where you would like to build new habits to strengthen you spiritually?
- Habits. Once in place, we do them without thinking. What habits do your family members or friends have that really annoy you? Do you think they do them on purpose? Do you have habits that annoy even yourself? Losing keys, perhaps, or stubbing your toe on the same place. If a person wanted to shift these habits, how might they do it?[107]

Prayer

God of all wisdom and power, you made the rhythms of birth and death, of seasons in life, the round of the passing years. Help us to perceive your hand at work in all creation. Help us to work with you in the wisdom of your rhythms to strengthen

---

107 Hint: It starts with *noticing*. Habit and vision completely interlock.

and establish life and goodness, to nurture truth and grace, to affirm the centrality of kindness and love. For we ask it in Jesus' name. Amen.

Hope 1

BIBLE PASSAGES

1 Peter 1:3–9, NRSVA

Blessed be the God and Father of our Lord Jesus Christ! By his great mercy he has given us a new birth into a living hope through the resurrection of Jesus Christ from the dead, and into an inheritance that is imperishable, undefiled, and unfading, kept in heaven for you, who are being protected by the power of God through faith for a salvation ready to be revealed in the last time. In this you rejoice, even if now for a little while you have had to suffer various trials, so that the genuineness of your faith – being more precious than gold that, though perishable, is tested by fire – may be found to result in praise and glory and honour when Jesus Christ is revealed. Although you have not seen him, you love him; and even though you do not see him now, you believe in him and rejoice with an indescribable and glorious joy, for you are receiving the outcome of your faith, the salvation of your souls.

Matthew 2:1–2, 9–10, NRSVA

In the time of King Herod, after Jesus was born in Bethlehem of Judea, wise men from the East came to Jerusalem, asking, "Where is the child who has been born king of the Jews? For we observed his star at its rising, and have come to pay him homage."

... When they had heard the king, they set out; and there, ahead of them, went the star that they had seen at its rising, until it stopped over the place where the child was. When they saw that the star had stopped, they were overwhelmed with joy.

Commentary

"I've just hung the laundry out so I hope it doesn't rain."

"I hope the train's on time today."

"I hope we took the right turning."

All these imply uncertainty and guesswork, and in ordinary conversation that's how we use the word "hope". Christian hope is not like that.

When we say our hope is in Christ, we aren't talking about having gambled everything on a horse that might after all come in last. In fact, it's quite the opposite. We're saying that, despite the grim or unpromising circumstances of our lives, we have sure and steadfast faith in a reality that others cannot see – but it is fully and really there.

Our Bible passage about the Magi has nothing to do with uncertainty. These men have been studying the stars all their lives and they know without doubt the significance of what they have seen – it's just a matter of finding their way to Jesus.

In our passage from 1 Peter comes this wonderful phrase – that we have been given "new birth into a living hope" through the resurrection of Jesus. This is particularly interesting for helping us understand Christian hope, because Peter has *already seen* the risen Lord: he's not merely hoping Jesus might rise from the dead; he's seen him risen and seen him ascend into heaven. Christ in in heaven now, but the certainty remains as Peter's inner witness – his hope. Also, the idea of being born into a living hope suggests that the hope is our context, bigger than us; we are inside it rather than its being a little flickering flame inside us. We now belong in this new world of hope and see life according to its light. We have permanently moved out of despair; we live somewhere else now, and see things differently.

Questions

- When you read these passages and think about the unshakeable confidence that Peter had in the risen Jesus and the Magi had in the birth of Christ, how does it make you feel about your own faith? Do you think "Yes! That's just like me!" – or, rather, "I wish I could feel so sure"?

- If you had to describe your faith and hope in Christ as a light, what sort of light would it be? All lit up like a football stadium? A candle flame in danger of being put out by the wind? A torch that could do with a new battery? A bedside lamp, comforting and warm, but not over-bright? A reading lamp, very focused? A streetlamp to show others the way? What sort of light?

- Later in his letter (1 Peter 3:15, NIVUK), Peter says: "Always be prepared to give an answer to everyone who asks you to give the reason for the hope that you have." Why do you believe in Jesus?

- Everyone has times when the light of their faith and hope falters.[108] What do you do when that happens to you? How do you strengthen your faith and hope?

Prayer

Beloved Jesus, who told your friend Peter that you had prayed for him that his faith might not fail – please pray for me. By your grace may I abide in the living hope of the gospel my whole life long; may I never let go of my end of the line that links me to the certain hope of your healing and victorious love. Amen.

---

108 See Matthew 11:2–6.

Hope 2

BIBLE PASSAGES

Romans 8:18–25, NRSVA

I consider that the sufferings of this present time are not worth comparing with the glory about to be revealed to us. For the creation waits with eager longing for the revealing of the children of God; for the creation was subjected to futility, not of its own will but by the will of the one who subjected it, in hope that the creation itself will be set free from its bondage to decay and will obtain the freedom of the glory of the children of God. We know that the whole creation has been groaning in labour pains until now; and not only the creation, but we ourselves, who have the first fruits of the Spirit, groan inwardly while we wait for adoption, the redemption of our bodies. For in hope we were saved. Now hope that is seen is not hope. For who hopes for what is seen? But if we hope for what we do not see, we wait for it with patience.

1 Corinthians 13:8–13, NRSVA

Love never ends. But as for prophecies, they will come to an end; as for tongues, they will cease; as for knowledge, it will come to an end. For we know only in part, and we prophesy only in part; but when the complete comes, the partial will come to an end. When I was a child, I spoke like a child, I thought like a child, I reasoned like a child; when I became an adult, I put an end to childish ways. For now we see in a mirror, dimly, but then we will see face to face. Now I know only in part; then I will know fully, even as I have been fully known. And now faith, hope, and love abide, these three; and the greatest of these is love.

2 Peter 1:19b, NRSVA

You will do well to be attentive to this as to a lamp shining in a dark place, until the day dawns and the morning star rises in your hearts.

Commentary

In our first study we looked at the certainty of the Christian hope – not wishful thinking but absolute confidence in the risen Jesus. We know him. We trust in him. We live in him.

In our Bible passages now, we examine the reason we describe this conviction as "hope" and "faith". It's because the ground of our hope is – although really there – not fully revealed.

The passage from 2 Peter puts it well: our hope in Christ is a real light, but it will no longer be necessary when the sun rises. As Paul expresses it in the passage from 1 Corinthians, our hope and faith belong to the partially revealed stage we live in at the moment; one day they will no longer be necessary (just as the wise men needed the star only until they found the infant Jesus).

There's a New Year cartoon[109] I love, which shows two characters chatting as one plants seeds in a garden of raised beds formed from the numbers of the coming year. The onlooker says, "Why be so optimistic about the year ahead? What do you think it will bring? Everything seems so messed up." The other replies, "I think it will bring flowers." The questioner asks, "Yes? How come?" The gardener replies, "Because I am planting flowers."

The realization of our Christian hope – its full flowering – will come to pass anyway, but we have a role to play; we can help. Just as our hearts are anchored to heaven by our hope in Jesus, so also heaven is firmly attached to our hearts. That means we don't have to wait; we can start now. We, here on earth, can plant the seeds of the tree of life that grows in our homeland. This is called building the kingdom.

Questions

- The US TV children's show host Fred Rogers encouraged his viewers to keep hope and faith alive in difficult times by looking for the helpers[110] – those who are, like our cartoon character, planting flowers. In your life, who are (or were) the helpers? Who planted your flowers?

- What part of the reign of Jesus do we already have in place and what part are we still waiting for? How much of what we are waiting for depends on us and how much is beyond our control?

- Our Romans passage says "… if we hope for what we do not see, we wait for it with patience." What is the place of patience? How might we cultivate it? Describe some instances from daily life that need patience to achieve a positive outcome. What is the difference between eagerness and impatience? How easy do you find it to be patient?

---

109 By Spanish artist J. M. Nieto. It originally appeared on 1 January 2017 in the Spanish paper *ABC.es*, where Nieto's work features daily.

110 "When I was a boy and I would see scary things in the news, my mother would say to me, 'Look for the helpers. You will always find people who are helping. To this day, especially in times of disaster, I remember my mother's words, and I am always comforted by realizing that there are still so many helpers – so many caring people in this world." Fred Rogers, in *Mister Rogers Talks with Parents*, published by Berkley Publishing Group in 1983.

Prayer

God of the wide skies and far distances, we are travelling home to you with hope in our hearts. Some of us are in training, others breathless and slow. All of us get footsore and weary. Thank you for leaving a lantern burning in the porch to guide us home. Thank you for Jesus walking along beside us. Thank you for keeping us going. Amen.

Redemption 1

BIBLE PASSAGES

Exodus 15:13, RSV

Thou hast led in thy steadfast love the people whom thou hast redeemed, thou hast guided them by thy strength to thy holy abode.

Psalm 31:5, RSV

Into thy hand I commit my spirit;
thou hast redeemed me, O Lord, faithful God.

Isaiah 1:27, RSV

Zion shall be redeemed by justice,
and those in her who repent, by righteousness.

Isaiah 43:1, RSV

But now thus says the Lord,
he who created you, O Jacob,
he who formed you, O Israel:
"Fear not, for I have redeemed you; I have called you by name, you are mine."

Isaiah 44:22, RSV

I have swept away your transgressions like a cloud,
and your sins like mist;
return to me, for I have redeemed you.

Isaiah 62:12, RSV

And they shall be called The holy people, The redeemed of the Lord; and you shall be called Sought Out, a city not forsaken.

1 Corinthians 6:19–20, RSV

Do you not know that your body is a temple of the Holy Spirit within you, which you have from God? You are not your own; you were bought with a price. So glorify God in your body.

Commentary

The idea of redemption has two aspects. The first comes up commonly in school reports: "Simon has redeemed himself a little in his exam results this year." This sense of redemption applies when someone has acted in a way unworthy of him- or herself, and has now taken action to restore the true standard. In our Bible passages, we see this meaning of the word in Isaiah 43:1 – Israel must, as schoolteachers say, pull its socks up, and return to a standard of integrity worthy of her calling as the people of God.

The second meaning of redemption is where the one redeemed is not the active agent, but has been redeemed by someone else. It comes from the world of property transactions, where the original owner buys back belongings or land he once owned that have passed into somebody else's hands. As a slave was also regarded as property, this applied to people too. The Christian theology of redemption principally derives from this sense of the word. The concept here is that we, who rightly belong to God and bear his image, became enslaved by Mammon, losing our free agency, helpless and bound. This happened because of our poor choices, but we lost our power to put things right. In Jesus, God came to buy us back – to redeem us; setting us free from slavery and returning us to our proper status as God's own people.

Belonging to God rather than Mammon is not just shuttling from one form of slavery to another: we are made by God in his image, and our redemption sets us free to be sons and daughter of God. It restores our true nature. Our 1 Corinthians 6 passage is not meant to imply that we are God's bond-slaves, but rather to remind us of our debt of gratitude in being set free.

Questions

- What do you know about modern-day slavery and people trafficking?[111] Think about those who drudge in inhumane conditions in sweatshops, or are literally sold into slavery. What can we do to join in God's work of redemption for them?
- Explore in the group what being redeemed by Jesus means to you. Is it something you think about often? How does it apply in your life and Christian experience?
- Is there any aspect of your life you think could do with more redeeming? Are there any areas where Mammon might still have a stronghold – a horrible little embassy still set up? If that is the case, how would you like to tackle it?

Prayer

Lord Jesus, thank you for setting us free from the bondage of sin and restoring us to the dignity for which we were born. Thank you for coming to save us. Teach us how to follow you, remind us to exercise our freedom in choosing goodness and life, strengthen and establish us in your free Spirit. Amen.

---

111 NB: Group leader – this is an important topic, but your group may not know much about it. You should read up about this in advance and be ready with information, pointers, and suggestions in case your group members draw a blank in discussing this one. "Stop the Traffik" and "Hope for Justice" are organizations working in this area.

Redemption 2

BIBLE PASSAGES

Isaiah 52:3, RSV

For thus says the Lord: "You were sold for nothing, and you shall be redeemed without money."

Galatians 3:13, RSV

Christ redeemed us from the curse of the law, having become a curse for us – for it is written, "Cursed be every one who hangs on a tree ... ".

Ephesians 1:7–8, RSV

In him we have redemption through his blood, the forgiveness of our trespasses, according to the riches of his grace which he lavished upon us.

Romans 3:21–26, RSV

But now the righteousness of God has been manifested apart from law, although the law and the prophets bear witness to it, the righteousness of God through faith in Jesus Christ for all who believe. For there is no distinction; since all have sinned and fall short of the glory of God, they are justified by his grace as a gift, through the redemption which is in Christ Jesus, whom God put forward as an expiation by his blood, to be received by faith. This was to show God's righteousness, because in his divine forbearance he had passed over former sins; it was to prove at the present time that he himself is righteous and that he justifies him who has faith in Jesus.

Commentary

There is a type of therapeutic psychology called Transactional Analysis.[112] It describes our interactions with one another as transactions in which we are rewarded (or not) by "strokes" that influence our future behaviour. This is a valid approach that has been very helpful to people learning to understand their life and relationships, even though at first it may seem a little chilling to consider our dealing with each other as a form of trade!

Elsewhere in the world of psychology, therapists have raised the topic of mutuality: if a relationship is all on one person's terms and the other gets nothing

---

112 Developed by Eric Berne in the 1950s.

out of it, it's either unhealthy or doomed. Healthy relationships are characterized by a degree of mutuality. This also imports a sense of transaction to our interactions – "What's in it for me?"

So the idea of redemption is not about commodifying us; it doesn't imply an understanding of God jealous for his chattels who happen to be people. It is all about relationship: setting right what has gone wrong; restoring to us our lost dignity.

In choosing meanness and cruelty, greediness and indifference, we grieved the heart of God and alienated ourselves from his highway of grace. We got lost. In Jesus, God came to find us, to put things right again, to give us a fresh start and restore the relationship to what it was supposed to have been in the first place.[113]

We believe that this transaction – this redemption, this buying us back – was done by God in Jesus dying on the cross. It's important to understand that this is a healing of a spoiled pattern, the restoration of something gone horribly wrong, that God does for us in Jesus. It isn't about an angry God torturing Jesus as a punishment because of our sin. The pain of the cross is borne by the heart of God, to set us free.

Questions

- Are you redeemed? Are you perfect? If you are redeemed, why are you not perfect? How does this work? In what ways is redemption instant and in what ways is it gradual? Do you think we grow into our redemption as we mature as Christians, like a baby growing up into adulthood? How do we realize our redemption and allow it to blossom and bear fruit?

- The mystery of redemption comes into our hymns and worship a lot, but it isn't easy to understand. In your group, share honestly the aspects of redemption that puzzle you, and try to make sense of it together. Please recognize that we don't all understand this the same way – you can all be proper Christians and still think differently!

- What are the signs of a redeemed life?

Prayer

Jesus, my Redeemer, help me to be worthy of you. May my day-to-day life be hallowed by grace and shine with your light. When other people disappoint and irritate me, help me to remember how patient and forgiving you have been with me. Jesus, my Redeemer, lead me in your way. Amen.

---

113 See also the study, in this book, called "Atonement 4 – Justification".

Faith and sight 1

BIBLE PASSAGES[114]

2 Corinthians 5:7, GNB

For our life is a matter of faith, not of sight.

2 Corinthians 4:16–18, GNB

For this reason we never become discouraged. Even though our physical being is gradually decaying, yet our spiritual being is renewed day after day. And this small and temporary trouble we suffer will bring us a tremendous and eternal glory, much greater than the trouble. For we fix our attention, not on things that are seen, but on things that are unseen. What can be seen lasts only for a time, but what cannot be seen lasts forever.

Hebrews 11:1–3, GNB

To have faith is to be sure of the things we hope for, to be certain of the things we cannot see. It was by their faith that people of ancient times won God's approval.

It is by faith that we understand that the universe was created by God's word, so that what can be seen was made out of what cannot be seen.

John 20:24–29, GNB

One of the twelve disciples, Thomas (called the Twin), was not with them when Jesus came. So the other disciples told him, "We have seen the Lord!"

Thomas said to them, "Unless I see the scars of the nails in his hands and put my finger on those scars and my hand in his side, I will not believe."

A week later the disciples were together again indoors, and Thomas was with them. The doors were locked, but Jesus came and stood among them and said, "Peace be with you." Then he said to Thomas, "Put your finger here, and look at my hands; then reach out your hand and put it in my side. Stop your doubting, and believe!"

Thomas answered him, "My Lord and my God!"

Jesus said to him, "Do you believe because you see me? How happy are those who believe without seeing me!"

---

114 Very helpful for extension material is the study called "Transfiguration – sight and insight", in *100 Stand-Alone Bible Studies*, the section on Mark's Gospel in "Themes from the four Gospels".

Commentary

I once heard it said that the purpose of life is to learn to hold our light steady amid the turbulent energies around us. This reminded me of a memorable trip to the wonderful island of Iona. The community there has such a rich and imaginative approach to worship – full of music, drama, and poetry. On one blustery night (it was October, and wild) our thoughts centred on the theme of being lights to the world. At the close of worship, we all went forth with our lighted candles, symbol of our mission. Only, of course, they all blew out the minute we crossed the threshold.

Learning to live by faith not sight is how we stop our inner candle being blown out. Our responsibility as disciples is to develop the skill of being motivated and sustained by the inner world, responding to cues coming from a dimension beyond the physical and apparent. This helps us to stand firm when our outer circumstances are troubled and distressing, because we are looking beyond this world; our gaze is fixed on eternity.

Questions

- Share your experience of a time when you felt convinced everything would be OK, despite all indications to the contrary; when the inner whisper of the Spirit sustained you. What happened?

- When you meet life's challenges, what do you do to strengthen your spirit and keep your light steady? What in particular, about the world as it is now, causes you misgivings and concern? Discuss in the group what responses to these problems might help steady and encourage your faith.

- How do you sustain and build up your spirit in normal times when things are going well, to help prepare for the inevitable struggles and difficulties that are part of every human life?

Prayer

O God, rock of our salvation, in you are our strength and peace. Your name is a strong tower within which we take refuge from the discouragement that daily assails us. Keep us steady in our faith, we pray; keep us on course and keep us moving. Help us to find you and follow you, to live by faith and not by sight, to lay hold on the eternal life you hold out to us. And in the moments when our footing slips and we stumble, please catch us and steady us again. For we ask it in Jesus' name. Amen.

Faith and sight 2

BIBLE PASSAGES[115]

John 1:38–39, GNB

> Jesus turned, saw them following him, and asked, "What are you looking for?"
> They answered, "Where do you live, Rabbi?" (This word means "Teacher.")
> "Come and see," he answered.

Mark 10:46–52, GNB

> They came to Jericho, and as Jesus was leaving with his disciples and a
> large crowd, a blind beggar named Bartimaeus son of Timaeus was sitting
> by the road. When he heard that it was Jesus of Nazareth, he began to shout,
> "Jesus! Son of David! Have mercy on me!"
> Many of the people scolded him and told him to be quiet. But he shouted
> even more loudly, "Son of David, have mercy on me!"
> Jesus stopped and said, "Call him."
> So they called the blind man. "Cheer up!" they said. "Get up, he is calling you."
> So he threw off his cloak, jumped up, and came to Jesus.
> "What do you want me to do for you?" Jesus asked him.
> "Teacher," the blind man answered, "I want to see again."
> "Go," Jesus told him, "your faith has made you well."
> At once he was able to see and followed Jesus on the road.

John 14:9–10, GNB

> Jesus answered, "For a long time I have been with you all; yet you do not know
> me, Philip?[116] Whoever has seen me has seen the Father. Why, then, do you say,
> 'Show us the Father'? Do you not believe, Philip, that I am in the Father and the
> Father is in me?"

Commentary

Our passage from Mark 10 records a very important moment. Mark's Gospel is
structured in three parts – opening chapters giving evidence of the divinity of Jesus,

---

115 Very helpful for extension material is the study called "The light of the world", in *100
Stand-Alone Bible Studies,* in the section on John in "Themes from the four Gospels"; the study
"Transformation 1" earlier in this section, pages 165-67; and the study "Transfiguration – sight
and insight" from the section on Mark in "Themes from the four Gospels" in *100 Stand-Alone
Bible Studies.*
116 See also the story of the road to Emmaus, Luke 24:13–32; any translation.

then a central block of teaching (chapters 8–10) challenging accepted teaching about the messiah and introducing the necessity of serving and suffering in the messianic destiny, and then the passion narrative.

In chapter 10, the healing of a blind man by Jesus is initially only partial, and must be reapplied. In the following passages, as Jesus reveals who he is, Peter responds enthusiastically – but recoils from Jesus' insistence that he must suffer and die. Jesus teaches about how essential this is, concluding the block of teaching by saying, "For the Son of Man came not to be served but to serve, and to give his life as a ransom for the many."[117]

At this point comes the healing of blind Bartimaeus. Jesus asks, "What do you want me to do for you?" Bartimaeus responds eagerly: "I want to see." This healing contrasts with the earlier two-stage healing of blindness. It is instant, and its completion is evidenced by Bartimaeus' "following Jesus in the way"; a phrase at first sight awkward, until you realize it means the Way with a capital "W" – that is, he became a disciple.

So Mark is proposing the concept of faith *as* sight, faith as a way of looking, as the ability to see in the sense of "understand". John offers the same idea, in describing Jesus calling his disciples: "What are you looking for? … Come and see."

Faith is the perception to grasp the meaning of events and discern underlying reality. This in turn allows us to so order our priorities as to become spiritually balanced and grounded – as the old hymn says:

> *oh, let me be*
> *grafted, rooted, built on thee.*[118]

Questions

- Who in your life blesses you with arresting insights? Sometimes it is little children as well as learned teachers! Sometimes even animals can show surprising insight.

- Can you think of instances where you see things very differently from a friend or family member (perhaps your taste in music or food, or your political outlook, or your views on how children should behave)? What strategies have you found for continuing in peace and friendship while holding such different opinions?

- During the time you have been a Christian, what has changed about the way you see life? How has your insight deepened? What new insights have you gained that you didn't have in the early days?

---

117 Mark 10:45, my paraphrase.
118 From the hymn "Bread of Heaven, on Thee we feed", by Josiah Conder (1789–1855).

Prayer

O dear Master, by your grace may our eyes be opened to see you as you really are; and by watching you, may we absorb your ways and become like you. Keep us close to you; keep us awake and watchful. Amen.

St John's signs

Water into wine
Healing at Capernaum
Healing at Bethesda
Feeding the five thousand
Walking on water
The man born blind
The raising of Lazarus
The great harvest of fish

Water into wine

BIBLE PASSAGES

John 2:1–11, RSV

On the third day there was a marriage at Cana in Galilee, and the mother of Jesus was there; Jesus also was invited to the marriage, with his disciples. When the wine gave out, the mother of Jesus said to him, "They have no wine." And Jesus said to her, "O woman, what have you to do with me? My hour has not yet come." His mother said to the servants, "Do whatever he tells you." Now six stone jars were standing there, for the Jewish rites of purification, each holding twenty or thirty gallons. Jesus said to them, "Fill the jars with water." And they filled them up to the brim. He said to them, "Now draw some out, and take it to the steward of the feast." So they took it. When the steward of the feast tasted the water now become wine, and did not know where it came from (though the servants who had drawn the water knew), the steward of the feast called the bridegroom and said to him, "Every man serves the good wine first; and when men have drunk freely, then the poor wine; but you have kept the good wine until now." This, the first of his signs, Jesus did at Cana in Galilee, and manifested his glory; and his disciples believed in him.

John 15:5,[119] RSV

"I am the vine, you are the branches. He who abides in me, and I in him, he it is that bears much fruit, for apart from me you can do nothing."

John 20:30–31, RSV

Now Jesus did many other signs in the presence of the disciples, which are not written in this book; but these are written that you may believe that Jesus is the Christ, the Son of God, and that believing you may have life in his name.

Commentary

Each of the Gospels was written to explain the significance of Jesus, and each evangelist has his own particular slant or emphasis.[120] John brings out who Jesus was in a number of ways. One is the seven "I Am" sayings[121] that correspond with seven miracles of Jesus; another is John calling Jesus' miracles "signs". He wants us to understand that, even more than the miracle itself, what the miracle points to is amazing. The miracle tells us something about Jesus.

---

119   See also John 15:1.
120   See the studies called "Themes from the four Gospels" in *100 Stand-Alone Bible Studies*.
121   See the study called "The *ego iemi*" in *100 Stand-Alone Bible Studies*.

John's Gospel is sometimes said to be divided into four parts: the Prologue (John 1:1–18), the Book of Signs (1:19 – 12:50), the Book of Glory (13:1 – 20:31, John describes the cross in terms of exaltation, Christ lifted up in glory), and the Epilogue (chapter 21). The seven miracles, all pointing to aspects of who Jesus is, come in the Book of Signs.

The first is the miracle at Cana in Galilee, where Jesus changes water into wine. The corresponding "I Am" saying comes later on, in chapter 15 – "I am the true Vine … " In each case, when he says "I Am", Jesus is taking to himself the *ego iemi* ("I AM THAT I AM"), the name and nature of God. It is a claim to Godhead.

In the book of Isaiah, Israel is portrayed as God's vineyard, which disappoints him by failing to bear fruit. Jesus, the True Vine, is faithful – the true Israel. This miracle shows how he supplies and fulfils what is lacking (faithfulness), transforming the ordinary into the special, the humble into the magnificent, inadequacy into triumph.

Questions

- In practical, everyday terms, what does it mean when Jesus says, "Abide in me"? Explore this in some depth together, considering the different aspects of your life it affects.

- That was a lot of water Jesus turned into wine! What does this mean about our attitude to life and celebration? How does it fit in with our Christian calling to a humble and simple life? When is the right time for water and when is the right time for wine? What could the water and what could the wine represent in our lives?

- If you could draw three things to Jesus' attention, just as Mary spoke to him about the wine, asking him to do something to help, what would they be? Can you pray together in your group about these things?

Prayer

Jesus, you are the living Vine, connecting us to one another, rooting us into God, the ground of our being. May we always be found in you, and may our lives always be fruitful through your grace and life and power that flow through us. Amen.

Healing at Capernaum[122]

BIBLE PASSAGES

John 4:46–54, NIVUK

Once more he visited Cana in Galilee, where he had turned the water into wine. And there was a certain royal official whose son lay ill at Capernaum. When this man heard that Jesus had arrived in Galilee from Judea, he went to him and begged him to come and heal his son, who was close to death.

"Unless you people see signs and wonders," Jesus told him, "you will never believe."

The royal official said, "Sir, come down before my child dies."

"Go," Jesus replied, "your son will live."

The man took Jesus at his word and departed. While he was still on the way, his servants met him with the news that his boy was living. When he enquired as to the time when his son got better, they said to him, "Yesterday, at one in the afternoon, the fever left him."

Then the father realised that this was the exact time at which Jesus had said to him, "Your son will live." So he and his whole household believed.

This was the second sign Jesus performed after coming from Judea to Galilee.

John 14:4–14, NIVUK

"You know the way to the place where I am going."

Thomas said to him, "Lord, we don't know where you are going, so how can we know the way?"

Jesus answered, "I am the way and the truth and the life. No one comes to the Father except through me. If you really know me, you will know my Father as well. From now on, you do know him and have seen him."

Philip said, "Lord, show us the Father and that will be enough for us."

Jesus answered: "Don't you know me, Philip, even after I have been among you such a long time? Anyone who has seen me has seen the Father. How can you say, 'Show us the Father'? Don't you believe that I am in the Father, and that the Father is in me? The words I say to you I do not speak on my own authority. Rather, it is the Father, living in me, who is doing his work. Believe me when I say that I am in the Father and the Father is in me; or at least believe on the evidence of the works themselves. Very truly I tell you, whoever believes in me will do the works I have been doing, and they will do even greater things than these, because I am going to the Father."

---

122 For this study, each group member will need a sheet of paper (at least A4, though A3 would be better) and a pen (or pens of several colours).

Commentary

This healing miracle is the sign for the "I Am" saying, "I Am the Way, the Truth and the Life".

Jesus sent the official off home, promising his son would recover. While the man was *on the way* his servants met him and confirmed *the truth* – the boy was restored to *life*.

In the early days, Christian faith was known as "the Way"; being a follower of Jesus was described as "walking in the Way".[123]

As Jesus expounds for his disciples the idea that he is the way, the truth, and the life (see chapter 14:1–14), he speaks of the Way in terms of the way to where he is going – into heaven, into the presence of the Father. This is the way that he will open for us by his death on the cross, the living way that connects the spiritual realm to the earthly realm: our way home.

He speaks of the Truth in terms of his true nature – who he really is – urging them to believe in this truth, and to accept the signs (miracles) as evidence. And he speaks of the Life in terms of the signs being done by the Father living in Jesus.

Come with me, the official begs Jesus, and heal my son. Jesus does not go, but sends him – to go where Jesus says, trusting the truth of his word, in the way that leads to life, and healing.

Questions

- Take a few minutes to think about the living Way as you have walked it. Draw a map of your journey with Jesus from the beginning to the present day: the milestones, the stony tracks, the swamps, where you got lost and felt like giving up, people who walked with you, the beautiful places. Draw a signpost indicating the way ahead. What will you write on it?

- Something we learn from this study is that Truth is not data – it's a *person*. Discuss in your group how to get the right balance between personal lived truth – our relationship with Jesus – and the creeds and doctrines the church teaches us.

- What do you think is meant by eternal Life? Life that goes on for ever, or a quality of life? It is said that the only connecting point with eternal life is the present moment (rather than the past or the future). Explore that idea together. What does it mean?

Prayer

Jesus, you are our truth, our living way; you are life itself. Help us to know and believe in you, to follow you, and to ground our lives in you. Amen.

---

123 See Mark 10:52 in the RSV or NRSVA or KJV (not the GNB or NIV – these miss the play on words).

Healing at Bethesda

BIBLE PASSAGES

John 5:2–9, NIVUK

Now there is in Jerusalem near the Sheep Gate a pool, which in Aramaic is called Bethesda and which is surrounded by five covered colonnades. Here a great number of disabled people used to lie – the blind, the lame, the paralysed. One who was there had been an invalid for thirty-eight years. When Jesus saw him lying there and learned that he had been in this condition for a long time, he asked him, "Do you want to get well?"

"Sir," the invalid replied, "I have no one to help me into the pool when the water is stirred. While I am trying to get in, someone else goes down ahead of me."

Then Jesus said to him, "Get up! Pick up your mat and walk." At once the man was cured; he picked up his mat and walked.

John 10:2–3, 7, 9, 11, 14, NIVUK

"The one who enters by the gate is the shepherd of the sheep. The gatekeeper opens the gate for him, and the sheep listen to his voice. He calls his own sheep by name and leads them out."

Therefore Jesus said again, "Very truly I tell you, I am the gate for the sheep.

I am the gate; whoever enters through me will be saved. They will come in and go out, and find pasture.

I am the good shepherd. The good shepherd lays down his life for the sheep.

I am the good shepherd; I know my sheep and my sheep know me."

Commentary

The connection between the healing at the Pool of Bethesda in chapter 5 and Jesus' teaching about himself as the good shepherd in chapter 10 might not have been immediately obvious. John makes the link for us by saying that the pool is near the Sheep Gate in Jerusalem – the Holy City, the centre for the people of God.

A strong thread about exodus and exile runs through the Old Testament's story of the people of Israel. Sometimes, being outside means escaping, being set free. Sometimes it means being marginalized, cast out, and excluded. A doorway can be a way in or a way out – it all depends how you look at it.

So when you join together these "I Am" sayings of Jesus – "I Am the gate … I Am the good shepherd …" – with the story of the healing at Bethesda, what emerges is teaching about freedom and inclusion. Jesus is the one whose love sets people free and leads them out of prison, but also welcomes them in – brings them home. He is both the shepherd and the gate, for the sheep.

This is most movingly made clear in his interaction with the paralyzed man at Bethesda. The man has been trying for years to get in to the pool; but he can't *get in* because he is *trapped* in his paralysis. And nobody will help him. Jesus sets him free from his imprisoning paralysis – the man hears his voice, and Jesus opens the gate for him and leads him out; he is free. He is restored to himself, and he is with Jesus; he has come home.

Questions

- Think about some of the human groupings you have known – schools, clubs, workplaces, churches. Were there "in-crowds", hard to get into? Where people were left out or passed by? Whose voices were loudest, and who was never heard? Who can you think of who might find it hard to come to church? How can we, in our local church and other places we belong, join in Jesus' ministry of inclusion and freedom, being the door for the sheep?

- At times in your life when you felt stuck, or when you felt left out, who helped you? Who stood by you?

- In the setting of modern human society around the globe, what can we identify that imprisons or marginalizes people today? Is there anything we as individuals can contribute to this vast arena of social and political interaction, to set people free and to bring them home?

Prayer

Jesus, Good Shepherd, you lead us out to freedom and you bring us home to rest. Thank you for searching for us, for finding us, for healing us, for setting us free. Help us to follow you and stay close to you; help us to be faithful to you. Amen.

Feeding the five thousand

BIBLE PASSAGES

John 6:5–15, NIVUK

When Jesus looked up and saw a great crowd coming towards him, he said to Philip, "Where shall we buy bread for these people to eat?" He asked this only to test him, for he already had in mind what he was going to do.

Philip answered him, "It would take more than half a year's wages to buy enough bread for each one to have a bite!"

Another of his disciples, Andrew, Simon Peter's brother, spoke up, "Here is a boy with five small barley loaves and two small fish, but how far will they go among so many?"

Jesus said, "Make the people sit down." There was plenty of grass in that place, and they sat down (about five thousand men were there). Jesus then took the loaves, gave thanks, and distributed to those who were seated as much as they wanted. He did the same with the fish.

When they had all had enough to eat, he said to his disciples, "Gather the pieces that are left over. Let nothing be wasted." So they gathered them and filled twelve baskets with the pieces of the five barley loaves left over by those who had eaten.

After the people saw the sign Jesus performed, they began to say, "Surely this is the Prophet who is to come into the world." Jesus, knowing that they intended to come and make him king by force, withdrew again to a mountain by himself.

John 6:35, 41, 47–51,[124] NIVUK

Then Jesus declared, "I am the bread of life."

"I am the bread that came down from heaven."

"Very truly I tell you, the one who believes has eternal life. I am the bread of life. Your ancestors ate the manna in the wilderness, yet they died. But here is the bread that comes down from heaven, which anyone may eat and not die. I am the living bread that came down from heaven. Whoever eats this bread will live for ever. This bread is my flesh, which I will give for the life of the world."

Commentary

There has been discussion about who was present at this miracle. Matthew 14:21, in telling of the same incident, says there were 5,000 men, not including women and children. In John's account here, we read of a large multitude all coming together,

---

124 I strongly recommend reading the whole section – there isn't room to give it here – John 6:25–59.

and the story speaks of *men* being fed. The story ends with Jesus withdrawing on seeing that they mean to make him their leader by force. It seems likely that this was (at least primarily) an increasing number of men determined on revolution – to overthrow the Roman occupation: a war band, with a political agenda.

It's important to understand this, because the exposition of the sign's significance does not follow on immediately, but comes after the account of the next sign (walking on the water), which teaches a clear distinction between the establishment of the reign of God and the appropriation of human political power.

Then unfolds Jesus' teaching about the Bread of Life. Jesus compares his coming with the manna in the desert. He is the sustenance of the people of God. He draws a distinction between those focused on material ends and those whose purpose is spiritual: "Very truly I tell you, you are looking for me, not because you saw the signs I performed but because you ate the loaves and had your fill. Do not work for food that spoils, but for food that endures to eternal life, which the Son of Man will give you" (John 6:26–27, NIVUK).

Questions

- Jesus said, "Do not work for food that spoils, but for food that endures to eternal life." We need to earn money to buy food, care for our families, pay our bills. How can we get the balance right in providing for both our physical and our spiritual needs?

- Jesus said, "I Am the bread of life." In what ways – honestly – do you feel that Jesus nourishes and sustains you? People often say, "God is an important part of my life." Is he the bread of life for them, or just the cherry on top of the cake? Think about this together.

- Jesus said, "Whoever eats this bread will live for ever." We understand that he is the bread, and have an idea of what eternal life means. What about the eating? What does eating this bread involve? In what ways do we take Jesus into our very viscera, so that we become one with him?

Prayer

Jesus, what you are and what you offer me is essential to life. Unless I feed upon what you hold out to me – your very being – my soul will die of starvation. Feed me, Lord, on your living bread. Amen.

Walking on water

BIBLE PASSAGES

John 6:14–21, NIVUK

After the people saw the sign Jesus performed, they began to say, "Surely this is the Prophet who is to come into the world." Jesus, knowing that they intended to come and make him king by force, withdrew again to a mountain by himself.

When evening came, his disciples went down to the lake, where they got into a boat and set off across the lake for Capernaum. By now it was dark, and Jesus had not yet joined them. A strong wind was blowing and the waters grew rough. When they had rowed about three or four miles, they saw Jesus approaching the boat, walking on the water; and they were frightened. But he said to them, "It is I[125]; don't be afraid." Then they were willing to take him into the boat, and immediately the boat reached the shore where they were heading.

John 1:1–3, NIVUK

In the beginning was the Word, and the Word was with God, and the Word was God. He was with God in the beginning. Through him all things were made; without him nothing was made that has been made.

Genesis 1:1–2, NIVUK

In the beginning God created the heavens and the earth. Now the earth was formless and empty, darkness was over the surface of the deep, and the Spirit of God was hovering over the waters.

Mark 4:41, NIVUK

They were terrified and asked each other, "Who is this? Even the wind and the waves obey him!"

Commentary

In translation into English, the full impact of this story is lost – it's like ruining the perfect punchline. There they are, out in the middle of the wild water in the dark; this is a picture of the beginning of creation, when the world was without form and void (*tohu wa boho* is the evocative Hebrew term used in Genesis 1). In the creation account, the spirit broods over the face of the deep; then the word of God

---

125 In the Greek – "I Am".

("Let there be light") issues forth to create order and creative peace. In this story, Jesus (the living Word full of the Spirit) comes *to them* across the face of the deep. He's not just walking around – he's heading their way. This image encapsulates the incarnation, the cosmic Christ, God's living Word with him from the beginning, coming to us.[126]

Jesus responds to his disciples' fear by calling out to them, "I Am!" The *ego iemi* again; the name of God. There could be no clearer or more powerful demonstration of just who Jesus is. It heightens the awe of the moment. And in English it vanishes, replaced by "It is I!"

We remember that this happens directly after the feeding of the five thousand, when Jesus withdrew as the focus of the crowd intensified towards making him a political leader. He would not let this happen.

So this incident shows Jesus' power and majesty, but also makes a clear and sharp differentiation between divine and worldly power. The reign of God is majestic and absolute, but not political.

Questions

- We shape our society politically. Our votes determine how we will care for the poor and marginalized, run our health and education services, etc. Yet Jesus refused to be a political leader. Discuss in the group how politics fits into our expression of Christian faith. Draw (or imagine) a Venn diagram showing what you consider to be the arena of politics, that of faith, and the overlap.

- Jesus would not be made a political leader, and he was not officially a rabbi, either. He held no status in any institution. Discuss in your group what this meant in his life – did it contribute to his arrest and death, was it part of his identification with all humanity, was it inappropriate for the Son of God to slot into a hierarchical structure and submit to human authority? Think together about organized religion – what are the positive aspects of organized church, and what are the drawbacks?

- An important aspect of this miracle – this sign – is that it demonstrates the power of Jesus over nature, indicating that he is divine. The relationship between God and the created order is a strong biblical theme: God has a covenant relationship with creation. In what ways can we as Christians express God's care for creation and fulfil the role God entrusted to us, as stewards of the earth?

Prayer

Holy God, holy and wise, holy and strong, holy and immortal, have mercy upon

---

126 To get the full flavour, you might like to read the Prologue of John's Gospel (John 1:1–18) and Genesis 1:1–5.

us. Lead us by the light of your Spirit shining in our hearts, direct us in the ways of your truth, help us to make wise and informed choices in the complicated pathways of the modern world. Amen.

The Man Born Blind

BIBLE PASSAGES[127]

John 9:1–7, NIVUK[128]

As he went along, he saw a man blind from birth. His disciples asked him, "Rabbi, who sinned, this man or his parents, that he was born blind?"

"Neither this man nor his parents sinned," said Jesus, "but this happened so that the works of God might be displayed in him. As long as it is day, we must do the works of him who sent me. Night is coming, when no one can work. While I am in the world, I am the light of the world."

After saying this, he spat on the ground, made some mud with the saliva, and put it on the man's eyes. "Go," he told him, "wash in the Pool of Siloam" (this word means "Sent"). So the man went and washed, and came home seeing.

John 9:13–16, NIVUK

They brought to the Pharisees the man who had been blind. Now the day on which Jesus had made the mud and opened the man's eyes was a Sabbath. Therefore the Pharisees also asked him how he had received his sight. "He put mud on my eyes," the man replied, "and I washed, and now I see."

Some of the Pharisees said, "This man is not from God, for he does not keep the Sabbath."

John 9:35–39, NIVUK

Jesus heard that they had thrown him out, and when he found him, he said, "Do you believe in the Son of Man?"

"Who is he, sir?" the man asked. "Tell me so that I may believe in him."

Jesus said, "You have now seen him; in fact, he is the one speaking with you."

Then the man said, "Lord, I believe," and he worshipped him.

Jesus said, "For judgment I have come into this world, so that the blind will see and those who see will become blind."

John 1:9–11, NIVUK

The true light that gives light to everyone was coming into the world. He was in the world, and though the world was made through him, the world did not recognise him. He came to that which was his own, but his own did not receive him.

---

127 See also John 8.12.
128 I recommend you read the whole chapter.

Commentary

The "I Am" saying of Jesus to go with the sign is incorporated into the story (in the first of our passages above): "I Am the Light of the World." This is the truth about Jesus to which the sign is pointing – but the story also deals with a related topic: spiritual sight and spiritual blindness.

In all four Gospels sight is a metaphor representing spiritual insight, and the healing of blind people points beyond physical healing to the *shalom* of God healing of the whole being, salvation expressed in faith.

A huge biblical theme is picked up in this story, about what Matthew called "blind guides".[129] The man healed of blindness comes to faith in Jesus – "'Lord, I believe.' And he worshipped him." By jarring contrast, we see the Pharisees ignoring the beautiful sign of this healing saying it can't be from God if it happened on the sabbath. They, who claim to be leaders, have no insight and cannot be trusted to show anyone the way.

They go so far as to throw the healed man out when he will not deny what was done for him. Jesus goes to find him. It is this context of rejection and marginalization that the healing is made complete and the man comes to faith in Christ.

Questions

- Physical blindness acts as a metaphor for insight in the Gospels, but we mustn't make the mistake of understanding that to mean people with disability are any more limited spiritually than the rest of us – physical limitations can help develop insight. Take time to share in the group your own experience of times when someone with chronic illness or disability showed spiritual strength and depth.

- Bad leadership creates problems in the household of faith. What should we do when our leaders let us down? Where have you seen this dealt with well? What do you consider the hallmarks of good leadership?

- Share with the group about special experiences of insight that came to you in life – light-bulb moments when you suddenly saw! What happened?

Prayer

Jesus, light of the world, open my eyes to your truth. Do not leave me lost in illusion, but save me from the cynicism of the disillusioned. Give me such a vision of your glory that my whole being will be illumined by who and what you are. Amen.

---

129 Matthew 15:14, and see also Luke 6:39.

The raising of Lazarus[130]

BIBLE PASSAGES

John 11:17–27, NRSVA

When Jesus arrived, he found that Lazarus had already been in the tomb for four days. Now Bethany was near Jerusalem, some two miles away, and many of the Jews had come to Martha and Mary to console them about their brother. When Martha heard that Jesus was coming, she went and met him, while Mary stayed at home. Martha said to Jesus, "Lord, if you had been here, my brother would not have died. But even now I know that God will give you whatever you ask of him." Jesus said to her, "Your brother will rise again." Martha said to him, "I know that he will rise again in the resurrection on the last day." Jesus said to her, "I am the resurrection and the life. Those who believe in me, even though they die, will live, and everyone who lives and believes in me will never die. Do you believe this?" She said to him, "Yes, Lord, I believe that you are the Messiah, the Son of God, the one coming into the world."

John 11:38–44, NRSVA

Then Jesus, again greatly disturbed, came to the tomb. It was a cave, and a stone was lying against it. Jesus said, "Take away the stone." Martha, the sister of the dead man, said to him, "Lord, already there is a stench because he has been dead for four days." Jesus said to her, "Did I not tell you that if you believed, you would see the glory of God?" So they took away the stone. And Jesus looked upwards and said, "Father, I thank you for having heard me. I knew that you always hear me, but I have said this for the sake of the crowd standing here, so that they may believe that you sent me." When he had said this, he cried with a loud voice, "Lazarus, come out!" The dead man came out, his hands and feet bound with strips of cloth, and his face wrapped in a cloth. Jesus said to them, "Unbind him, and let him go."

Commentary

In this miracle, or sign, the "I Am" saying of Jesus comes in the middle of the story. Jesus says to Martha, "I Am the resurrection and the life," directly asking if she believes. Her answer, "Yes, Lord, I believe that you are the Messiah, the Son of God, the one coming into the world", expresses faith in his divine nature; she is responding to his revelation of his divine nature in using the "I Am", the name of God.

---

130 It's helpful to look at the whole of John 11.

The raising of Lazarus is a turning point in John's Gospel. It is a climactic moment, because it is a sign that Jesus has power over life and death – by definition, the power uniquely God's. The miracle causes a number of people to put their faith in Jesus, but also triggers the moment his enemies run out of patience, and begin plotting his arrest.[131] This is the last sign in the Book of Signs section. Chapter 12 relates the incident in which Jesus is anointed at Bethany and then enters Jerusalem, and debate about who he is intensifies. The Book of Glory, the unfolding of the story of his crucifixion, then follows.

Questions

- Listen together to the Bible passages read aloud. As you listen, make a note of something that especially catches your attention and stands out for you, something that puzzles you, and something that you feel is of particular application to your life at the moment. Discuss these together.

- This story records Jesus' tears and distress. When he arrives and sees Mary's grief, he is troubled and moved to tears (11:33–35). Our second passage above describes him as "greatly disturbed". Yet, at the beginning of the chapter, he confidently tells his disciples that Lazarus's illness won't end in death. Explore together why Jesus was so moved. Was it simply the grief of bereavement, or was it dread at what he was about to trigger? Is this John's parallel to the account of Jesus' tears in Gethsemane in the Synoptic Gospels? What do you think?

- The signs of Jesus created division among those who witnessed them, and the Gospels note the divisive effect he had.[132] Yet Jesus is a healer, a man of peace, who came to bring the *shalom* of God, reconciling all creation. Explore in your group why he causes division. When is truth unwelcome? What is it about Jesus that provokes such strongly contrasting reactions?

Prayer

Yes, Lord Jesus, I believe that you are the messiah, the Son of God, the one who was coming into the world for our salvation. Come into my world, into my heart, into my life, and establish your reign in me. Amen.

---

131 See John 11:45–57.
132 See Matthew 10:34–36 or John 10:19–21.

The great harvest of fish

BIBLE PASSAGES

John 21:1–14, NIVUK

Afterwards Jesus appeared again to his disciples, by the Sea of Galilee. It happened this way: Simon Peter, Thomas (also known as Didymus), Nathanael from Cana in Galilee, the sons of Zebedee, and two other disciples were together. "I'm going out to fish," Simon Peter told them, and they said, "We'll go with you." So they went out and got into the boat, but that night they caught nothing.

Early in the morning, Jesus stood on the shore, but the disciples did not realise that it was Jesus.

He called out to them, "Friends, haven't you any fish?"

"No," they answered.

He said, "Throw your net on the right side of the boat and you will find some." When they did, they were unable to haul the net in because of the large number of fish.

Then the disciple whom Jesus loved said to Peter, "It is the Lord!" As soon as Simon Peter heard him say, "It is the Lord," he wrapped his outer garment round him (for he had taken it off) and jumped into the water. The other disciples followed in the boat, towing the net full of fish, for they were not far from shore, about a hundred metres. When they landed, they saw a fire of burning coals there with fish on it, and some bread.

Jesus said to them, "Bring some of the fish you have just caught." So Simon Peter climbed back into the boat and dragged the net ashore. It was full of large fish, 153,[133] but even with so many the net was not torn. Jesus said to them, "Come and have breakfast." None of the disciples dared ask him, "Who are you?" They knew it was the Lord. Jesus came, took the bread and gave it to them, and did the same with the fish. This was now the third time Jesus appeared to his disciples after he was raised from the dead.

Matthew 13:47–49, NIVUK

The kingdom of heaven is like a net that was let down into the lake and caught all kinds of fish. When it was full, the fishermen pulled it up on the shore.

---

133 This may or may not be a symbolic number. There is no scholarly consensus.

Commentary

This story is in the twenty-first chapter of John – in the Epilogue, not the Book of Signs. The preceding seven signs and corresponding seven "I Am" sayings belong to the unfolding revelation before his crucifixion of who Jesus is. This sign points ahead.

Luke's Gospel also tells of a miraculous large catch after an unsuccessful night of fishing (Luke 5:4–11). That occasion is about the call of the disciples, the beginning of ministry, when Jesus invites them to become "fishers of men".

John's Gospel, the last to be written, explores the question, "What now?" in the resurrection stories. In the story of Doubting Thomas (chapter 20), he speaks of finding Jesus in the midst of the weekly church meeting – Thomas misses him when he fails to attend. John takes us beyond the time of Jesus' physical earthly presence, to the company of believers as the Body of Christ – where we find him now.

In this story of the great catch of fish, we see his disciples returning to their ordinary occupations and finding the Lord there, but also glimpse the promise of fulfilment of what Jesus began – the swelling of the church, the fishing for men, the call to be no longer disciples only, but apostles. This is not the end, John is telling us; this is only the beginning. As Matthew's Gospel says, "I Am with you always" (Matthew 28:20).

Questions

- In the dawn light when Jesus called to them, the disciples didn't recognize him. Then Peter twigged: "It is the Lord!" When in your life have you been at a low ebb, and then felt the tide of faith lifting again – "It is the Lord"?

- We are all called to share the gospel, to be "fishers of men". How we do it will vary according to temperament. What ways of making Jesus known and loved work best for you?

- John Wimber said, of new Christians finding it hard to fit in to church life, "You have to catch 'em before you can clean 'em." How can we make our church community open and welcoming, hospitable to newcomers, a safe space, and a nurturing environment? What drew you to faith in Jesus?

Prayer

To our small and unsuccessful efforts, Lord Jesus, please add your mighty power. Even the winds and the waves obey you – may we hear and obey you too. May we be confident and courageous in your service. Help us to remember that you are always with us. Amen.

Spiritual charisms

Wisdom
Knowledge
Prophecy
Teaching
Service
Faith
Healing
Miracles
Discernment
Tongues
Interpretation
Helping
Administration
Pastoral guidance
Encouragement
Giving
Leadership
Apostleship
Evangelism
Intercession
Hospitality
Mercy
Willingness to face martyrdom
Celibacy
Understanding
Counsel
Fortitude
Reverence
Fear of the Lord

Wisdom[134]

BIBLE PASSAGES

1 Corinthians 2:4–14, NIVUK

My message and my preaching were not with wise and persuasive words, but with a demonstration of the Spirit's power, so that your faith might not rest on human wisdom, but on God's power.

We do, however, speak a message of wisdom among the mature, but not the wisdom of this age or of the rulers of this age, who are coming to nothing. No, we declare God's wisdom, a mystery that has been hidden and that God destined for our glory before time began. None of the rulers of this age understood it, for if they had, they would not have crucified the Lord of glory. However, as it is written:

"What no eye has seen,
  what no ear has heard,
and what no human mind has conceived" –
  the things God has prepared for those who love him –
these are the things God has revealed to us by his Spirit.

The Spirit searches all things, even the deep things of God. For who knows a person's thoughts except their own spirit within them? In the same way no one knows the thoughts of God except the Spirit of God. What we have received is not the spirit of the world, but the Spirit who is from God, so that we may understand what God has freely given us. This is what we speak, not in words taught us by human wisdom but in words taught by the Spirit, explaining spiritual realities with Spirit-taught words. The person without the Spirit does not accept the things that come from the Spirit of God but considers them foolishness, and cannot understand them because they are discerned only through the Spirit.

1 Corinthians 1:22–25, NIVUK

Jews demand signs and Greeks look for wisdom, but we preach Christ crucified: a stumbling-block to Jews and foolishness to Gentiles, but to those whom God has called, both Jews and Greeks, Christ the power of God and the wisdom of God. For the foolishness of God is wiser than human wisdom, and the weakness of God is stronger than human strength.

---

134 See also the study in this book on "Discernment".

James 1:5, NIVUK

> If any of you lacks wisdom, you should ask God, who gives generously to all without finding fault, and it will be given to you.

Commentary

In this section of Bible studies we corral together from different places all the charisms – gifts – of the Holy Spirit. There are many, but when we begin to list the attributes of saintly people wisdom is one of the first that springs to mind.

Wisdom is mentioned throughout the Bible numerous times,[135] sometimes identifying "the fear of the Lord" as the beginning of wisdom. Indeed, a whole section of the Bible is designated as Wisdom Literature (Job, Proverbs, Ruth, Ecclesiastes, the Song of Songs, Esther). This part of the Bible is notable for its inclusive and compassionate outlook – in these books more than in the books of history, the Law and the Prophets, God spreads his wing over the foreigner and the dispossessed. The outlook of the Wisdom books aligns more easily with that of modern-day thinking.

Writing about God's wisdom in the New Testament, Paul contrasts it with the world's wisdom. He speaks of the inability of those in power to recognize God's wisdom when it comes clothed in weakness, suffering, or disadvantage. He identifies the cross as God's wisdom in action, yet seeming to be sheer folly to ordinary human reason.

Holy Wisdom[136] in ancient Jewish tradition (*Hagia Sophia*) connects to the *Logos*[137] of Greek tradition, considered by some to be the same as the Holy Spirit, the second person of the Trinity.

So wisdom as a spiritual gift is an every-believer charism; where the Holy Spirit dwells in a person's heart, wisdom will manifest – but this might appear as foolishness to the world.

Questions

- Think of examples you have witnessed or experienced, where spiritual logic and worldly logic were completely different – where what seemed clever in the world's eyes was spiritually dim, or where spiritual wisdom looked gauche, naïve, and foolish to the world.

- Because the Spirit's wisdom can speak through uneducated or unsophisticated people, children sometimes surprise us with their insight.[138] What examples have you noticed of this?

---

135 For further study I especially recommend 2 Chronicles 1:1–12; Job 28; Proverbs 8; Psalm 111:10.
136 See Proverbs 8.
137 See John 1:1.
138 The story of "The Emperor's New Clothes", for example.

- How do you try to cultivate wisdom in your own life? What wisdom have you learned that you would love to pass on?

Prayer

Lead me into all truth, wise and loving God. May I be humble, may I be simple, may I be lowly; may my life reflect the wisdom of my crucified Lord. Amen.

Knowledge

BIBLE PASSAGES

1 Corinthians 12:8, NIVUK

To one there is given through the Spirit a message of wisdom, to another a message of knowledge by means of the same Spirit.

1 Corinthians 13:2, NIVUK

If I have the gift of prophecy and can fathom all mysteries and all knowledge, and if I have a faith that can move mountains, but do not have love, I am nothing.

Acts 9:10–19, GNB

There was a believer in Damascus named Ananias. He had a vision, in which the Lord said to him, "Ananias!"

"Here I am, Lord," he answered.

The Lord said to him, "Get ready and go to Straight Street, and at the house of Judas ask for a man from Tarsus named Saul. He is praying, and in a vision he has seen a man named Ananias come in and place his hands on him so that he might see again."

Ananias answered, "Lord, many people have told me about this man and about all the terrible things he has done to your people in Jerusalem. And he has come to Damascus with authority from the chief priests to arrest all who worship you."

The Lord said to him, "Go, because I have chosen him to serve me, to make my name known to Gentiles and kings and to the people of Israel. And I myself will show him all that he must suffer for my sake."

So Ananias went, entered the house where Saul was, and placed his hands on him. "Brother Saul," he said, "the Lord has sent me – Jesus himself, who appeared to you on the road as you were coming here. He sent me so that you might see again and be filled with the Holy Spirit." At once something like fish scales fell from Saul's eyes, and he was able to see again. He stood up and was baptized; and after he had eaten, his strength came back.

Commentary

Knowledge, as a spiritual gift, is when for purposes of ministry the servant of God becomes aware of information they could not otherwise know; similar to, but different from, prophecy, wisdom, and discernment.[139]

---

139 You might find it helpful to look up those three studies, which also appear in this section.

Perhaps someone spiritually blocked doesn't realize that something they have or do is hindering their spiritual path; or someone has an illness God wants to heal.[140] This information is revealed to God's servant, to help the other change or be healed. Knowledge can come in dreams, a sense of certainty, or an image springing to mind that turns out to mean a lot to the person who needs help.

Someone I knew exercised the gift of knowledge frequently and effectively. In our ministry team, we asked him how the "words of knowledge" came to him. Simply and candidly, "I just make them up," he said. This was really interesting. Obviously he wasn't just inventing things, as they were proved true in the context of our meetings – people got healed and set free under his ministry. But it felt the same as just making it up. He trusted, he opened himself to God's Spirit, and he humbly offered what came into his mind to the meeting to be tested.

This was a healthy use of the gift of knowledge, but the whole area of charismatic ministry is fertile ground for dominance games and abuse. If someone is using "knowledge from the Lord" to shame or exclude people; if the result of their "knowledge" is anything other than healing, peace, and well-being; if what they claim to know doesn't ring true; if there is any secrecy or superiority or prestige or manipulation of any kind – then that isn't the charism of knowledge, it's a power trip.

Our passage from Acts is a good example of the gift of knowledge: it's not interpretative, unlike wisdom; it is about rather than for someone, unlike prophecy; it's straight facts, not about underlying or hidden characteristics, unlike discernment. It is information received by no other means than the Spirit of God, with the purpose and outcome of healing, freedom, and faith. That's the gift of knowledge.

Questions

- Share any experience you have (in others or yourself) of the gift of knowledge. What happened? Were there any occasions when something like this came to you, but you felt too shy or embarrassed to say anything?

- Abusive people could pretend to have a gift like this to gain power over others. What safeguards or checks could be put in place to stop destructive individuals taking advantage in this way?[141]

- How might you try some of these gifts in a group setting? What ground rules would you need?[142]

---

140 God wants to heal all illness, but there's a question about when and how.
141 Include the possibility of teamwork in your suggestions.
142 Include trust, transparency, and confidentiality in your thinking.

Prayer

O Lord, you have searched us and you know us. Nothing is hidden from you. Help me to be humble and kind, because there is so much about other people's struggles I do not know; help me to be open to your Spirit, in case you ever want to share some knowledge with me that will heal and help others. Amen.

Prophecy

BIBLE PASSAGES

1 Corinthians 14:1, 3–6, NIVUK

Follow the way of love and eagerly desire gifts of the Spirit, especially prophecy … the one who prophesies speaks to people for their strengthening, encouraging and comfort. Anyone who speaks in a tongue edifies themselves, but the one who prophesies edifies the church. I would like every one of you to speak in tongues, but even more to prophesy. The one who prophesies is greater than the one who speaks in tongues, unless someone interprets, so that the church may be edified. [I]f I come to you and speak in tongues, what good will I be to you, unless I bring you some revelation or knowledge or prophecy or word of instruction?

1 Corinthians 14:22–25, NIVUK

Tongues, then, are a sign, not for believers but for unbelievers; prophecy, however, is not for unbelievers but for believers. So if the whole church comes together and everyone speaks in tongues, and enquirers or unbelievers come in, will they not say that you are out of your mind? But if an unbeliever or an enquirer comes in while everyone is prophesying, they are convicted of sin and are brought under judgment by all, as the secrets of their hearts are laid bare. So they will fall down and worship God, exclaiming, "God is really among you!"

1 Peter 4:10–11, NIVUK

Each of you should use whatever gift you have received to serve others, as faithful stewards of God's grace in its various forms. If anyone speaks, they should do so as one who speaks the very words of God.

Matthew 7:21–23, NIVUK

Not everyone who says to me, "Lord, Lord," will enter the kingdom of heaven, but only the one who does the will of my Father who is in heaven. Many will say to me on that day, "Lord, Lord, did we not prophesy in your name and in your name drive out demons and in your name perform many miracles?" Then I will tell them plainly, "I never knew you. Away from me, you evildoers!"

Commentary

In the Old Testament, the prophetic gift rested on individuals like Moses and Elijah, who acted as go-betweens for God and his people. Then in the Gospels,

Jesus was himself the living Word of God – in his life and teaching, his death and resurrection, he imparted and made known God's truth. In his death Jesus opened a new and living way between earth and heaven. At his ascension he returned to the Father, thus taking humanity into heaven. Then at Pentecost the Holy Spirit was poured out on humanity, consolidating the link of the new and living way.

Because the Holy Spirit was poured out in this way, there is no longer any need for a go-between; the Temple veil was torn in two at the death of Jesus, signifying the coming of direct communication between God and his people. This means that the prophetic role is now shared by the whole people of God. All of us are called to a prophetic life of announcing God's kingdom by our choices, words, behaviour, demeanour, and attitudes.

That said, there are some who emerge as having a special gift of prophecy. They are able to see right through the cultural accretions of the mainstream culture and identify what God is saying to the times in which they live. They often challenge us where we have gone astray (e.g. into racism, materialism, modern slavery, injustice). They speak truth to power with courage. They reveal reality. Their calling is to immerse themselves deeply in the presence of God, hear his word for the present age deep in their hearts, and bring its challenge or reassurance clearly to the attention of God's people for weighing and testing.

As our Matthew passage makes clear, the prophetic calling is about how we live, not just what we say.

Questions

- Who would you say have been the prophets of this age, of our lifetime?
- In the group, draw up a list of the characteristics of a prophetic life, that speaks to our world about the truth of Jesus.
- John the Baptist, a great prophet, withdrew to live in the desert, as did the Early Church Fathers. How did that help them get close to God's truth and power? What can we take from the way they lived, to put in place in our own lives?

Prayer

Spirit of truth and power, rest upon me. Sift me and refine me, blow away my chaff, skim away my impurities. By the wind and fire of your influence, may I become more like Jesus. Amen.

Teaching

Exodus 18:20, NIVUK

Teach them his decrees and instructions, and show them the way they are to live and how they are to behave.

Exodus 35:30–35, NIVUK

Then Moses said to the Israelites, "See, the Lord has chosen Bezalel son of Uri, the son of Hur, of the tribe of Judah, and he has filled him with the Spirit of God, with wisdom, with understanding, with knowledge and with all kinds of skills – to make artistic designs for work in gold, silver and bronze, to cut and set stones, to work in wood and to engage in all kinds of artistic crafts. And he has given both him and Oholiab son of Ahisamak, of the tribe of Dan, the ability to teach others. He has filled them with skill to do all kinds of work as engravers, designers, embroiderers in blue, purple and scarlet yarn and fine linen, and weavers – all of them skilled workers and designers."

James 3:1–2a, NIVUK

Not many of you should become teachers, my fellow believers, because you know that we who teach will be judged more strictly. We all stumble in many ways.

1 Timothy 3:14–15, NIVUK

Although I hope to come to you soon, I am writing to you with these instructions so that, if I am delayed, you will know how people ought to conduct themselves in God's household, which is the church of the living God, the pillar and foundation of the truth.

Proverbs 27:17, NIVUK

As iron sharpens iron, so one person sharpens another.

Acts 2:42, NIVUK

They devoted themselves to the apostles' teaching and to fellowship, to the breaking of bread and to prayer.

2 Timothy 3:16, NIVUK

All Scripture is God-breathed and is useful for teaching, rebuking, correcting and training in righteousness, so that the servant of God may be thoroughly equipped for every good work.

---

143 See also Romans 12:7; Ephesians 4:11; Corinthians 12:28; Matthew 28:19–20.

Commentary

Someone once asked a primary-school teacher, "And what do you teach?" She replied, "Children."

If you research the spiritual gift of teaching, what you find is about teaching facts and knowledge, and teaching the Bible: expounding and imparting knowledge and correcting false information. Our passage from 2 Timothy speaks of teaching in that way. But, even in that passage, the knowledge imparted is intended for practical not merely theoretical purposes – equipping and training the servants of God *for the life they lead*. To be righteous rather than to be right, if you see the distinction. We teach not things but people.

In our Acts 2 passage, we see teaching bedded into a holistic pattern of life, spiritual formation by participation in community of which words are only a part. Our Proverbs 27 passage likewise envisages us teaching one another, mutually honing our practice – presumably by example as much as by didactic impartation. Our Exodus 20 passage integrates the teaching of words and the teaching of example: "show them how to live."

Our passage from Exodus 35 adds the interesting dimension that the spiritual gift of teaching need not only be about teaching religion as a separate topic. In the fully integrated spiritual life, craftsmanship is also a holy pursuit undertaken in God's name, and some are gifted to teach such skills *by God*.

James warns that the vocation of teacher is no light undertaking; we are responsible before God for what we have taught others to believe and to do.

Questions

- What are the most useful things you have learned, to help you live happily and effectively? Who taught you these things?
- How do you personally learn best?[144]
- Who are the best teachers you have known, of the faith or in life generally? What made them so good?

Prayer

> *Show me your ways, Lord,*
>   *teach me your paths.*
> *Guide me in your truth and teach me,*
>
>   *for you are God my Saviour,*
>   *and my hope is in you all day long.*
> **(Psalm 25:4–5, NIVUK)**

---

144 E.g. by watching, listening, reading, following instructions, alone, in a group, or by doing.

Service[145]

BIBLE PASSAGES

Mark 10:42–45, NIVUK

Jesus called them together and said, "You know that those who are regarded as rulers of the Gentiles lord it over them, and their high officials exercise authority over them. Not so with you. Instead, whoever wants to become great among you must be your servant, and whoever wants to be first must be slave of all. For even the Son of Man did not come to be served, but to serve, and to give his life as a ransom for many."

John 13:3–5, NIVUK

Jesus knew that the Father had put all things under his power, and that he had come from God and was returning to God; so he got up from the meal, took off his outer clothing, and wrapped a towel round his waist. After that, he poured water into a basin and began to wash his disciples' feet, drying them with the towel that was wrapped round him.

2 Corinthians 11:7–9, NIVUK

Was it a sin for me to lower myself in order to elevate you by preaching the gospel of God to you free of charge? I robbed other churches by receiving support from them so as to serve you. And when I was with you and needed something, I was not a burden to anyone, for the brothers who came from Macedonia supplied what I needed. I have kept myself from being a burden to you in any way, and will continue to do so.

Ephesians 4:11–13, NIVUK

So Christ himself gave the apostles, the prophets, the evangelists, the pastors and teachers, to equip his people for works of service, so that the body of Christ may be built up until we all reach unity in the faith and in the knowledge of the Son of God and become mature, attaining to the whole measure of the fullness of Christ.

Commentary

The charism of service is often the thing people think they mean by the charism of helping. Where helping is about empowering and enabling others to grow into their

---

145 It may be useful to look at the study on the charism of "Helping" in this book alongside this.

own strength, service is about doing for others what they cannot do for themselves. It may involve having the humility to take on lowly and menial tasks that others need to have done, as our passage from John 13 shows, or it may mean putting our skills at the service of others to build up the church, as Paul describes in the passages from 2 Corinthians and Ephesians.

It's interesting to reflect on the ways in which we serve *one another* – it's not a one-way flow. The list of forms of service in the church in the Ephesians passage very likely includes people having their meals cooked and their bathrooms cleaned for them, and the 2 Corinthians passage points out that, in order for Paul to serve their church, other churches had to give financially to support him in doing this work.

It's important to avoid the pitfall of thinking that doing everything for someone is the gift of service. I remember an elderly man whose wife died leaving him incapable of knowing how to do his own washing, and a widow who had no idea which electricity supplier she had, or how to pay the bill. To do everything for someone makes them vulnerable; it infantilizes them, it isn't kind. When Jesus washes the disciples' feet, he doesn't offer to take it on for ever; he makes it clear that they should all take turns at the chores – "You should wash one another's feet".

The spiritual gift of service is about freely putting at God's disposal whatever you are good at. Even in the context of earning a living, this applies; you can go above and beyond the requirements of your job, elevating it to a form of loving service.[146]

Questions

- To what extent do you think the gift of service is an every-believer ministry, and to what extent is it a special charisma in some people's lives? What dangers might we want to avoid in believing that some people have a special gift of service? Is there anyone who is not called to serve?[147]

- Where do your gifts of service lie? In what ways do you feel called to serve God in the church, at home, and in the wider community? Is there any way you feel called to serve that you have not yet tried?

- To what extent does the gift of service come from the aptitude and ability of the person serving, and to what extent does it depend more on what needs to be done, regardless of how well fitted we feel for the tasks?

---

146 See Ephesians 6:5–8.

147 For instance, very severely disabled people, small children, and aged folk, who bring precious gifts of a different nature, and bring out the servant spirit in others?

Prayer

Servant King, thank you for living and dying for us, for washing our feet and washing our souls clean from sin. Help us to serve as humbly and gladly as you showed us to do. Give us the grace to pick up the towels and get on with it, when we see the need arise. Amen.

Faith

BIBLE PASSAGES

1 Corinthians 12:4, 6b, 7–8, 11, NIVUK

There are different kinds of gifts, but the same Spirit distributes them ... and in everyone it is the same God at work.

Now to each one the manifestation of the Spirit is given for the common good. To one there is given through the Spirit a message of wisdom, to another a message of knowledge by means of the same Spirit, to another faith by the same Spirit ... All these are the work of one and the same Spirit, and he distributes them to each one, just as he determines.

Mark 11:22–25, NIVUK

"Have faith in God," Jesus answered. "Truly I tell you, if anyone says to this mountain, 'Go, throw yourself into the sea,' and does not doubt in their heart but believes that what they say will happen, it will be done for them. Therefore I tell you, whatever you ask for in prayer, believe that you have received it, and it will be yours."

John 14:1, NIVUK

"Do not let your hearts be troubled. You believe in God; believe also in me."

Ephesians 2:8–9, NIVUK

For it is by grace you have been saved, through faith – and this is not from yourselves, it is the gift of God – not by works, so that no one can boast.

James 2:14–17, NIVUK

What good is it, my brothers and sisters, if someone claims to have faith but has no deeds? Can such faith save them? Suppose a brother or a sister is without clothes and daily food. If one of you says to them, "Go in peace; keep warm and well fed," but does nothing about their physical needs, what good is it? In the same way, faith by itself, if it is not accompanied by action, is dead.

Commentary

We have to make the distinction between the saving faith of all believers — the thing that makes us Christian — and the charism or spiritual gift of Faith.

Our Ephesians passage sets out the basis for our salvation — the grace of God's unconditional love and mercy received by faith. Something freely given that we cannot earn. Our passage from James builds on that, clarifying that though we cannot earn God's saving love by anything we do, nevertheless the reality of a living faith is evidenced by the way we live and the choices we make.

So a person with the gift of faith does have that kind of saving faith in Jesus by which they receive the grace of God's love and forgiveness; but in addition they regularly show that they have the mountain-moving faith of our Mark passage.

Remember that the gifts of the Spirit are for the building up of the church. The gift of faith is essential for all aspects of mission, but especially for cutting new ground – starting a new outreach to students or street people, planting a new church, or beginning an ambitious teaching or prayer programme. The impulse to act is received from God by faith, and then sustained all the way through to completion by faith. As Isaiah (45:2, NIVUK) says, "I will go before you and will level the mountains." It's by faith that the mountain-moving power of God works through us to extend the reach of his kingdom.

Questions

- How would you describe your own experience of faith? When did it begin? What sustains it? How important to you does it feel?

- Think of an example of someone in the Bible, or personally known to you, or whose life you have heard about, who you believe has the gift of faith.

- Do you think faith is for every aspect of our life or just for some things? We hear of people "living by faith", and praying in the resources they need. What is the right balance, do you think, of faith with common sense and forward planning? Does the person who prays in what they need have more faith than the person who has a job to pay their bills – or just a different calling?

Prayer

> *Give me the faith which can remove*
> *And sink the mountain to a plain;*
> *Give me the childlike praying love,*
> *Which longs to build Thy house again;*
> *Thy love, let it my heart overpower,*
> *And all my simple soul devour.*
> **(Charles Wesley, *Hymns and Sacred Poems*, 1749, number 186)**

Healing

BIBLE PASSAGES

Mark 1:30–34, NIVUK

Simon's mother-in-law was in bed with a fever, and they immediately told Jesus about her. So he went to her, took her hand and helped her up. The fever left her and she began to wait on them.

That evening after sunset the people brought to Jesus all who were ill and demon-possessed. The whole town gathered at the door, and Jesus healed many who had various diseases.

Luke 4:40, NIVUK

At sunset, the people brought to Jesus all who had various kinds of illness, and laying his hands on each one, he healed them.

Matthew 15:30, NIVUK

Great crowds came to him, bringing the lame, the blind, the crippled, the mute and many others, and laid them at his feet; and he healed them.

Acts 5:12–16, RSV

Now many signs and wonders were done among the people by the hands of the apostles. And they were all together in Solomon's Portico. None of the rest dared join them, but the people held them in high honour. And more than ever believers were added to the Lord, multitudes both of men and women, so that they even carried out the sick into the streets, and laid them on beds and pallets, that as Peter came by at least his shadow might fall on some of them. The people also gathered from the towns around Jerusalem, bringing the sick and those afflicted with unclean spirits, and they were all healed.

James 5:14–16, NIVUK

Is anyone among you ill? Let them call the elders of the church to pray over them and anoint them with oil in the name of the Lord. And the prayer offered in faith will make the sick person well; the Lord will raise them up. If they have sinned, they will be forgiven. Therefore confess your sins to each other and pray for each other so that you may be healed. The prayer of a righteous person is powerful and effective.

Commentary

Of all the spiritual charisms, healing is the one most churches are willing to try in public worship. Many churches now include a time of laying on of hands for healing, often after people have received the bread and wine of Holy Communion. Most church communities feel optimistic about prayer for healing, and report encouraging results from having prayed for the sick. Within these forays into the ministry of the Holy Spirit, sometimes individuals emerge for whom this gift develops into a charism. Outside the jurisdiction of religious organizations, there are also people with a natural gift for healing, but when we speak of the charism of healing, we mean healing in the name of Jesus.

It's important to be humble and open-minded about this (and all the gifts). People who are sick or disabled should never be made to feel uncomfortable or lacking in faith when their problems persist. Our criterion in serving God is obedience, not success. We know Jesus healed and so did the Christians in Bible days, and so have believers through all the generations since. We join in, offering prayer and laying on of hands, knowing that God wants all of us to be well and happy; and sometimes, as part of that, we will see a miracle.

Meanwhile, the whole people of God should be a healing community, working for the *shalom* of human society and all creation.

Questions

- Have you experienced healing or prayer for healing – whether ministering to others or receiving ministry? What happened? How did you feel about it?
- What do you think could be the pitfalls for a healing ministry? Do you know anyone who had bad experiences of it? How could you be adventurous with healing while also safeguarding against inadvertently hurting people?
- In what ways does your church participate in the healing ministry of the Holy Spirit? Do you regard yourselves as a healing church? In what ways? Would you like to try some kinds of healing you have not so far explored?

Prayer

Lord Jesus, we put our trust in you. Move us to compassion for those who suffer in sickness or disability; use our hands to help and heal them. Place your healing hands upon us gathered here, too; heal us from all that harms or hinders us, and may the wholeness of your Spirit breathe into our life together. Amen.

Miracles

BIBLE PASSAGES

John 5:19, RSV

Jesus said to them, "Truly, truly, I say to you, the Son can do nothing of his own accord, but only what he sees the Father doing; for whatever he does, that the Son does likewise."

Acts 19:11–15, RSV

God did extraordinary miracles by the hands of Paul, so that handkerchiefs or aprons were carried away from his body to the sick, and diseases left them and the evil spirits came out of them. Then some of the itinerant Jewish exorcists undertook to pronounce the name of the Lord Jesus over those who had evil spirits, saying, "I adjure you by the Jesus whom Paul preaches." Seven sons of a Jewish high priest named Sceva were doing this. But the evil spirit answered them, "Jesus I know, and Paul I know; but who are you?"

Ephesians 4:25–28, NIVUK

Therefore each of you must put off falsehood and speak truthfully to your neighbour, for we are all members of one body. "In your anger do not sin": do not let the sun go down while you are still angry, and do not give the devil a foothold.

John 14:30–31, NIVUK

"[The prince of this world] has no hold over me,[148] but he comes so that the world may learn that I love the Father and do exactly what my Father has commanded me."

Commentary

Because miracles are not magic tricks, their occurrence cannot be guaranteed, but there are certain conditions that invite miracles where others don't.

The most obvious is need. Miracles rescue us. For a miracle of supply to occur, there must first be a lack. A miracle o§f healing happens only when someone is ill. So the more organized, comfortable, stable, and predictable our lives, the fewer miracles we encounter. This isn't a problem, just a fact. Miracle territory is always close to the edge – sometimes right over it. If you want manna, go into the desert.

---

148   "He has no hold over me" – other translations: "[He] hath nothing in me" (KJV), "He has no power over me" (NRSVA), "He does not have anything in me" (DLNT).

Even then, you can't force God's hand. It is possible to guarantee the conditions of suffering, but not the rescuing miracle. We are God's subjects, not the other way round.

The second precondition is truth, in the largest sense – spoken truth, but also lived truth. Honesty, authenticity, openness, 100% commitment with nothing held back, no prevarication. We are made in the image of God,[149] and he spoke the world into being. When Jesus spoke a command of healing, it happened. He did nothing except what he saw the Father do, he aligned himself perfectly with the flow of God's grace, holding back nothing from God; in him there was no untruth. As our passages express it, he gave the devil no "foothold". Because his life and words gave an unequivocal message, nature organized itself faithfully around him. As long as we deal with half-truths, half-commitment, hypocrisy, hesitation, and giving the devil a foothold, we have not set the precondition for miracles – because we give the natural order mixed messages. But even with all this said, remember there are no guarantees of outcomes. There was no rescuing miracle for Jesus on the cross, because his suffering and death were part of the miracle God was doing. We do not always see the pattern, but we can always trust him.

Questions

- Jesus did nothing but what he saw the Father do. In what ways can we watch what the Father is doing, and how can we put it into practice?
- Jesus said the prince of this world has no foothold in him. What mistakes give a foothold to the devil, and how might we guard against this?
- Can you think of any instances you have experienced or heard of, where in times of great need God miraculously provided? Can you think of any examples from the Bible?

Prayer

God of all power and goodness, help us so to align ourselves with your truth and grace that your love may flow through us into the circumstances of our lives. By the power of the cross of Jesus, may we be cleansed of all our sin, and may we walk in the light of your truth, with our lives offering no foothold to the devil. For we ask it in Jesus' name. Amen.

---

149 Romans 8:29 (NIVUK): "For those God foreknew he also predestined to be conformed to the image of his Son, that he might be the firstborn among many brothers and sisters."

Discernment[150]

BIBLE PASSAGES

Malachi 3:18, NRSVA

Then once more you shall see the difference between the righteous and the wicked, between one who serves God and one who does not serve him.

1 Kings 3:9–12, RSV

"Give thy servant therefore an understanding mind to govern thy people, that I may discern between good and evil; for who is able to govern this thy great people?"

It pleased the Lord that Solomon had asked this. And God said to him, "Because you have asked this, and have not asked for yourself long life or riches or the life of your enemies, but have asked for yourself understanding to discern what is right, behold, I now do according to your word. Behold, I give you a wise and discerning mind, so that none like you has been before you and none like you shall arise after you."

1 Kings 19:11–13, RSV

And behold, the Lord passed by, and a great and strong wind rent the mountains, and broke in pieces the rocks before the Lord, but the Lord was not in the wind; and after the wind an earthquake, but the Lord was not in the earthquake; and after the earthquake a fire, but the Lord was not in the fire; and after the fire a still small voice. And when Elijah heard it, he wrapped his face in his mantle and went out and stood at the entrance of the cave.

Acts 16:17–18, NIVUK

She followed Paul and the rest of us, shouting, "These men are servants of the Most High God, who are telling you the way to be saved.' She kept this up for many days. Finally Paul became so annoyed that he turned round and said to the spirit, 'In the name of Jesus Christ I command you to come out of her!"

Hebrews 4:12, RSV

For the word of God is living and active, sharper than any two-edged sword, piercing to the division of soul and spirit, of joints and marrow, and discerning the thoughts and intentions of the heart.

---

150   See also the study on "Wisdom" in this book.

1 John 4:1, RSV

Beloved, do not believe every spirit, but test the spirits to see whether they are of God; for many false prophets have gone out into the world.

Commentary

In *The Princess and Curdie*, George MacDonald's 1883 fantasy novel for children, the mysterious grandmother in the tower gives twelve-year-old Curdie a special gift: the ability to discern what someone is becoming by taking their hand (or paw) in his. When he holds the paw of the dog Lina, so ugly she is terrifying to behold, he feels the hand of a little child. When he takes the hand of some human adults, he feels the slithering belly of a snake, the paw of a monkey, or the claw of a bird of prey. C. S. Lewis, who loved MacDonald's work, took up this idea of a human being progressing or regressing – developing more or less resemblance to the image of God.

This is a wonderful fictional representation of the charism of discernment: the ability to sense what sits beneath or behind presenting appearances, perceiving the underlying reality.

In our passages, Elijah discerns the presence of God in the silence rather than in the stormy wind and fire; Paul discerns a malign presence underlying the apparent affirmation and encouragement of the girl calling after them; Solomon receives the gifts of wisdom and discernment to help him make sound and perceptive judgments in governing the people.

The story of Solomon shows how intertwined are the gifts of wisdom and discernment – yet there is a difference. Discernment has the particular characteristic of seeing beyond first appearances to an underlying motivation or hidden reality.

Questions

- In what circumstances do you think the gift of discernment could be particularly useful?

- Our quotation from 1 John 4 speaks of "testing the spirits", to guard against false prophets (or what Jesus called "blind guides"[151]). Where in modern times has a lack of discernment allowed false prophets and blind guides to arise in the people of God? How might we encourage the development of the gift of discernment to guard the church's integrity?

- Our quotation from Hebrews speaks of discerning the thoughts and intentions of the heart. Discuss in your group how to find a healthy balance of discernment and proper caution, while avoiding overthinking and paranoid suspicion.

---

151 Matthew 15:7–14; Matthew 23:13–33.

Prayer

Wise and loving Father, you look into our hearts and see who we really are. May I walk so close to you that the Spirit's discernment takes residence in the eyes of my spirit, the insight of my understanding. God be in my eyes, and in my looking. Amen.

Tongues[152]

BIBLE PASSAGES

Mark 16:17, RSV

And these signs will accompany those who believe: in my name they will cast out demons; they will speak in new tongues ...

Acts 2:5–12, RSV

Now there were dwelling in Jerusalem Jews, devout men from every nation under heaven. And at this sound the multitude came together, and they were bewildered, because each one heard them speaking in his own language. And they were amazed and wondered, saying, "Are not all these who are speaking Galileans? And how is it that we hear, each of us in his own native language? Parthians and Medes and Elamites and residents of Mesopotamia, Judea and Cappadocia, Pontus and Asia, Phrygia and Pamphylia, Egypt and the parts of Libya belonging to Cyrene, and visitors from Rome, both Jews and proselytes, Cretans and Arabians, we hear them telling in our own tongues the mighty works of God." And all were amazed and perplexed, saying to one another, "What does this mean?"

Acts 19:6, RSV

And when Paul had laid his hands upon them, the Holy Spirit came on them; and they spoke with tongues and prophesied.

1 Corinthians 14:2–5, RSV

One who speaks in a tongue speaks not to men but to God; for no one understands him, but he utters mysteries in the Spirit. On the other hand, he who prophesies speaks to men for their upbuilding and encouragement and consolation. He who speaks in a tongue edifies himself, but he who prophesies edifies the church. Now I want you all to speak in tongues, but even more to prophesy. He who prophesies is greater than he who speaks in tongues, unless some one interprets, so that the church may be edified.

1 Corinthians 14:18, RSV

I thank God that I speak in tongues more than you all ...

152 For supplementary reading, Don Basham's book *Face Up With A Miracle*, published by Whitaker House in 1971, is very helpful, as is Jackie Pullinger's book *Chasing the Dragon*, published by Hodder in 1980.

1 Corinthians 14:39–40, RSV

So, my brethren, earnestly desire to prophesy, and do not forbid speaking in tongues; but all things should be done decently and in order.

Commentary

The gift of tongues is sometimes referred to as *glossolalia* – a linguists' term meaning something that sounds like language but is in reality nonsense. However, this is not the New Testament understanding of the gift. All languages sound like nonsense if we don't understand them, and what is spoken when the gift of tongues is exercised can be an ancient language or one spoken by a small minority, or it can be an angelic language.[153] As our Acts passage makes clear, if a group of people who spoke numerous different languages were present, they would be able to identify what sounds like nonsense – and it has sometimes happened that someone from overseas has understood when a prayer in tongues was given in worship.

Tongues will always be used for prayer ("one who speaks in a tongue speaks not to men but to God"), not for a message from God; that would be prophecy, knowledge, or wisdom. Sometimes called "praying in the Spirit", this gift has the particular benefit of allowing the believer to pray with the Spirit's understanding when unsure what to ask for or how to direct the prayer. Another benefit is that tongues can deepen or accelerate the spiritual quality of a meeting, encouraging the flow of spiritual gifts and experience. It is also very powerful for personal transformation – in her work among drug addicts in Hong Kong, the evangelist Jackie Pullinger has seen numerous new Christians freed from addiction through exercising the gift of tongues regularly and at length in their prayer.

Questions

- What has been your personal experience (in yourself or others) of speaking in tongues? What was your response to it or, if you have never come across it, what do you think about it?

- Jackie Pullinger recommends praying in tongues for half an hour every morning, and the apostle Paul prayed in tongues frequently, "more than you all". What advantages can you see to allowing the Spirit to pray through you in a language you do not know?

- Would you like to pray in tongues? Why or why not? There are two usual ways to begin, once we have humbly asked God for this gift: the first is just to start speaking, allowing words to come even if they sound like nonsense; the second is for someone who already exercises the gift to start praying in tongues, and join in. Why not have a go?

---

153 1 Corinthians 13:1.

Prayer

Spirit of God, thank you for the beauty and mystery of your power. Please, by your grace, allow me to exercise your gift of tongues, to deepen my experience of you. Amen.

Interpretation

BIBLE PASSAGES

1 Corinthians 12:8a, 10b, RSV

> To one is given through the Spirit ... various kinds of tongues, to another the interpretation of tongues.

1 Corinthians 12:30, RSV

> Do all speak with tongues? Do all interpret?

1 Corinthians 14:6, 13–19, RSV

> Now, brethren, if I come to you speaking in tongues, how shall I benefit you unless I bring you some revelation or knowledge or prophecy or teaching?
>   ... Therefore, he who speaks in a tongue should pray for the power to interpret. For if I pray in a tongue, my spirit prays but my mind is unfruitful. What am I to do? I will pray with the spirit and I will pray with the mind also; I will sing with the spirit and I will sing with the mind also. Otherwise, if you bless with the spirit, how can any one in the position of an outsider say the "Amen" to your thanksgiving when he does not know what you are saying? For you may give thanks well enough, but the other man is not edified. I thank God that I speak in tongues more than you all; nevertheless, in church I would rather speak five words with my mind, in order to instruct others, than ten thousand words in a tongue.

1 Corinthians 14:26–28, RSV

> What then, brethren? When you come together, each one has a hymn, a lesson, a revelation, a tongue, or an interpretation. Let all things be done for edification. If any speak in a tongue, let there be only two or at most three, and each in turn; and let one interpret. But if there is no one to interpret, let each of them keep silence in church and speak to himself and to God.

Commentary

Paul's instructions about the interpretation of tongues are given in the context of the substantial section on the ordering of public worship in 1 Corinthians. In the last of our passages above, he says, "If there is no one to interpret, let each of them keep silence in church and speak to himself and to God." Interpretation might be interesting but is not necessary when someone is praying alone; the power of the Spirit working through the person is not diminished by the mind's lack of understanding. It is still possible to feel the emotion and urgency of the prayer, to be fully engaged in spirit even if the mind does not know the meaning of the words.

However, in the context of public worship, other people praying in tongues can be inspiring but it is a lot more useful when what is being said is understood. Paul is also concerned about not opening ourselves to ridicule or scandal: "If, therefore, the whole church assembles and all speak in tongues, and outsiders or unbelievers enter, will they not say that you are mad?" (1 Corinthians 14:23).

In that context, his recommendation is not for the whole church to speak in tongues simultaneously, but for one or two individuals to pray in tongues and then an interpretation to be given. This implies prearrangement (or at least reliability): knowing that one will be speaking in tongues, knowing whether or not one who can interpret will be there, and knowing the interpretation will be given. This tells us that the gift of tongues is not an incontinent outpouring and the interpretation is not a matter of chance, but rather that these elements of public worship can be structured in. The same Spirit who can give such wondrous gifts on Sunday morning can let us know on Thursday afternoon that he plans to do so. Then all can proceed decently and in order. There is nothing especially spiritual about spontaneity.

Questions

- Have you any experience of the gift of interpretation? What happened? Would the exercise of this gift in any way change how you feel about the exercise of tongues in public worship or in private prayer?
- Speaking in tongues and giving interpretations in public worship may seem a tall order. How would you feel about a workshop group to explore and experiment with the gifts of the Spirit in your church? How could such a group be planned and organized ?
- In what way does your church allow for the inclusion in public worship of the exercise of spiritual gifts? How might this be increased and planned for?

Prayer

Mighty God, your work in us is exciting and beyond our understanding. May we be open to your Spirit's leading, willing to follow, obedient to your call; but help us also to retain our common sense. Pour out your gifts upon us, and may they be effective for conversion, unity, and inclusion in our church. Amen.

Helping

BIBLE PASSAGES

1 Corinthians 12:28, RSV

And God has appointed in the church first apostles, second prophets, third teachers, then workers of miracles, then healers, helpers, administrators, speakers in various kinds of tongues.

Genesis 2:20–23, KJV

And Adam gave names to all cattle, and to the fowl of the air, and to every beast of the field; but for Adam there was not found an help meet for him.

And the Lord God caused a deep sleep to fall upon Adam, and he slept; and he took one of his ribs, and closed up the flesh instead thereof;

And the rib, which the Lord God had taken from man, made he a woman, and brought her unto the man.

And Adam said, This is now bone of my bones, and flesh of my flesh: she shall be called Woman, because she was taken out of Man.

John 14:16,[154] GNB

"I will ask the Father, and he will give you another Helper, who will stay with you forever."

John 15:26, GNB

"The Helper will come – the Spirit, who reveals the truth about God and who comes from the Father. I will send him to you from the Father, and he will speak about me."

John 16:7, GNB

"But I am telling you the truth: it is better for you that I go away, because if I do not go, the Helper will not come to you. But if I do go away, then I will send him to you."

1 John 2:1, GNB

I am writing this to you, my children, so that you will not sin; but if anyone does sin, we have someone who pleads with the Father on our behalf – Jesus Christ, the righteous one.

---

154 Also verse 26.

Commentary

Sometimes known as "helps", this beautiful charism enables or empowers others to blossom and reach their full potential.

It is sometimes confused with the charism of service, because the term "helping" or "helps" can be understood to mean "lending a helping hand".

A Christian women's group had the task of identifying their spiritual gifts. Most (not all) were homemakers, deriving an income from low-paid, part-time work with their primary sense of vocation vested in bringing up their children and cooking and cleaning for their families. It was striking to notice how many said they had "the gift of helping"; because they'd be the ones to make the hot drinks, wash the cups, run the crèche, mop the floor, change the nappies, launder the dish towels. That's not the gift of helps – it's more simple necessity, long familiarity with being left to take responsibility for the chores that belong to everyone; and in some cases lack of confidence.

The only time the term occurs in the Bible is in 1 Corinthians 12:28. The Greek word, *antílēpsis*, literally means "to take hold of, succour, rescue, participate, help, support". So it's about joining in positively for someone else's benefit. Or it could mean reaching out to them.

It is noticeably similar to the way Eve is described in relation to Adam – a "help meet" for him. The two Hebrew words from which the term "help meet" derives mean someone who is like you, an appropriate companion, and someone to save or rescue or be strong for you. There are also similarities with the term "paraclete" (Greek root), used by John to describe the work of the Holy Spirit and Jesus in coming alongside to help us,[155] and to advocate for us in prayer.

Gathering up these diverse strands, the meaning of a "helper" begins to emerge: someone who reaches out to you, is on your side, assists you in becoming your best self.[156] This with the gift of helps play a strong part in building up and strengthening the faith community. Notice that this is nothing subservient; the charism of helping is not about being at someone else's disposal; on the contrary, it's about supporting others where they are vulnerable, fragile, or weak.

Questions

- Think of someone you know who has this gift, and share how you have seen it in action at home or in church or in your neighbourhood.

- In what ways has the help of God come to find you at times when you were struggling?

---

155 See also the study on "Encouragement".
156 See also the study on "Encouragement", and the similar role of Barnabas.

- The gift of helps intuitively seems like a very personal, hands-on charism. But how can podcasts, books, phone calls, TV programmes, or initiatives like the Samaritans and the Citizens Advice Bureau offer inspiring models for the gift of helps?

Prayer

Holy Spirit of God, our help and strength, you lift us up on your pinions and carry us beyond where we could possibly go. Inspire us to help one another, to reach out, to lift the fallen, to help those who are stuck or stumbling to find fresh strength and make a new start. Amen.

Administration

BIBLE PASSAGES

1 Corinthians 12:27–31, RSV

Now you are the body of Christ and individually members of it. And God has appointed in the church first apostles, second prophets, third teachers, then workers of miracles, then healers, helpers, administrators, speakers in various kinds of tongues. Are all apostles? Are all prophets? Are all teachers? Do all work miracles? Do all possess gifts of healing? Do all speak with tongues? Do all interpret? But earnestly desire the higher gifts.

Titus 1:4–5, RSV

To Titus, my true child in a common faith:
Grace and peace from God the Father and Christ Jesus our Saviour.
This is why I left you in Crete, that you might amend what was defective, and appoint elders in every town as I directed you.

Matthew 20:8, RSV

And when evening came, the owner of the vineyard said to his steward, "Call the labourers and pay them their wages, beginning with the last, up to the first."

Luke 12:42, RSV

And the Lord said, "Who then is the faithful and wise steward, whom his master will set over his household, to give them their portion of food at the proper time?"

Genesis 1:26, NRSVA

Then God said, "Let us make humankind in our image, according to our likeness; and let them have dominion over the fish of the sea, and over the birds of the air, and over the cattle, and over all the wild animals of the earth, and over every creeping thing that creeps upon the earth."

Genesis 2:15, RSV

The Lord God took the man and put him in the garden of Eden to till it and keep it.

Commentary

The Greek for the spiritual gift of administration, *kubernesis*, is most often used of a captain or master, on a ship.[157] This role involves a significant level of leadership – we aren't just talking about filing and answering the phone – but it doesn't carry final authority. The administrator has delegated authority to organize and manage.

It's interesting to find administration included as a charism of the Holy Spirit. I personally do not have the spiritual gift of administration. I find paperwork mind-numbing; even dogs don't do what I tell them; data never stays long in my mind; I easily forget (anything). As a result, both as the mother of a big family and as the pastor of as many as six churches at one time, I've had to learn and to persevere at admin, filing everything meticulously, organizing my time carefully, planning in detail, watching budgets and property, finding courage for managing difficult people. I got very good at it – but that's not the same as its being my spiritual gifting.

The presence of the Holy Spirit is characterized by grace, freedom, and joy. Those with the charism of administration carry out oversight conscientiously, but joyously. They have a light touch. There is humour, patience, and kindness in their attitude. They take the trouble to get things right, and they are good listeners. Of all the charisms, this is the one you most often find carried out by someone who lacks the gifting and does it badly. The gift of administration, often belittled as boring, is pure gold.

Questions

- Note that in our passage from 1 Corinthians 12, Paul makes it clear that different members of the body should fulfil different roles. In many churches, the administrator has the caretaker's role thrown in as well, or the preacher and teacher has evangelism and administration added on. Think about your church. What are the areas of administration? Who carries them out? Where is the gifting? For which areas of service should you pray in someone new?

- We sometimes speak of "every-believer" ministries. The stewardship of the earth surpasses that: it's an every-*human* ministry. We are – all of us without exception – called to the faithful stewardship of creation. How can your church, and you personally, respond to God's calling to this role?

- Share in your group what you believe your own gifting to be, and what you perceive the gifts of each other to be.

---

157 See Acts 27:11.

Prayer

O Lord, all the world belongs to you. I own nothing; I am only the steward of what is yours. Help me with this big responsibility. May I be faithful in administering the material goods, professional tasks, domestic duties, and relational roles with which you have entrusted me. Help me to do this steadily and with a quiet mind, so that I may bring the peace and order of heaven into every area of responsibility in my life. Amen.

Pastoral guidance

BIBLE PASSAGES[158]

Acts 20:28–31, GNB

So keep watch over yourselves and over all the flock which the Holy Spirit has placed in your care. Be shepherds of the church of God, which he made his own through the blood of his Son. I know that after I leave, fierce wolves will come among you, and they will not spare the flock. The time will come when some men from your own group will tell lies to lead the believers away after them. Watch, then, and remember that with many tears, day and night, I taught every one of you for three years.

Ezekiel 34:2–6, NIVUK

Son of man, prophesy against the shepherds of Israel; prophesy and say to them: "This is what the Sovereign Lord says: woe to you shepherds of Israel who only take care of yourselves! Should not shepherds take care of the flock? You eat the curds, clothe yourselves with the wool and slaughter the choice animals, but you do not take care of the flock. You have not strengthened the weak or healed those who are ill or bound up the injured. You have not brought back the strays or searched for the lost. You have ruled them harshly and brutally. So they were scattered because there was no shepherd, and when they were scattered they became food for all the wild animals. My sheep wandered over all the mountains and on every high hill. They were scattered over the whole earth, and no one searched or looked for them."

Psalm 23:1–4, RSV

The Lord is my shepherd, I shall not want;
    he makes me lie down in green pastures.
He leads me beside still waters;
    he restores my soul.
He leads me in paths of righteousness
    for his name's sake.
Even though I walk through the valley of the shadow of death,
    I fear no evil;
for thou art with me;
    thy rod and thy staff,
    they comfort me.

---

158 These passages mention fierce wolves and liars who prey on and fracture the flock. I have kept the questions positive, but your group could find it helpful to take the opportunity to discuss spiritual/sexual predators/abuse in the church, or other aspects of bad pastoring. If you do this, make sure it's not the last thing you discuss. End the meeting with a positive topic.

Commentary

The gift of pastoral guidance – the role of a pastor – is about nurturing and tending the flock, overseeing the well-being of God's people. Like all the charisms it is for building up the church, so we have to remember that it is a *spiritual* gift; the role of pastor is not that of a church social worker or club manager.

In most churches, the pastor is also a preacher and teacher, heading up the evangelism and taking care of the administration, but the New Testament keeps these roles and charisms distinct.

Perhaps the closest we can come to the biblical role of pastor is in our home-group leaders. These people provide for the spiritual nourishment of the members by ensuring a good programme of study, fellowship, and shared prayer. They are usually the first to know when someone has a problem, and they follow up those who drift off. They provide a context in which church members can learn and grow – but they also help them to feel they belong, they are part of the family, they are known and loved.

In times of sickness, bereavement, hardship, or personal difficulties, the pastor is someone you can confide in, who will remember you in prayer and visit you at home.

Good pastoral care is essential in keeping the flock together and in good heart. Nothing is more likely to make the sheep give up and wander off than church leaders who don't know them and don't care about them.

Questions

- Who have you known with the gift of pastoral guidance? Describe how you saw this gift in them.
- How are the different charisms reflected in the different ministries in your church? Do you have one church leader who covers everything, or different people responsible for different areas? Does this work well – for the leader and for the people? What are the structures through which pastoral guidance flows in your church? How well is it working? Can you think of any ideas to help it be even better?
- How do you see the role of pastor and the role of evangelist working together for the building up and nurturing of the people of God?[159]

---

159 If the evangelist steadily brings new people in and the pastor nurtures, there may be issues of social/cultural difference to consider as part of the continuous process of integration. Should they join existing home groups? Should there be a buddy system? Should there be a special nurture group for new Christians? If no new people ever come, or if the integration of different kinds of people is something never considered in your church, that could be worth thinking about too.

Prayer

God of love, Shepherd of our souls, thank you for watching over us, for caring for us and guiding us. Help us to grow together as one flock, comfortable with one another, trusting each other. Bless our leaders and pastors in their responsibility of caring for us, and fill them continually with your Holy Spirit. Amen.

Encouragement[160]

BIBLE PASSAGES[161]

Galatians 6:1–2, 9–10, RSV

Brethren, if a man is overtaken in any trespass, you who are spiritual should restore him in a spirit of gentleness. Look to yourself, lest you too be tempted. Bear one another's burdens, and so fulfil the law of Christ ...

And let us not grow weary in well-doing, for in due season we shall reap, if we do not lose heart. So then, as we have opportunity, let us do good to all men, and especially to those who are of the household of faith.

Acts 11:22–24, RSV

[T]he church in Jerusalem ... sent Barnabas[162] to Antioch. When he came and saw the grace of God, he was glad; and he exhorted them all to remain faithful to the Lord with steadfast purpose; for he was a good man, full of the Holy Spirit and of faith. And a large company was added to the Lord.

Acts 14:19b–23, RSV

[T]hey stoned Paul and dragged him out of the city, supposing that he was dead. But when the disciples gathered about him, he rose up and entered the city; and on the next day he went on with Barnabas to Derbe. When they had preached the gospel to that city and had made many disciples, they returned to Lystra and to Iconium and to Antioch, strengthening the souls of the disciples, exhorting them to continue in the faith, and saying that through many tribulations we must enter the kingdom of God. And when they had appointed elders for them in every church, with prayer and fasting, they committed them to the Lord in whom they believed.

1 Thessalonians 5:11, RSV

Therefore encourage one another and build one another up, just as you are doing.

---

160 See also the study on "Fortitude" and the one on "Helping" in this book.

161 See also Nehemiah 2:17–20; 1 Samuel 23:15–18; 1 Thessalonians 5:14; Hebrews 3:13; Hebrews 10:24.

162 Check out Barnabas in the book of Acts. When encouragement is needed, he's usually there.

Commentary

To understand a word, we look at the route it has travelled to get to us. The French for "heart" is *coeur*, and the word "encourage" – meaning "en-hearten" – came into the English language with the Norman invasion, displacing English words such as *bealden*[163] ("to make bold"), *herten*[164] ("hearten"), and the Old English *onhyrdan* ("enhearten"). So encouragement puts new heart into someone else, strengthening and emboldening them.

It can mean "motivate", to give someone strength or hope ("We went to the match to encourage the players"); enhance or further ("We have always encouraged good behaviour in the Sunday school"); help or foster ("We are encouraging the re-establishment of beavers in this area"). This is about bringing your own positive strength and enthusiasm alongside a weaker person or someone who has grown tired or dispirited, to help them keep on or start again.

The Greek world for this gift is *parakaleo* – which also means "exhort" or "beseech" or "call upon"; we take our word "paraclete"[165] from this. This introduces the idea of how we speak to someone, to help them keep going.

Surely every Christian needs encouragement. To continue patiently and cheerfully when times look desperate, to go on believing when others sneer at faith in God, to choose simplicity and service in a materialistic and individualistic society, to keep a discipline of prayer and study – none of this is easy; all of it is more inclined to falter without the encouragement of fellow believers. And some people so persistently and warmly encourage others that we see it has become their charism. These are the people who lift you up when you are down, who remind you of why something is worthwhile. Not usually leaders: they face you when addressing the crowd you are in, or go ahead of you at the front of the platoon. The encourager walks beside you, travels with you, becomes – for a stretch of the way – your companion on the journey.

Questions

- Who has encouraged you in your Christian life and in your own particular calling?
- What area of life or service do you think would benefit from encouragement in your church? Is there any area where you are strong as a church community, and could offer encouragement to others? How could you go about that?
- In your own personal life, is there any area of tiredness, fear, defeat, or despair where you could do with some encouragement right now?

---

163 Middle English alternative *balden*, Old English *bealdian*.
164 Old English *hiertan, hyrtan*.
165 John 14:16–17.

Prayer

Strengthen and establish us in the gospel, Lord Jesus. Make us bold to serve and proclaim you, and steadfast in encouraging our brothers and sisters in the faith. Amen.

Giving

BIBLE PASSAGES

Luke 21:1–4, NIVUK

As Jesus looked up, he saw the rich putting their gifts into the temple treasury. He also saw a poor widow put in two very small copper coins. "Truly I tell you," he said, "this poor widow has put in more than all the others. All these people gave their gifts out of their wealth; but she out of her poverty put in all she had to live on."[166]

2 Corinthians 9:6–12, NIVUK

Remember this: whoever sows sparingly will also reap sparingly, and whoever sows generously will also reap generously. Each of you should give what you have decided in your heart to give, not reluctantly or under compulsion, for God loves a cheerful giver. And God is able to bless you abundantly, so that in all things at all times, having all that you need, you will abound in every good work. As it is written:

> "They have freely scattered their gifts to the poor;
>   their righteousness endures for ever."[167]

Now he who supplies seed to the sower and bread for food will also supply and increase your store of seed and will enlarge the harvest of your righteousness. You will be enriched in every way so that you can be generous on every occasion, and through us your generosity will result in thanksgiving to God.

This service that you perform is not only supplying the needs of the Lord's people but is also overflowing in many expressions of thanks to God.

Matthew 10:8b, NIVUK

Freely you have received; freely give.

Luke 6:38, NIVUK

Give, and it will be given to you. A good measure, pressed down, shaken together and running over, will be poured into your lap. For with the measure you use, it will be measured to you.

---

166 See also 1 Kings 17:7–16.
167 Psalm 112:9.

Matthew 6:3–4, NIVUK

[W]hen you give to the needy, do not let your left hand know what your right hand is doing, so that your giving may be in secret.

Commentary

The spiritual charism of giving is characterized by attitude. There is no sense of guilt or compulsion in it – rather, it brings joy and freedom. Grace is a foundational concept in Christian faith – God's free and unconditional gift of himself – and the outworking of salvation expresses the unblocked flow of grace in our lives. This makes giving, in the widest sense, central to Christian practice. All Christians are called to give sacrificially, because they are called to follow Jesus, and that's what he did. Since giving is so important a feature of Christian life, it's not immediately easy to identify how the spiritual charism of giving differs from Christian giving in a general sense.

The sign of giving as a Holy Spirit charism is the focus on and delight in giving. Those who have this charism are not just willing to give when necessary or dutiful in paying their tithe – they live to give. Their joy in life is being a channel for God's blessing in this way. Often living very simply and frugally, their delight is in giving to others. Mother Teresa showed this charism in pouring out all her resources, and a lot of other people's too, to help the destitute.

I knew an elderly widow who had lived in poverty all her life – from a workhouse childhood to the army pension of a chronically ill husband injured in the war and needing constant attention, and then to the small old-age state pension. Yet she would save up and from her tiny store she would quietly and privately bring me from time to time some money to send to a man in prison, so he could buy himself some cigarettes. Such kindness, such understanding and imaginative compassion – that's the charism of giving.

Questions

- Our giving should be generous, but intelligent. How do you feel we should respond to beggars in the town centre? What is the most constructive way of helping them?

- Many of us share our resources with others – for example, if we are parents, we have a responsibility to our children in how we dispose of our income. What balance do you aim for in budgeting to fulfil your home and family commitments and also giving towards the Lord's work?

- John Wesley said, "Earn all you can, save[168] all you can, give all you can." Share in the group your thoughts about blending appropriate self-care (time and

---

168 By "save" he meant not "stash away" but "refrain from spending".

opportunities to relax and enjoy life[169]), while also living simply and giving generously. How does this work in practice in your own life?

Prayer

Source of all joy, in your service is perfect freedom. May your grace guide us, your unconditional love inspire and shape us, and your kindness motivate and direct us. Amen.

---

169 E.g. holidays, meals out with your friends or partner, or participating in a sport or hobby.

Leadership

BIBLE PASSAGES

1 Thessalonians 5:12–13, GNB

We beg you, our friends, to pay proper respect to those who work among you, who guide and instruct you in the Christian life. Treat them with the greatest respect and love because of the work they do. Be at peace among yourselves.

1 Timothy 3:2–7, GNB

A church leader must be without fault; he must have only one wife, be sober, self-controlled, and orderly; he must welcome strangers in his home; he must be able to teach; he must not be a drunkard or a violent man, but gentle and peaceful; he must not love money; he must be able to manage his own family well and make his children obey him with all respect. For if a man does not know how to manage his own family, how can he take care of the church of God? He must be mature in the faith, so that he will not swell up with pride and be condemned, as the Devil was. He should be a man who is respected by the people outside the church, so that he will not be disgraced and fall into the Devil's trap.

1 Peter 5:1–4, NIVUK[170]

To the elders among you, I appeal as a fellow elder and a witness of Christ's sufferings who also will share in the glory to be revealed: be shepherds of God's flock that is under your care, watching over them – not because you must, but because you are willing, as God wants you to be; not pursuing dishonest gain, but eager to serve; not lording it over those entrusted to you, but being examples to the flock. And when the Chief Shepherd appears, you will receive the crown of glory that will never fade away.

Romans 12:6, 8, NIVUK

We have different gifts, according to the grace given to each of us. If your gift is … to lead, do it diligently …

Commentary

The New Testament is firm on this point: church leaders must be humble. The passage from 1 Timothy explores this a little further, mentioning the "Devil's trap" that accompanies church leadership. This snare seems to occur in two

---

170 See also Mark 10:42–45.

areas – one is egoism, the other is scandal. There's a third area of temptation for church leaders implied in our Romans 12 passage ("If your gift is … to lead, do it diligently") – laziness.

Church leaders to a very considerable extent set their own agenda and manage their own timetable. Oversight is scanty, and there is a high degree of trust. As part of the esteem and respect in which they are held, church congregations rarely require top–down accountability. Of course the leader's church denomination will have put in place an appraisal system, but this often depends heavily on self-assessment or information voluntarily supplied by the leader.

This means the leader relies strongly on self-motivation to get the balance right: neither to neglect their family nor to let family concerns marginalize church duties; to be active in the wider community but not to let this become an excuse for neglecting crucial administrative responsibilities; neither to take refuge in study and ignore pastoral oversight, nor to spend so much time on cultivating relationships as to neglect study and preaching/teaching preparation. And a church leader must also be skilled in conflict resolution.

It's easy to see how vital it is that this be a true vocation – a spiritual charism, not a bright idea. Faith communities always reflect the qualities of their leaders, and real effectiveness comes from authentic, Spirit-led calling. We should pray for our leaders!

Questions

- Imagine you have to place an advertisement for a church leader, including a description of the qualities you are looking for. "The successful applicant will be …" What would you say?
- No church leader is perfect. What areas of leadership weakness do you think your church could cover, and what would be non-negotiable necessities for a leader in your church?
- Imagine your faith community really messed up, appointing an absolutely dire leader for your church. What do you think makes an atrocious leader? What could you do as a faith community to support that individual, filling in the gaps to keep your fellowship in good heart?

Prayer

Father, we pray for the leaders of our home group and our church, and for our denomination's regional and national leaders. Pour your Spirit into them, we pray; bless them and hold them, inspire and strengthen them. We thank you for them and we place them into your loving care. Amen.

Apostleship

BIBLE PASSAGES

Ephesians 2:19, 20–22, NIVUK

[Y]ou are ... built on the foundation of the apostles and prophets, with Christ Jesus himself as the chief cornerstone. In him the whole building is joined together and rises to become a holy temple in the Lord. And in him you too are being built together to become a dwelling in which God lives by his Spirit.

1 Corinthians 12:27–28, NIVUK

Now you are the body of Christ, and each one of you is a part of it. And God has placed in the church first of all apostles, second prophets, third teachers, then miracles, then gifts of healing, of helping, of guidance, and of different kinds of tongues.

Acts 11:1–4, 18, NIVUK

The apostles and the believers throughout Judea heard that the Gentiles also had received the word of God. So when Peter went up to Jerusalem, the circumcised believers criticised him and said, "You went into the house of uncircumcised men and ate with them."

Starting from the beginning, Peter told them the whole story.

... When they heard this, they had no further objections and praised God, saying, "So then, even to Gentiles God has granted repentance that leads to life."

Acts 11:22–26, NIVUK

News of this reached the church in Jerusalem, and they sent Barnabas to Antioch. When he arrived and saw what the grace of God had done, he was glad and encouraged them all to remain true to the Lord with all their hearts. He was a good man, full of the Holy Spirit and faith, and a great number of people were brought to the Lord.

Then Barnabas went to Tarsus to look for Saul, and when he found him, he brought him to Antioch. So for a whole year Barnabas and Saul met with the church and taught great numbers of people. The disciples were called Christians first at Antioch.

Commentary

We refer to the original twelve disciples Jesus called and sent forth to minister as "apostles", but this is distinct from the role of apostle in the church as it developed.

The role of apostle comes "first of all" in the list from 1 Corinthians 12 – it is of primary importance in the church. It involves oversight on a large scale, not of a local meeting only but of a much wider grouping, and the travel implicit in that; in the book of Acts we see apostles going from one community to another to evangelize, instruct, nurture, and resolve disputes. The role includes missionary work and church planting, with an ongoing responsibility for overseeing the establishment of the new church communities in the true faith. Sometimes there are culturally contextual questions to be answered, and the apostles deal with those,[171] helping the local church to evolve a faith practice appropriate to their cultural context.

The apostles work together to provide leadership oversight that holds the church together in unity. They lead the leaders, minister to the ministers, and constitute the final decision-making body.

It is essential that those who serve in this capacity are called to do so by the Spirit of God and are gifted by him. If personal advancement and aggrandizement creep into motivation to apostleship, the church is undone, becoming an empty shell from which the life has departed.

Questions

- In the modern church, who would you say are the apostles? Are they the regional leaders within a denomination, or are they the primary leaders of all the denominations working together, or the church planters, or … ?

- Look at the first of our two passages from Acts 11. Explore the relationship between Peter and the other apostles. Notice the balance of freedom to act with accountability to the others. With this in mind, what qualities do you think an apostle would need? Discuss how this benefits the church community, and what the modern counterparts of this might be.

- Looking at our second passage from Acts 11, we see the aspect of being sent out that is integral to the apostolic calling. Notice that Barnabas is chosen by agreement of the church, but that he has the freedom to seek out Saul to help him. What does this tell you about the need to delegate and call on the skills of others in the work of an apostle? How might this principle work on a smaller scale in local church leadership?

---

171 For example, the section on head covering in 1 Corinthians 11:2–16, or the decisions about Gentile converts in Acts 21:17–26.

Prayer

Spirit of God, come into all those who bear the responsibility today of acting as apostles in your church. Come as a consuming fire and burn up all personal ambition; come as a rushing wind and blow away all small-minded preoccupations; give to them your vision, your faith, and your love, that they may serve you well. Amen.

Evangelism

BIBLE PASSAGES

Ephesians 4:11–13, NIVUK

So Christ himself gave the apostles, the prophets, the evangelists, the pastors and teachers, to equip his people for works of service, so that the body of Christ may be built up until we all reach unity in the faith and in the knowledge of the Son of God and become mature, attaining to the whole measure of the fullness of Christ.

Acts 1:8, NIVUK

… you will receive power when the Holy Spirit comes on you; and you will be my witnesses in Jerusalem, and in all Judea and Samaria, and to the ends of the earth.

Matthew 28:18–20, NIVUK

Then Jesus came to them and said, "All authority in heaven and on earth has been given to me. Therefore go and make disciples of all nations, baptising them in the name of the Father and of the Son and of the Holy Spirit, and teaching them to obey everything I have commanded you. And surely I am with you always, to the very end of the age."

Luke 9:1–6, NIVUK

When Jesus had called the Twelve together, he gave them power and authority to drive out all demons and to cure diseases, and he sent them out to proclaim the kingdom of God and to heal those who were ill. He told them: "Take nothing for the journey – no staff, no bag, no bread, no money, no extra shirt. Whatever house you enter, stay there until you leave that town. If people do not welcome you, leave their town and shake the dust off your feet as a testimony against them." So they set out and went from village to village, proclaiming the good news and healing people everywhere.

Luke 15:1–6a, GNB

One day when many tax collectors and other outcasts came to listen to Jesus, the Pharisees and the teachers of the Law started grumbling, "This man welcomes outcasts and even eats with them!" So Jesus told them this parable:

"Suppose one of you has a hundred sheep and loses one of them – what do you do? You leave the other ninety-nine sheep in the pasture and go looking for the one that got lost until you find it. When you find it, you are so happy that you put it on your shoulders and carry it back home."

Commentary

We usually envisage evangelism as addressing crowds or encouraging individuals to accept Christian faith; a verbal gift (telling people about Jesus and his gospel), and also a relational gift – building bridges and making connections between church and world.

Distinctions are drawn between the every-believer call to bear witness (being willing to give account of our faith) and the charism of evangelism, where gifted individuals are known for their unusually high rates of success in drawing people to faith in Christ.

There could be a different perspective on this gift. The "evangel" is the gospel, so evangelizing is extending the influence and range of the gospel – building the kingdom. As Jesus said (see Matthew 28 passage), "Make disciples of all nations". This suggests a deeper, more thorough conversion than simply obtaining acquiescence, leading someone to Christ. Evangelism influences character and attitudes as well as encouraging belief. The aim isn't more and more Christians regardless of lifestyle, but increased numbers with lives bearing the fruit of the Spirit, changing the world into a more peaceful, kind, and healthy place. Evangelism is for advancing the reign of God's *shalom*.

So the work of an evangelist may not include addressing crowds or getting people to respond to altar calls. But if you look at their life you will see that they leave a trail of people with solid, lasting, unshakeable faith in Jesus, and lives that make the world kinder, more peaceful, and – according to their range of influence – healed.

Questions

- Who have you known personally whom you believe to have had the gift of evangelism? Describe them and why you think this.
- In what ways do you personally feel called to share the gospel? Are there some kinds of evangelism you favour above others? Explain why. Are there any approaches to evangelism you find unhelpful? Explain why.
- Jesus lived in absolute simplicity. Our Luke 9 passage suggests a correlation between the commission to share the good news (in words and deeds) with the strict observance of a simple lifestyle. Why is this? To ensure the world converts to the faith, rather than the world distracting the faithful? For focus? Because those who live simply can relate to poor as well as rich? To eliminate the possibility of people accepting a creed just to obtain handouts? What is the connection between living simply and communicating the gospel?

Prayer

You have entrusted us to carry the torch of the gospel for our generation. May we bear and share the flame faithfully, until the whole world shines to the praise of your name. Amen.

Intercession

BIBLE PASSAGES[172]

Romans 8:26–27, NRSVA

... the Spirit helps us in our weakness; for we do not know how to pray as we ought, but that very Spirit intercedes with sighs too deep for words. And God, who searches the heart, knows what is the mind of the Spirit, because the Spirit intercedes for the saints according to the will of God.

Luke 18:1–7, NRSVA

Jesus told them a parable about their need to pray always and not to lose heart. He said, "In a certain city there was a judge who neither feared God nor had respect for people. In that city there was a widow who kept coming to him and saying, 'Grant me justice against my opponent.' For a while he refused; but later he said to himself, 'Though I have no fear of God and no respect for anyone, yet because this widow keeps bothering me, I will grant her justice, so that she may not wear me out by continually coming.'" And the Lord said, "Listen to what the unjust judge says. And will not God grant justice to his chosen ones who cry to him day and night? Will he delay long in helping them? I tell you, he will quickly grant justice to them."

Luke 22:31–32, NRSVA

"Simon, Simon, listen! Satan has demanded to sift all of you like wheat, but I have prayed for you that your own faith may not fail; and you, when once you have turned back, strengthen your brothers."

Matthew 18:18–20, NRSVA

"Truly I tell you, whatever you bind on earth will be bound in heaven, and whatever you loose on earth will be loosed in heaven. Again, truly I tell you, if two of you agree on earth about anything you ask, it will be done for you by my Father in heaven. For where two or three are gathered in my name, I am there among them."

Commentary

It can be easier to define something by isolating what it's not. A legend has grown up about Michelangelo being asked how he sculpted his lifelike statues, in which he replies that the task is simple – you just chip away everything that doesn't look like the subject.

---

172 It's also helpful to read chapter 17 of John's Gospel.

For every one of the charisms there is a lesser occupation or habit that echoes – but is not – it.

It is important and appropriate that we should pray for the church and the world, for the sick and the needy, in our formal prayers when we meet for public worship. But though these prayers are intercessions (prayer offered for others), they are only a pale reflection of the gift of intercession.

Those called to intercession grab God by the coat collar and *will not let him go*. They beg, they plead, they weep, they persist, they fall to the ground and prostrate themselves before him; they find the passion of their heart harnessed and engaged like the horses pulling the chariot of Ben Hur. They feel the power of the Spirit surging through them and sweeping them up in its force. They can pray for causes in which they have no personal interest and with which they have no personal connection, impelled by the swell of the Spirit's sea. When they are called to pray, the Spirit of God picks them up and prays in them until the job is done. It can be both exhilarating and exhausting. Obviously this is not quite the same as the intercessions in church on Sunday – though there's no real reason why it couldn't be.

When Jesus intercedes for us, it's the passionate sort, not the formality. That should encourage us.

Questions

- If anyone in the group feels called to the charism of intercession, listen to their experience of what this is like. Everyone else – think of a time when you felt called to pray for something you really cared about. What happened? Describe your experience.

- The world and its people need our prayers. Intercession is like the blood of life. There are times – August, especially, and Christmas – when we are on vacation or busy, and there's a lull in our intercession. Discuss in your group the possibility of prayer triplets meeting to cover these times when everyone's busy or away and far fewer are praying.

- Discuss ways of helping you be specific and faithful in intercession. Might you create an altar corner where you can write down prayers and revisit them daily? Might you meet in a group to pray? Might one person be willing to organize a prayer chain? What ideas do you have and what has been helpful in your experience?

Prayer

Thank you, Jesus, for praying for me. Give me the grace to be faithful in praying for others. Amen.

Hospitality

BIBLE PASSAGES

Hebrews 13:1–2, NIVUK

Keep on loving one another as brothers and sisters. Do not forget to show hospitality to strangers, for by so doing some people have shown hospitality to angels without knowing it.

1 Peter 4:8–10, NIVUK

Above all, love each other deeply, because love covers over a multitude of sins. Offer hospitality to one another without grumbling. Each of you should use whatever gift you have received to serve others, as faithful stewards of God's grace in its various forms.

Romans 12:13, NIVUK

Share with the Lord's people who are in need. Practise hospitality.

1 Timothy 5:8–10, NIVUK

Anyone who does not provide for their relatives, and especially for their own household, has denied the faith and is worse than an unbeliever.

No widow may be put on the list of widows unless she is over sixty, has been faithful to her husband, and is well known for her good deeds, such as bringing up children, showing hospitality, washing the feet of the Lord's people, helping those in trouble and devoting herself to all kinds of good deeds.

Genesis 18:2–5, NIVUK

Abraham looked up and saw three men standing nearby. When he saw them, he hurried from the entrance of his tent to meet them and bowed low to the ground.

He said, "If I have found favour in your eyes, my lord, do not pass your servant by. Let a little water be brought, and then you may all wash your feet and rest under this tree. Let me get you something to eat, so you can be refreshed and then go on your way – now that you have come to your servant."

Commentary

The charism of hospitality makes people feel at home. We particularly associate it with welcoming others into our houses, and giving them something to eat and drink; including them in our family circle. The ability of some Christians to do this with warmth and kindness, thinking nothing of the work and expense involved, is truly inspirational.

But the gift of hospitality can still be exercised with no home to receive guests in and no food to offer them. Hospitality was at work in the trenches and the concentration camps when one person took another under their wing in kindness, sharing what little they had. Hospitality makes room for a fellow passenger to sit down on a crowded bus, or invites a new child in the playground to join in a game.

Hospitality is about sharing, making a guest or a stranger feel loved and included like one of the family. It's more to do with relationship than with material goods. When someone fallen on hard times goes to the food bank for help, the hospitality is not the dispensing of donated groceries; it's the understanding and kindly welcome, the invitation to sit down and join others in enjoying a cup of tea. Even refugees subsisting in the cold in makeshift tents can show hospitality to others, insisting on sharing what little they have with the volunteers from aid organizations who come to help them. In reaching out to help others, the one showing hospitality is also enriched and encouraged – and this is a true sign of grace at work.

Questions

- Our 1 Timothy passage identifies the exercise of hospitality as something very appropriate for a widow. Why do you think this might be? Have you found women more likely to practise hospitality than men? In what ways, less obvious than inviting folk round for meals, might men be quietly offering hospitality, unremarked?

- Who have you known with the gift of hospitality? What do you remember about them?

- In recent years the church has increased its emphasis on eating together and social interaction. This can sometimes be difficult for introverts. If you are not a group person, is the gift of hospitality not for you, or are there other ways of exercising it?

Prayer

You welcome us with kindness, and you prepared a place for us in heaven. Gracious God, may our lives reflect your goodness and your love. Amen.

Mercy

BIBLE PASSAGES[173]

Psalm 51:1-2, NRSVA

> Have mercy on me, O God,
>   according to your steadfast love;
> according to your abundant mercy
>   blot out my transgressions.
> Wash me thoroughly from my iniquity,
>   and cleanse me from my sin.

Luke 10:36-37, NRSVA

> "Which of these three, do you think, was a neighbour to the man who fell into the hands of the robbers?" He said, "The one who showed him mercy." Jesus said to him, "Go and do likewise."

Matthew 18:32-33, NRSVA

> "You wicked slave! I forgave you all that debt because you pleaded with me. Should you not have had mercy on your fellow-slave, as I had mercy on you?"

Lamentations 3:22-23, NRSVA

> The steadfast love of the Lord never ceases,
>   his mercies never come to an end;
> they are new every morning;
>   great is your faithfulness.

Micah 6:8, KJV

> He hath shewed thee, O man, what is good; and what doth the Lord require of thee, but to do justly, and to love mercy, and to walk humbly with thy God?

Commentary

All Christians are called to show mercy. All of us have done things we are ashamed of, which estrange us from our spiritual nature and calling, and it is because of God's mercy and loving-kindness that we are healed and restored, made whole again. Because our life in Christ starts in mercy, it must proceed with mercy –

---

173   The book of Jonah is also a glorious, funny, delightful story about mercy.

henceforth we live from this beginning. The way to remain in the mercy on which we depend is to exercise that mercy in our lives.

We are called to love but cannot always feel it; when that happens, the way forward is to choose kindness – for all practical purposes, it comes out the same. Similarly, we are called to mercy but can't always feel it, especially when we are hurt and angry, when we have been wronged. When that happens, the way forward is to choose restraint, which is the unsung twin of mercy. When you could sue, but don't. When you could hit or shout, but don't. When you could expose the secret, steal the unguarded purse, mock the stupid remark, draw attention to the indiscretion, but don't. If you aren't sure how to practise mercy, start with restraint.

But we're thinking of mercy as a charism, as a spiritual gift. The signs of a charism are that exercising it energizes you – it brings you joy, peace, and lightness; that when you practise the gift the results are particularly effective; that other people recognize this gifting in you.

These spiritual charisms are the gifts of the Holy Spirit – his, not ours – and he dwells in you. If you look at our Bible passages, something you notice is that God always has mercy; it's his very nature, the sign of his presence. So mercy is a special gift in that it belongs to the whole people of God without exception; by mercy we are born again, by mercy we live. This is a gift to which every one of us is called. It is the air of heaven.

Questions

- We are called to be merciful, but not to be doormats. Discuss in your group how to both show mercy and set wise boundaries (e.g. when to overlook bad behaviour and when to report it; when to allow late payments and when to call them in; when to be gracious about rudeness or unkindness and when to draw a relationship to a close). How can you be merciful and still say "No"?

- Share in your group about a time when someone showed mercy to you. What happened? How did you feel? How did mercy change the dynamic?

- What are the areas in your life where you need others to show you mercy, or you are struggling to show mercy to others?

Prayer

Merciful God, thank you for accepting me as I am, for loving me without condition; no strings attached. Loving God, I belong to you. May your Holy Spirit dwell in me, fill me, overflow in me, so that your mercy spills out of my life like a mountain spring. Amen.

Willingness to face martyrdom

BIBLE PASSAGES

John 10:17–18, GNB

"I am willing to give up my life, in order that I may receive it back again. No one takes my life away from me. I give it up of my own free will. I have the right to give it up, and I have the right to take it back. This is what my Father has commanded me to do."

Hebrews 11:32–38, NRSVA

For time would fail me to tell of Gideon, Barak, Samson, Jephthah, of David and Samuel and the prophets – who through faith conquered kingdoms, administered justice, obtained promises, shut the mouths of lions, quenched raging fire, escaped the edge of the sword, won strength out of weakness, became mighty in war, put foreign armies to flight. Women received their dead by resurrection. Others were tortured, refusing to accept release, in order to obtain a better resurrection. Others suffered mocking and flogging, and even chains and imprisonment. They were stoned to death, they were sawn in two, they were killed by the sword; they went about in skins of sheep and goats, destitute, persecuted, tormented – of whom the world was not worthy. They wandered in deserts and mountains, and in caves and holes in the ground.

Matthew 26:38–39, RSV

Then he said to them, "My soul is very sorrowful, even to death; remain here, and watch with me." And going a little farther he fell on his face and prayed, "My Father, if it be possible, let this cup pass from me; nevertheless, not as I will, but as thou wilt."

Luke 9:23–25, RSV

And he said to all, "If any man would come after me, let him deny himself and take up his cross daily and follow me. For whoever would save his life will lose it; and whoever loses his life for my sake, he will save it. For what does it profit a man if he gains the whole world and loses or forfeits himself?"

Luke 14:33,[174] RSV

So therefore, whoever of you does not renounce all that he has cannot be my disciple.

174 See also 1 Corinthians 7:29–31.

Commentary

When I began to research the spiritual gifts to make sure I didn't miss any, I was shocked to find this included in the list. It felt viscerally repugnant to me. The Bible urges us to choose life.[175] When I was a child, the passage about people being sawn in half terrified and repelled me.

But I suppose this is exactly why the willingness to face martyrdom is a spiritual gift. Jesus himself was crucified, and of his twelve disciples only John is thought to have died a natural death of old age – and even he was exiled on Patmos. Even today there are places in the world where asking for Christian baptism reduces your life expectancy to six months.

It is hard to make sense of this, or to imagine how anyone could find the courage, without factoring in willingness to face martyrdom as a charism – a gift bringing joy and peace when it is exercised.[176] Not that this should make us blasé about religious persecution; it is a terrible and wicked thing, abhorrent to God, whether done to Christians or done by them.

I also came across Voluntary Poverty (a life of simplicity) listed as a spiritual gift, and I'm including it here for those of us who live safe and comfortable lives. We too are called to give up self-interest, and to lay down personal advancement as a goal in life. We too are called to take up our cross and follow Jesus.

Questions

- When you think about martyrdom, how does it make you feel? How do you respond to our passage from Hebrews about suffering for the sake of the gospel?[177]

- When you read about Jesus' call to take up your cross daily and follow him, how does it make you feel? What do you think it means, for you, in practical terms? Being completely honest, at the present time in your faith do you feel there is a level of surrender you cannot manage?[178]

- Discuss how to get the balance right between choosing life, and renouncing everything to follow Jesus. Is it about swapping one kind of happiness for another?

---

175 See Deuteronomy 30:19–20.

176 See also Acts 16:22–25, for the attitude.

177 NB: In your group, please don't get into swapping modern-day horror stories and capping tales of frightful things you've read about, or airing knowledge you may have of statistics about modern martyrdom. Keep the conversation at a level at which everyone can contribute.

178 If that's true, don't worry. People change over time, and circumstances can call out surprising courage in us all. It's best always to begin by being honest. God understands.

Prayer

Father, you made me and called me into life. Yet I know this world is not my eternal home; all this is passing away. Give me the courage I need to live my days in faithfulness, and to lay it down with dignity and trust when the time comes to do so; for I belong to you. Amen.

Celibacy

BIBLE PASSAGES

1 Corinthians 7:5–9, NRSVA

Do not deprive one another except perhaps by agreement for a set time, to devote yourselves to prayer, and then come together again, so that Satan may not tempt you because of your lack of self-control. ... I wish that all were as I myself am. But each has a particular gift from God, one having one kind and another a different kind.

To the unmarried and the widows I say that it is well for them to remain unmarried as I am. But if they are not practising self-control, they should marry. For it is better to marry than to be aflame with passion.

Matthew 19:8–12, GNB

Jesus answered, "Moses gave you permission to divorce your wives because you are so hard to teach. But it was not like that at the time of creation. I tell you, then, that any man who divorces his wife for any cause other than her unfaithfulness, commits adultery if he marries some other woman."

His disciples said to him, "If this is how it is between a man and his wife, it is better not to marry."

Jesus answered, "This teaching does not apply to everyone, but only to those to whom God has given it. For there are different reasons why men cannot marry: some, because they were born that way; others, because men made them that way; and others do not marry for the sake of the Kingdom of heaven. Let him who can accept this teaching do so."

Psalm 68:6, KJV

God setteth the solitary in families: he bringeth out those which are bound with chains ...

Commentary

Some church traditions include celibacy as a spiritual gift, but not without debate. In our 1 Corinthians passage it's thought to be implied by Paul's use of the word "gift" (charism), yet he is not using the term as he does elsewhere (e.g. the lists in Romans 12 and 1 Corinthians 12) to mean specifically gifts of the Holy Spirit.[179]

---

179 There's an interesting internet article on this at: http://helpmewithbiblestudy. org/3HolySpirit/WorksGiftsCelibacyMarriage.aspx#sthash.FGLUb3eG.dpbs

Yet, because celibacy is present in the church as a sacred path to follow, it's good for us to consider it as one of the spiritual charisms, especially as the Holy Spirit's gifts are for the building up of the church, and celibacy does this by freeing individuals from family responsibilities that take up time and attention.

A spiritual gift cannot be compelled; you can't make rules for the Holy Spirit to follow. If monks, nuns, and Catholic priests have to be celibate as a requirement of their dedication, is that a spiritual gifting from God? Is the sexual fidelity of a married couple as a condition of Christian marriage a spiritual gift? Or is a gift of the Spirit more a particular personal ministry, calling, or gifting? Where disabled people in the church have been considered by their carers to be unsuitable for marriage and sexual relationship, is this a spiritual calling inherent in their condition, or more a requirement imposed by society?

Some people are naturally asexual, but most monastics (and other Christians called to abstain from marriage) say the celibate path is a struggle at times, requiring the empowerment of the Holy Spirit to make of it a grace and to reveal it as a gift.

For some Christians, celibacy is a path to which they feel called for a season, then feel called at a later point to marriage and family life – or people who have been married and widowed may enter monastic life. Our 1 Corinthians passage mentions temporarily fasting from sex. The other spiritual gifts are usually a feature of a person's whole life and character, in some sense defining them.

Questions

- Psalm 68 says God sets the solitary in families. Single and celibate people in the church still need friendship and the support of companions. How can our faith community include and encourage both single and married people?

- Celibate Christians are free from many of the family ties and commitments that would otherwise be a practical and financial priority, and of the emotional priority of what is sometimes called a "primary relationship". What advantages and disadvantages can you see in this, to the individual and to the community? Why might a married couple choose to observe a period of celibacy?

- What do you feel about requiring celibacy of others – e.g. of people who need care because of disability, or those who feel called to the Catholic priesthood? How do you experience God's call in your own role as a single person or sexual partner?

Prayer

Set me free to serve you as the person you made me to be, and help me to be faithful in my calling. Amen.

Understanding

BIBLE PASSAGES

Isaiah 11:2–3, NRSVA

The spirit of the Lord shall rest on him,
the spirit of wisdom and understanding,
the spirit of counsel and might,
the spirit of knowledge and the fear of the Lord.
His delight shall be in the fear of the Lord.

1 Kings 3:7–12, NRSVA

"[Solomon said] O Lord my God, you have made your servant king in place of my father David, although I am only a little child; I do not know how to go out or come in. And your servant is in the midst of the people whom you have chosen, a great people, so numerous they cannot be numbered or counted. Give your servant therefore an understanding mind to govern your people, able to discern between good and evil; for who can govern this your great people?"

It pleased the Lord that Solomon had asked this. God said to him, "Because you have asked this, and have not asked for yourself long life or riches, or for the life of your enemies, but have asked for yourself understanding to discern what is right, I now do according to your word. Indeed I give you a wise and discerning mind; no one like you has been before you and no one like you shall arise after you."

1 Kings 4:29, NRSVA

God gave Solomon very great wisdom, discernment, and breadth of understanding as vast as the sand on the seashore.

Nehemiah 8:2, NRSVA

[T]he priest Ezra brought the law before the assembly, both men and women and all who could hear with understanding.

Psalm 119:130, NRSVA

The unfolding of your words gives light;
it imparts understanding to the simple.

Luke 2:47, NRSVA

And all who heard him were amazed at his understanding and his answers.

Matthew 15:16, NRSVA

Then he said, "Are you also still without understanding?"

Colossians 1:9, NRSVA

[W]e have not ceased praying for you and asking that you may be filled with the knowledge of God's will in all spiritual wisdom and understanding.

Commentary

It's maybe not surprising that the Wisdom books of the Bible (look in Proverbs and Job) make frequent reference to understanding. In the Bible, it has three main applications.

First, the ability to interpret spiritual teaching intelligently, particularly the word of God in the Scriptures. In 2 Timothy 2:15 (KJV) Paul speaks of "rightly dividing the word of truth". The Greek phrase used is about cutting a path through rough scrub to create a direct route rather than skirting around the edges; getting to the point, the meaning. Our passage from Luke is an instance of this. It refers to the time when the child Jesus was found in the Temple, discussing matters of faith with the religious elders. The depth of his insight astounded those who heard him.

Second, the ability to make wise choices. Our Colossians passage is an instance of this. Knowing what to do, choosing the right path, seeing the implications of what is before you – this is understanding. "Discerning what is right", as our 1 Kings 3 passage says. In our Matthew passage, Jesus expresses exasperation at the stubborn lack of insight persisting despite all the signs of God at work.

Third, the ability to relate effectively to other people – to hear their point of view for the purpose of social justice and wise governance (see our passage from Nehemiah).

Questions

- What has most helped you to understand and interpret the meaning of passages of Scripture? How useful have you found study groups, podcasts, sermons, books, talking with friends? Discuss what has been helpful to you, and might benefit your group.

- Anybody's understanding can be developed and increased, but the spiritual charism of understanding is insight as a special gift. Share with your group about individuals you have come across who you believe had this gift.

- The gift of understanding, eagerly sought and diligently nurtured, would increase world peace. Here's how to begin: in your group, take it in turns to answer the question: "What is it like to be you?"

Prayer

Teach me, O Lord, the way of your statutes,
and I will observe it to the end.
Give me understanding, that I may keep your law
and observe it with my whole heart.
Lead me in the path of your commandments,
for I delight in it. Amen.
(Psalm 119:33–35, NRSVA**)**

Counsel

BIBLE PASSAGES

Matthew 10:16–20, NIVUK

"I am sending you out like sheep among wolves. Therefore be as shrewd as snakes and as innocent as doves. Be on your guard; you will be handed over to the local councils and be flogged in the synagogues. On my account you will be brought before governors and kings as witnesses to them and to the Gentiles. But when they arrest you, do not worry about what to say or how to say it. At that time you will be given what to say, for it will not be you speaking, but the Spirit of your Father speaking through you."

Psalm 16:7–8, NIVUK

I will praise the Lord, who counsels me;
    even at night my heart instructs me.
I keep my eyes always on the Lord.
    With him at my right hand, I shall not be shaken.

Isaiah 50:4–5, NIVUK

The Sovereign Lord has given me a well-instructed tongue,
    to know the word that sustains the weary.
He wakens me morning by morning,
    wakens my ear to listen like one being instructed.
The Sovereign Lord has opened my ears;
    I have not been rebellious,
    I have not turned away.

Wisdom 9:13–17, NRSVA

For who can learn the counsel of God?
Or who can discern what the Lord wills?
For the reasoning of mortals is worthless,
and our designs are likely to fail;
for a perishable body weighs down the soul,
and this earthy tent burdens the thoughtful mind.
We can hardly guess at what is on earth,
and what is at hand we find with labour;
but who has traced out what is in the heavens?
Who has learned your counsel,

unless you have given wisdom
and sent your holy spirit from on high?

Commentary

The spiritual gift of counsel is like prudence, intuition, and common sense plugged into the mains. It is the instinct of the Holy Spirit operating in us so that we know what to say and how to act in any given situation – but especially when life takes us by surprise.

The charism of counsel is the situational operation of the logic of the gospel. It has connections with the gift of wisdom, but counsel is the putting into practice in real-life circumstances of that inner reservoir of wisdom.

When someone trains to be a counsellor, it's impressed on them that they aren't there to give people the benefit of their advice, but to listen so that their clients can discern and discover their own true north. Similarly, the gift of counsel is not about being ready with religious opinions to hand out at every opportunity, but about allowing the Spirit's wisdom to emerge in context. Our passage from Isaiah brings this out very clearly – that the counsel offered springs from an ingrained habit of listening to the inner voice of the Spirit.

The gift of counsel is luminous, bringing enlightenment when things are muddled and confused. I once knew someone who described her method of making decisions when confronted with different options or a choice of courses of action as "looking for the one the light shines on". The gift of counsel has to do with making wise choices – knowing what to do and what to say; but this is more than just being a sensible person. It's about following the inner leading and guiding of the Holy Spirit, because sometimes there can be more to the situations in which we find ourselves than we could possibly know; but he knows.

Questions

- Share with your group about a time when you were prompted or guided to choose to do or say something just right, even though you didn't have the information to know it would be the right thing. For which situations in your life would you really value the gift of counsel now?
- Who have you known who you believe had the gift of counsel, and why?
- How do you think we could strengthen and develop the gift of counsel?[180]

---

180 You might like to include prayer, reading the Bible, reading the work of spiritual writers, and the company we keep.

Prayer

Fount of all knowledge, source of all wisdom, guide me in what I say, what I choose, and how I respond to other people. Lead me in paths of peace and kindness; help me to listen to your Spirit's voice and to what other people are really saying to me. Help me to feel my way beneath the superficial to get at the truth of things, and to choose just the right form of words to bring healing and light. Amen.

Fortitude

BIBLE PASSAGES

Mark 4:3–8, NIVUK

"Listen! A farmer went out to sow his seed. As he was scattering the seed, some fell along the path, and the birds came and ate it up. Some fell on rocky places, where it did not have much soil. It sprang up quickly, because the soil was shallow. But when the sun came up, the plants were scorched, and they withered because they had no root. Other seed fell among thorns, which grew up and choked the plants, so that they did not bear grain. Still other seed fell on good soil. It came up, grew and produced a crop, some multiplying thirty, some sixty, some a hundred times."

Philippians 4:12–13, NIVUK

I have learned the secret of being content in any and every situation, whether well fed or hungry, whether living in plenty or in want. I can do all this through him who gives me strength.

John 4:31–34, NIVUK

Meanwhile his disciples urged him, "Rabbi, eat something."

But he said to them, "I have food to eat that you know nothing about."

Then his disciples said to each other, "Could someone have brought him food?"

"My food," said Jesus, "is to do the will of him who sent me and to finish his work."

Matthew 24:9–13, NIVUK

"Then you will be handed over to be persecuted and put to death, and you will be hated by all nations because of me. At that time many will turn away from the faith and will betray and hate each other, and many false prophets will appear and deceive many people. Because of the increase of wickedness, the love of most will grow cold, but the one who stands firm to the end will be saved."

Commentary

"Fortitude" is a very rich concept, as we can see when we find it hiding in other words. It comes from the Latin *fortis*, meaning "strong". A fort, or fortress, or fortified building will be sturdy and well defended against attack. "Comfort" literally means "with strength", and is about helping restore someone who is weak, building up their spirits. So there are connotations of building up, of standing strong, of resisting incursion – and the usual definition of "fortitude" is "courage".

"Courage" springs from the Latin word for the heart (*cor*), as does the word "core" (we might speak of our "core values", or say we were "shaken to the core"), and the medieval word "corage", which meant "heart" in the sense of vigour or enthusiasm.[181]

The spiritual gift of fortitude is the ability to keep the fire burning, to resist all incursions of the enemy, to hold commitment in place, to endure through boredom and disappointment, to be brave under attack and resilient in discouragement.

In the human body, the liver is remarkable for its power to regenerate after surgical or chemical damage. From as little as 25 per cent, it can grow back. The charism of fortitude is like this physical power of regeneration – it's like an organ at the centre of the soul's viscera that struggles back to health and strength with astonishing determination and tenacity.

Questions

• In times of doubt or discouragement, what (or who) has strengthened you?

• When people are upset or shocked, a common response from friends and neighbours is to offer them a cup of tea – this is often very helpful. Some people reach for a stiff drink (whisky, maybe!) when they need something to fortify them. What ordinary, practical thing would you do or offer, if a friend of yours had a severe shock or bad news?

• "The name of the Lord is a fortified tower; the righteous run to it and are safe."[182] What do you think this means, in practice?

Prayer

O God my rock and my fortress, you are my strength and stay. When I am most afraid, I put my trust in you. Keep me rooted strongly in your Spirit's power; keep me planted firm and deep in your salvation; for I ask it in Jesus' name. Amen.

---

181 See also the study on "Encouragement" in this book.
182 Proverbs 18:10, NIVUK.

Reverance

BIBLE PASSAGES

Hebrews 12:18–28, NIVUK

You have not come to a mountain that can be touched and that is burning with fire; to darkness, gloom and storm; to a trumpet blast or to such a voice speaking words that those who heard it begged that no further word be spoken to them, because they could not bear what was commanded: "If even an animal touches the mountain, it must be stoned to death." The sight was so terrifying that Moses said, "I am trembling with fear."

But you have come to Mount Zion, to the city of the living God, the heavenly Jerusalem. You have come to thousands upon thousands of angels in joyful assembly, to the church of the firstborn, whose names are written in heaven. You have come to God, the Judge of all, to the spirits of the righteous made perfect, to Jesus the mediator of a new covenant, and to the sprinkled blood that speaks a better word than the blood of Abel.

See to it that you do not refuse him who speaks. If they did not escape when they refused him who warned them on earth, how much less will we, if we turn away from him who warns us from heaven? At that time his voice shook the earth, but now he has promised, "Once more I will shake not only the earth but also the heavens." The words "once more" indicate the removing of what can be shaken – that is, created things – so that what cannot be shaken may remain.

Therefore, since we are receiving a kingdom that cannot be shaken, let us be thankful, and so worship God acceptably with reverence and awe, for our "God is a consuming fire."

Isaiah 11:1–2, AMP

And the Spirit of the Lord will rest on Him –
  The Spirit of wisdom and understanding,
The Spirit of counsel and strength,
  The Spirit of knowledge and of the [reverential and obedient] fear of the Lord.

Commentary

Our Hebrews passage about the holy mountain reminds us that we live in the presence of unseen but immense spiritual power, like villagers whose home is at the foot of a live volcano. God is with us.

We usually think of reverence as a reflexive response to the experience of the deeply holy. So, for example, when the Magi came into the presence of Jesus they knelt down and paid him homage. Their reverence was primarily about what was in him, and only secondarily about what was in them. Reverence is called forth in us in worship sometimes – think of films you may have seen of worship at Taizé, with the simple chants sung in harmony, the soft light of candles, the big gathering of people singing to God. Our response to the sense of the numinous is reverence.

But when we come to reverence as a spiritual gift, we take things a step further. The charism of reverence is an attitude of mind that quietly and continuously reminds others of the presence of God and the holiness of all life. It is like the fragrance of incense burning, arising from our life, subtly calling others to worship. So it has an evangelistic component to it, recalling those around us to the way of holiness.

There are no English words for this charism as accurate as the Sanskrit (Indian) word *yoga*, which is about a state of connection, and a disciplined practice of awareness that keeps us in connection. The yoga of reverence is the faithful practice of connection to God, which doesn't wait for an experience outside us (a wonderful sunset, a moving church service, a beautiful song) to call it forth. The charism of reverence sustains awareness of God's presence, consistently living in its light. It's a very disciplined, focused practice – not easy to do; keeping your eyes upon Jesus regardless of what is happening all around.

Questions

- What has helped you to enter a state of reverence? What moves you to worship and helps you to believe in the unseen God?
- Who have you known with the ability to hold awareness of God faithfully and consistently, so that to be with them is to be reminded of Jesus?
- What do you think might help you to develop and practise this discipline of keeping your eyes on Jesus?

Prayer

Holy God, holy and wise, holy and immortal, holy and strong, have mercy upon us. How easily distracted we are, how shallow and frivolous we can be. Help us develop the muscle of reverence, to strengthen our focus on your presence that is always with us. Amen.

Fear of the Lord

BIBLE PASSAGES

Isaiah 11:2, NIVUK

The Spirit of the Lord will rest on him –
    the Spirit of wisdom and of understanding,
the Spirit of counsel and of might,
    the Spirit of the knowledge and fear of the Lord.

2 Chronicles 19:6–7, 9, NIVUK

"Consider carefully what you do, because you are not judging for mere mortals but for the Lord, who is with you whenever you give a verdict. Now let the fear of the Lord be on you. Judge carefully, for with the Lord our God there is no injustice or partiality or bribery ... You must serve faithfully and wholeheartedly in the fear of the Lord."

Psalm 33:8, NIVUK

Let all the earth fear the Lord;
    let all the people of the world revere him.

Psalm 34:7, NIVUK

The angel of the Lord encamps around those who fear him,
    and he delivers them.

Psalm 111:10, NIVUK

The fear of the Lord is the beginning of wisdom;
    all who follow his precepts have good understanding.
To him belongs eternal praise.

Psalm 128:1, NIVUK

Blessed are all who fear the Lord,
    who walk in obedience to him.

Proverbs 2:3–8, NIVUK

[I]f you call out for insight
    and cry aloud for understanding,
and if you look for it as for silver
    and search for it as for hidden treasure,

then you will understand the fear of the Lord
   and find the knowledge of God.
For the Lord gives wisdom;
   from his mouth come knowledge and understanding.
He holds success in store for the upright,
   he is a shield to those whose way of life is blameless;
he guards the course of the just
   and protects the way of his faithful ones.

Proverbs 22:4, NIVUK

Humility is the fear of the Lord;
   its wages are riches and honour and life.

Commentary

The spiritual gift of fear of the Lord is about respecting boundaries. The Old Testament Law warned against opportunistic ruthlessness, lack of integrity, and injustice. The people of God were to be upright and honourable, so that you could be safe in their company and trust their word.

The way of blessing has to do with honesty and kindness, integrity and compassion. It remembers that people judge by image and appearances, but God looks on the heart.[183] Walking in this way, you follow the flow of grace in the world, attracting goodness. This doesn't mean no adversity will befall you. The rings of a tree are formed from the soft wood of fast summer growth, which gives flexibility, and the slow hard growth of winter, which gives strength. People need adversity as well as ease, to develop character. But the fear of the Lord – walking in the way of blessing and respecting its boundaries – will keep your heart and mind and soul safe even in adversity.

This is no light matter. In a world where people may be imprisoned, tortured, and killed, faith sometimes needs immense courage. But, for whatever life brings, the fear of the Lord develops steadiness and wholesomeness; it arms us with real strength within. It sharpens our wits and allows us to learn from experience. The fear of the Lord is about staying on the path of holiness, not allowing yourself to be distracted or to forget who you are and where you're heading.

Questions

• Some people react against associating the word "fear" with God. How about you? Are there other words you would prefer? Why do you think the Bible uses the word "fear"? What are the positive aspects of picking so extreme a term? How is the fear of the Lord at work in your life?

---

183 See 1 Samuel 16:7.

- Thinking of our national life, where would you like to see the fear of the Lord applied in politics and society? Where do you see it now, and where is it missing? What part can we as Christians play?
- Notice in our quotation from Psalm 33 that all the earth fears the Lord. What do you think this means? In what sense do other species, who are in a covenant relationship with God,[184] fear him?

Prayer

Keep me in your way, wise and loving God. In my everyday choices, may I draw back from what offends you and embrace what gladdens your heart. May my life please you and my spirit be shaped by your goodness and grace. Amen.

---

184 Genesis 9:12–17.